6.3

IMMIGRANT ASSOCIATIONS IN EUROPE

EUROPEAN SCIENCE FOUNDATION

The European Science Foundation (ESF) is an international non-governmental organization with its seat in Strasbourg (France). Its members are academies and research councils with national responsibility for supporting scientific research, and which are funded largely from governmental sources. The term 'science' is used in its broadest sense to include the humanities, social sciences, biomedical sciences, the natural sciences and mathematics. The ESF currently has 49 members from 18 European countries.

The tasks of the ESF are:

to assist its Member Organizations to co-ordinate research programmes;

to identify areas in need of stimulation, particularly those of an interdisciplinary nature;

to further co-operation between researchers by facilitating their movement between laboratories, holding workshops, managing support schemes approved by the Member Organizations, and arranging for the joint use of special equipment;

to harmonize and assemble data useful to the Member Organizations;

to foster the efficient dissemination of information;

to respond to initiatives which are aimed at advancing European science;

to maintain constructive relations with the European Communities and other relevant organizations.

The ESF is funded through a general budget to which all Member Organizations contribute (according to a scale assessed in relation to each country's net national income), and a series of special budgets covering additional activities, funded by those organizations which choose to participate. The programmes of the ESF are determined by the Assembly of all Member Organizations. Their implementation is supervised by an elected Executive Council, assisted by the office of the Foundation which consists of an international staff directed by the Secretary General.

Further information on ESF activities can be obtained from:

European Science Foundation
1 Quai Lezay Marnésia
67000 Strasbourg
France

Immigrant Associations in Europe

Edited by

JOHN REX
Centre for Research in Ethnic Relations, University of Warwick
DANIELE JOLY
Centre for Research in Ethnic Relations, University of Warwick
and
CZARINA WILPERT
Technical University, Berlin

Gower

Aldershot · Brookfield USA · Hong Kong · Singapore · Sydney

Published by
Gower Publishing Company Limited
Gower House
Croft Road
Aldershot
Hants GU11 3HR
England

Gower Publishing Company
Old Post Road
Brookfield
Vermont 05036
USA

British Library Cataloguing in Publication Data

Immigrant associations in Europe. ——
    (Studies in European migration; no. 1)
    1. Minorities —— European —— Societies, etc.
    I. Rex, John   II. Joly, Daniele
    III. Wilpert, Czarina   IV. Series
    305.8'0094   D1056

Library of Congress Cataloging-in-Publication Data

Immigrant associations in Europe.
    Bibliography: p.
    Includes index.
    1. Europe—Foreign population—Societies, etc.
2. Europe—Emigration and immigration.   I. Rex, John.
II. Joly, Daniele.   III. Wilpert, Czarina.
D1056.I48   1987   305.8'006'04   87-357

ISBN: 0 566 05474 4

Printed in Great Britain at the University Press, Cambridge

Contents

Preface

The international and interdisciplinary study 'International Migration and the Cultural Sense of Belongingness of the Second Generation' was launched at the initiative of the European Science Foundation (ESF) in 1980. The objectives of the projects affiliated with the ESF initiative were to study the evolution of the immigrant worker communities and the ethnic identity options of the offspring of the immigrant workers in eight European countries: Austria, Belgium, France, the Federal Republic of Germany, the Netherlands, Sweden, Switzerland and the United Kingdom. At least two different immigrant nationalities were studied in each country. One of the products of the study is the present series of three volumes which address complementary aspects about the future of the new ethnic minorities in a changing European context. This study has been under the leadership of an international and interdisciplinary board of scholars since its inception, among these were Michel Oriol (France), Henri Tajfel (the United Kingdom), and Czarina Wilpert (the Federal Republic of Germany). In addition Julian Pitt-Rivers, Emil Temime and Michael Posner have acted in an advisory capacity.

The first book of the series, *Immigrant Associations in Europe,* studies the social organization and institution building of certain immigrant nationalities in France, the Federal Republic of Germany, the Netherlands, Sweden, Switzerland, and the United Kingdom. This is the first publication on a European level to analyse the internal organization of the immigrant communities and to discuss the ideological alternatives they offer to the following generations. One of the interesting features of this work is that the studies show that immigrant associations are not a transitional phenomenon, but that they gain renewed strength as they come to fulfill changing functions as communities become more established and settled. (Editors: John Rex, University of Warwick, Daniele Joly, University of Warwick and Czarina Wilpert, Technical University of Berlin.)

The second book in the series, *Entering the Working World; Following the descendants of Europe's immigrant labour force,* examines the labour market experiences of the offspring of the immigrant workers, while taking into consideration the different contexts of the labour market framework, economic and policy conditions in each of the European countries in question. At the same time it includes original findings on the training, occupational status, work and mobility orientations of this new generation in comparison to their indigenous peers and the generation of their parents. This book focuses on immigrant and ethnic minority youth in Austria (Turkish and Yugoslav), Belgium (Moroccan and Turkish), the Federal Republic of Germany (Turkish and Yugoslav), Great Britain (Asian and West Indian), and Switzerland (Italian and Spanish youth). (Editor: Czarina Wilpert, Technical University, Berlin.)

The third book in the series, *New Identities in Europe; Immigrant ancestry and the ethnic identity of youth*, presents findings from studies of identification patterns and identity structures of the descendants of immigrants: Finns, Turks and Yugoslavs in Sweden, Muslim Pakistanis and Greek Cypriots in Britain, Turks in the Federal Republic of Germany and Spaniards in the Netherlands. The authors are social psychologists and sociologists. One common point of reference in their studies is the conceptual framework of Identity structure analysis which also offers instruments for empirical research. (Editor: Karmela Liebkind, Helsinki University.)

1 Introduction: The Scope of a Comparative Study

John Rex

The chapters which follow report the findings of a number of teams of social scientists working in different European countries on the nature of immigrant associations. These teams formed part of a larger enterprise concerned with the comparative study of the problem of so-called 'second-generation ethnic identity'. Nearly all the teams involved in this larger enterprise found it necessary to focus their attention in part on the study of associations, and it seemed to them that the topic was important in its own right and that it merited a separate report.

The original intention of the collaborative study was to compare different relatively short-distance migrations of groups with similar cultures (for example Spaniards, Portuguese and Italians to Switzerland, France, Germany and the Netherlands) both with each other and with other migrant groups coming from longer distances, from colonial conditions and from culturally different backgrounds (for example, Pakistanis in Britain, Algerians in France, Afro-Caribbeans in Britain and France, Turks in Germany).

In the event, not all of the studies envisaged were possible within the framework of the collaboration, and evidence on associations was available in the cases of Pakistanis and Greek Cypriots in Britain, Portuguese and Italians in France, Turks in Germany, Spaniards in the Netherlands and Switzerland, and Finns in Sweden. There turned out to be important recurrent themes in all these cases, as will be indicated below, but the differences between them should first also be noted.

The Italian migration to France and the Finish migration to Sweden represent long-established processes of migration between neighbouring and culturally similar countries. The Spanish migration to Switzerland and the Netherlands and that of the Portuguese to France are of more recent origin and typify the period in which north-western European economies grew relatively faster than those of the south, making the southern countries and their people dependent upon the north-west. The migration of Pakistanis to Britain and

Turks to Germany (including West Berlin) was influenced in their associational life at least by the fact of Islam. Pakistanis also came from a formerly colonial background, as did the Greek Cypriots, although in the latter case the religious difference was that between Orthodox and Protestant Christianity rather than between another world religion and Christianity. These differences between the migrations studied might have been expected to produce differences between the types of associational life to be found in the different cases.

A more detailed account of the differences between the various countries can be gained from the quantitative, legal, and institutional background data supplied by the various teams which is now summarized.

Migration to Great Britain
In Great Britain minorities are distinguished according to whether they come from the British Commonwealth or from foreign countries. Additionally, a distinction is made between old and new Commonwealth countries. The latter group of countries are mostly distinguished by the fact that their people had dark skin colour, although they also included people from Cyprus, Malta and Gibraltar, who are usually thought of as white and European. It should also be noted that Pakistan has now left the Commonwealth, but that the British census now groups together those born in the new Commonwealth and Pakistan. In order to count those of new Commonwealth and Pakistani descent, the census gives figures for those living in households with a new Commonwealth or Pakistani head. Obviously the very categories used in the statistics collected reflect the preoccupation of the British government with race and race relations.

Relevant statistics from the 1981 census are shown in Table 1.1 where it can be seen that Pakistanis are the third largest group from the new Commonwealth, numbering with their children 295,461. The number of immigrants born in Cyprus is 84,327 and the total number, together with their British-born children, is about 100,000. The Irish-born number 607,428. Irish immigration to Britain is comparable to Finnish migration to Sweden.

Immigration in Britain was crucially affected by the Commonwealth Immigration Acts of 1962, 1968 and 1971. Before 1962 Commonwealth citizens could settle freely in Britain. After that date vouchers were required. Thus before 1962 there was large-scale migration of workers. After that date only small numbers of voucher holders and dependants of those settled were admitted.

2

Table 1.1 Numbers of immigrants and dependents by national origin

Residents born outside the United Kingdom	3,359,825
Born in the old Commonwealth, resident in Great Britain	152,747
Born in the Irish Republic, resident in Great Britain	607,428
Born in the new Commonwealth or Pakistan, resident in Great Britain	1,513,373
Born in Pakistan, resident in Great Britain	188,198
Born in India, resident in Great Britain	391,874
Born in the Caribbean, resident in Great Britain	295,175
Living in households with new Commonwealth or Pakistani heads	2,207,245
Living in households with Pakistani head	295,461
Born in the Mediterranean new Commonwealth	129,620
Born in Cyprus	84,327
Living in households with a Mediterranean new Commonwealth head	170,078

Source: OPCS census 1981, country of birth, Tables 1 and 3.

Turkish migration to West Germany

'Guestworker', the special term for foreign workers in the Federal Republic of Germany, conveys the notion of the invited and temporary nature of manpower recruitment dependent on the needs and goodwill of the host society. This policy was first institutionalized through a series of treaties between the Federal Republic and the governments of countries in the southern European periphery (Italy 1955, Spain 1960, Greece 1960, Turkey 1961, Portugal 1964, Tunisia 1965, Morocco 1966 and Yugoslavia 1968). Recruitment was at its height in 1973, the year the federal government closed the borders to the entry of any further foreign workers. To carry out the recruitment the German Labour Bureau had established offices in major urban centres of the countries concerned.

A rapid increase of Turkish workers coming into Germany occurred in the five-year period 1968 to 1973. In 1971 the Turks became the largest foreign worker group, when their number first surpassed the Yugoslavs and the Italians. In 1973 the Turkish population reached over 900,000. Return migration, at a rate of 100,000 a year, was more than offset by other Turks sending for their families. As a result, in the fifteen-year period between 1967 and 1982 the Turkish population grew from 172,000 to one and a half million.

Table 1.2   Foreign population in Germany by nationality, 1982

	Foreign-born population (%)	
EEC countries	1,167,037	25.7
Greeks	292,349	6.4
Italians	564,960	12.5
Yugoslavians	612,798	13.5
Moroccons	44,192	1.0
Portuguese	99,529	2.2
Spaniards	165,998	3.7
Turks	1,546,280	34.2
Tunisians	25,269	0.6
Others	1,177,440	26.0

Source: *Bericht zur Ausländerpolitik März* 1984: 74.

Table 1.2 shows the numbers and percentages of the foreign population in Germany according to nationality in 1982.

Italian and Portuguese immigration to France

At the time of the 1982 census, the number of Portuguese citizens resident in France (764,860) ranked second only to the number of Algerians (795,000) among over three and a half million foreigners residing there. Italian citizens (333,740) formed the fourth largest group.

The 3.7 million foreigners[1] recorded in March 1982 represent an increase of 6.9 per cent over the figure recorded in 1975. The relative share of the six largest contingents of foreigners can be seen in Table 1.3.

Italian migration to France had been going on for more than a century. In 1851 there were 63,307 Italians in France, and by 1901 the number had risen to 330,465. The highest recorded number was in 1931, when it was 808,038. It drooped to 450,764 in 1946 and reached a post-war peak of 682,956 in 1962, dropping to 462,940 in 1975 and 333,740 in 1982.

Until about 1960 the most important migration stream into France was from Italy. Taking into consideration persons of Italian origin who have become naturalized French citizens, the size of the Italian community in France is more than one million persons. And, if all the population with Italian origins in previous generations, that is with parents or grandparents born in Italy were included, the Italian 'community' would reach much larger proportions. However, since many Italians have become naturalized, the numbers appearing in the census are relatively low.

Table 1.3   Numbers of foreign residents by country of origin

	Foreign-born population (%)	
Algerians	795,920	21.6
Portuguese	764,860	20.8
Moroccans	431,120	11.7
Italians	333,740	9.1
Spaniards	321,440	8.7
Tunisians	189,400	4.1

Source: *SOPEMI*, 1984, OECD, Paris, p. 23.

Portuguese immigration to France first grew in significance in the 1960s when Italian migration was already on the decline. There was a certain amount of competition among the labour-recruiting countries during this period to obtain foreign manpower. Because of its lower wages and mediocre housing conditions, France lost the Italian and Spanish 'market' to Switzerland and West Germany. As a result, France looked to its former colonies and Portugal for its labour reserves. The political standstill created by Salazarism restricted the free movements of Portuguese abroad forcing the Portuguese emigrants to leave clandestinely. The French, despite their policy of rigid and systematic controls, in order to attract them overlooked their illegal arrival.

Living very often in difficult conditions, but none the less with more autonomy than foreigners officially recruited, more than 880,000 Portuguese lived in France between 1960 and 1974 (560,000 workers, and 314,000 dependants). The period after 1974 saw the closure of the French frontiers to immigration, and in the period between 1975 and 1982 the Portuguese population increased by only 6000. It has now stabilized. The natural increase is offset by the number of losses through return migration and naturalization. As a result the Portuguese population remains young. Forty-five per cent of the Portuguese living in France are under twenty-five years of age.

With respect to their legal status, the Italians profit from their right to free circulation as members of the European Community, whereas the Portuguese, who entered the European community only on 1 January 1986, continue for the time being to be subject to the 'general regulations for foreigners in France' during a transitional period of seven years. Their stay is dependent on procuring a work permit before they depart for France. The accompaniment of family members is equally dependent on preliminary authorization. French authorities are *de facto*, however, often more lenient with the Portuguese than with other foreign nationalities.

5

Finnish migration to Sweden

Finns in Sweden offer an example of a long-established migration by a people to a relatively friendly neighbouring country. There are about a quarter of a million Finnish immigrants living in Sweden. Most of them arrived during the 1960s as a result of extensive change in the industrial structure of Finland and of the difficult employment and housing situation caused by the coming of age of the many people born after the Second World War. From 1946 a total of 445,000 Finns moved to Sweden. This movement, however, was accompanied by return migration. At times, including the present, the return flow is actually larger than the migration to Sweden. During the post-war period, 201,900 migrants have returned to Finland. The flow of migration was at its peak during the 1960s, when the gross migration to Sweden was almost 100,000. In 1969 and 1970 alone some 80,000 Finns moved to Sweden.

It should be noted that the labour market agreement ratified in 1954 guaranteed free labour mobility among the Nordic countries.

There is some difficulty in defining a Swedish Finn. In 1981 there were 246,362 Finnish-born persons living in Sweden. If, however, Finnish citizens born in Sweden are also counted, the number rises to 290,000. If Finnish citizens born in Finland but living in Sweden are considered, together with those who have at least one parent born in Finland, Swedish Finns total about 380,000.

Swedish Finns form the largest group of immigrants in Sweden. They account for about half of the total. The next largest groups are the Yugoslavs, the Danes, the Turks, the Poles, the Greeks and the West Germans. All these groups number less than 40,000.

Spanish migration to Switzerland and the Netherlands

Latin America was the primary destination of Spanish emigrants prior to 1960. Between 1905 and 1914 they numbered 1.6 million. In the period 1950 to 1960 there were still half a million such emigrants.

Since 1960, however, Spanish migration to other European countries has grown rapidly. By 1971 about one million Spanish people had migrated to European countries including 569,144 to France, 147,447 to West Germany, 112,996 to Switzerland, 67,563 to Belgium, 51,329 to Great Britain and 29,442 to the Netherlands.

Switzerland

In 1981 Switzerland had 26,721 Spanish immigrants with Permission A (for nine months only), 25,567 with Permission B (to be renewed yearly) and 73,099 with Permission C (permission to stay without limitation).

The Spanish were the second largest group after the Italians who numbered 483,066.

Spanish immigrants come from Galicia (24 per cent) Castile (15 per cent) Andalucía (11 per cent) and León (11 per cent), i.e. predominantly from the least developed Spanish regions.

Swiss policy on immigration is based upon the needs of the Swiss economy, and the Swiss government recognizes at least a part of its migrant labour force as only temporary and subject to repatriation. This has led to the departure of 280,000 immigrants, including 77,000 Spaniards. Legislation on immigration is still based upon the First Law on Foreign People passed after the First World War. A new and more liberal law was proposed in 1974 but was rejected in a referendum in 1982. An extreme right-wing party, Action Nationale, actively stirred up xenophobic feelings in opposing this law.

The Netherlands
Spanish migration to the Netherlands started moderately in the decade 1950 to 1960, reached its peak in the next decade and then went down slowly in the decade 1970 to 1980 after the closure of the frontiers to new immigrants. There has also been return emigration, so the Spanish immigrant population went down from 39,000 in 1970 to 24,000 in 1980.

Until recently, official government policy rested upon two fundamental ideas:

—guestworkers are only temporarily in the Netherlands, functioning as an economic buffer;
—the Netherlands is not an immigration country.

The first of these ideas was modified in a policy statement presented to parliament in 1983, which suggests that most minority people have come to stay, and that they should have an equal place in society and full opportunities for development. The objectives of this policy involve recognizing the cultures of minority groups, preventing discrimination and encouraging development in social and economic terms.

The second idea, however, is still maintained. There is therefore a very strict policy with regard to the admission of foreigners.

Common themes in the study of associations
Despite the differences in the structure of the various migrations discussed in the chapters which follow it is possible to detect recurrent themes in all of them.

Perhaps the first point to notice is that associational life in the migrant communities exists within what perhaps is the most fundamental structural element of all, namely the structure of kinship. Those who migrate retain links with their homeland, those who remain in the homeland are concerned with the fate of their migrant kin, and a complex process involving holiday visits, letters and verbally transmitted messages and the return of the dead of the homeland for burial arises to sustain and reproduce the kinship structure in a new form.

Such kinship links at first make the business of forming formal associations redundant, but there are from the outset larger structures which are extended from the homeland to the country of settlement which help to systematize provision for migrant needs. This is particularly true of churches and political bodies.

Migration in nearly all cases involves some degree of difference between the religion of the migrants and that of the country of settlement. This is most obviously so in the case of Muslim migrants to a Christian country, but it is also the case within Christianity. The Greek Orthodox Cypriots in Britain confront western Protestant Christianity, and Roman Catholic migrants may settle in Protestant countries and find their religion alien. Even when Protestants migrate to Protestant countries and Catholics to Catholic countries, however, there is a sense of belonging to different congregations.

In these cases, migrants will combine with their fellows to establish familiar forms of prayer and worship in their new environments, and the religious organization of the homeland will take active steps to ensure the continued adherence and faithfulness of their migrating members. The first duty of a migrating Muslim is to establish places of prayer in his land of settlement, and it is not long before mosques and centres of Qur'anic instruction proliferate where they settle. Similarly Orthodox and Catholic missions quickly arise amongst immigrant communities.

The state of origin may also act to provide for the needs of migrants abroad and to assume consular duties on their behalf. Together with this, however, it may seek to supervise the migrants politically. This will be particularly necessary from the state's point of view where some of the migrants see themselves in part at least as political refugees. The state will also be concerned that the migrant community does not become a political base for revolution. Apart from this, however, the state will be under pressure from the migrants' kinfolk to act on their behalf and it may be involved, together with the government of the country of settlement, in the recruitment and welfare of labour.

The refugee aspect of migration is very often present even when the primary motive for migration is economic. All of the countries of immigrant origin discussed here, apart from Finland, have had or still have military dictatorships, and all have or have had clandestine political parties, which have an opportunity to flourish in exile that is denied to them at home. Communist parties also arise in all cases (including the Finns), as may be expected amongst workers who have suffered political persecution and hardship at home and severe exploitation abroad. In fact the Communist party is often the source of immigrant association formation and vies with the church in its attempt to organize the workers.

By no means all associations, however, have these political or religious sources. Immigrants have directly experienced needs and will organize to provide for these themselves or to persuade the government of the country of settlement to provide for them. This will be the case in regard to the search for jobs, housing, sports facilities and education for their children. Apart from such material needs, however, they will also be concerned with providing a link above the level of kinship between migrant communities and their home villages or regions. Such associations will seek to reproduce in the new country aspects of the homeland culture through festivals, the provision of meeting places and the maintenance of homeland customs. They will also help to organize travel and burial clubs to ensure, what the Franco–Italian report called, the 'bilaterality of references'.

Of these associations much the most powerful are those concerned with educational facilities. On the one hand, they will seek to enhance and enlarge the opportunities provided by education within the community of settlement. On the other, they will provide supplementary schooling to ensure the maintenance of the mother tongue and cultural and religious distinctiveness. Religious organizations and parties of the right and the left will compete to control organizations of this kind.

The maintenance of kinship links, the intervention of homeland religious and political organizations and the flourishing of spontaneously formed associations amongst migrants all serve to create a striking possibility, namely that the very boundaries of political organization as they have been understood in the nation state will be undermined and that, apart from citizens of states of the normal sort, it will have to be accepted for many generations that there are whole communities maintaining links with two countries or living in a diaspora which is a more important focus for identity than any nationality.

In its origins the present collaborative research programme was concerned precisely with this problem of identity. In the view of some of the collaborating teams, the striking fact about their migration studies is precisely the emergence of a new immigrant identity. Others would emphasize that the migrant lives within and perhaps between two cultures, apparently integrated with the country of settlement and its political system, yet at the same time maintaining an outside loyalty.

9

The study of associations is particularly important in this respect. The associations may be seen *inter alia* as offering newly defined identity options to migrants, each individual association having its own particular nuance in the options which it offers. There remains, however, the question of whether particular migrants and more especially migrants' children accept these options. This theme is one which will be taken up in a separate set of reports produced for the European Science Foundation, but it is dealt with in part both in the British studies and in the studies of Spanish immigrants to Switzerland and the Netherlands reported here.

The final point to be noted, however, is that the governments of the countries of settlement do not remain passive so far as the formation of immigrant associations is concerned. They will seek to provide for the needs which immigrant associations exist to satisfy, and they may well seek to supervise and police the activities of the associations. Thus, after the first decade or so of immigration one usually finds the emergence of new state welfare associations and a new focus for the activity of immigrant associations, whose main activity often becomes that of gaining any benefits which are on offer. In this way the potentially secessionist tendency within the immigrant community is overcome through a new pattern of clientage and patronage.

Another aspect of the integration of the migrant group into the nation of the country of settlement results from the growth of migrants' involvement in the economy. The needs of migrants lead to the growth of new specialized businesses which provide for food needs, for cultural items of all kinds and for travel, at the same time as filling niches within the host economy. The existence of such businesses, if they transcend pariah status, may well give rise to class differentiation within the migrant community and to the possibility of businessmen on the one hand and workers on the other forming alliances with their equivalents in the country of settlement.

The process of incorporating the immigrant minority community into the state and the transcendence of ethnic bonds by those of class, however, has hardly begun and it is by no means certain that either of these processes will be strong enough to destroy what seem to be resilient forms of ethnic community and association. For this reason, the studies of associations which follow represent a valuable contribution to the political sociology of contemporary Europe.

Notes

1   These figures are based on census data as reported by the French National Office for Statistics (INSEE) to the OECD. The figures available from the Ministry of Internal Affairs (SOPEMI, 1984, OECD, p. 100), which estimate the foreign population on the basis of valid resident permits for foreigners over sixteen years of age, are larger. This was 4,459,000 in 1982.

2 Asian and Greek Cypriot Associations and Identity

John Rex and Sasha Josephides

The theoretical problem in the British study*
The study of associations within the European Science Foundation's Additional Activity on Second Generation Identity emerged in an unusual way, and it is even possible that the British studies of the Pakistani and Kashmiri and the Greek Cypriot community were based upon a misunderstanding. It is well, therefore, that these studies should be introduced by indicating what it was in the original study, undertaken by the Institut d'Études et de Recherches Interethniques et Interculturelles (IDERIC) team in Nice, that attracted the attention of British collaborators and how they reinterpreted the problem.

The IDERIC team undertook to study second-generation identity by means of a three-fold approach including socio-historical, social anthropological and socio-institutional studies. The third of these approaches was to focus on immigrant associations amongst Italian and Portuguese immigrants in France.

The British response to the request for collaboration with the IDERIC team was to take up particularly its emphasis upon the study of associations and to seek to relate this to 'second-generation identity'. It was suggested that *inter alia* associations might be seen as proposing 'identity options' and that, if these were made clear, it would then be possible to investigate how far samples of 'second-generation' people, or young people born or educated in the country of settlement, accepted these options. To some extent it was also envisaged that there would be aspects here too of the social-anthropological approach and the socio-historical approach of the French studies. From the outset, it was felt that formal associations represented too restricted a focus, and that a study of these should be supplemented by a study of representative families and their networks. Apart from the verbalized identity options formulated by associations, it was thought there was also much to be gained by studying the way in which the social life and the psychological orientations of migrants

---

* by John Rex

were affected by and affected the meanings of cultural symbols transmitted from the migrants' homeland. This latter interest seemed to coincide with the particular meaning attached to the notion of a socio-historical approach by the IDERIC team.

Whether there are common themes involved in the study of associations or in the study of social networks or in the study of transmitted symbols will emerge both in the British reports and in related chapters produced by various collaborating teams. The aim of this section will be to consider the sociological meaning attaching to some of the terms which are assumed in the naïve statement of the research problem given above. The fact of the matter is that, although the notion of associations and their effect on identity is widely accepted as pointing to a real problem, that problem is not clearly defined and hence leads to much argument of an ideological sort. A discussion of the precise meaning to be attached to some of the central sociological terms will, it is hoped, help to dispel some of this ideological confusion. Necessarily any such attempt at this stage can only provide a basis for discussion rather than finally determining all the issues, but it is to be hoped that a clear statement of one British view will stimulate others in the European teams to make their own theoretical positions clear. This may help in clarifying the basis for future comparative research.

An initial issue which must be faced is the possibility of a division of opinion along the lines of the major split in European social science methodology, namely that between structuralist explanations and those of a 'methodologically individualist' sort. This chapter is written by a sociologist (Rex 1961) much influenced by the work, theories and methodology of Max Weber (1968) and obviously belongs within the camp of methodological individualism. When it refers to social structure and social relations it uses these terms in the sense in which they are used in anthropology by Radcliffe-Brown (1952) as meaning the network of social relations between individual human beings (or typical individual human beings) engaged in meaningful action. In principle, such a view of structure is very different from that popularized both by structuralists such as Claude Lévi-Strauss (1966; see also Glucksmann 1974) and by structural functionalists like Talcott Parsons (1952) who are ultimately concerned with the relations between parts of a system, even though in practice they make reference to the relations between actors engaged in meaningful action.

This approach to the theory of associations involves a choice and may not satisfy those who feel that explanation is achieved only when reference is made to the structure of a system. But, as one distinguished positivist (Lundberg 1939) once put it, 'the need for explanation ceases when the curiosity comes to rest'. For the present writer, curiosity is not satisfied by explanations of a structuralist or systemic sort. Even when explanations are given in these terms it appears to me that the concepts of structure and system need to be further unpacked so that they yield what Weber called 'explanations which are adequate on the level of meaning', that is to say explanations in terms of the action of individual hypothetical actors.

What then is the problem of second-generation identity and how may it be better defined sociologically in terms of concepts defined in this way?

Most of us share the view that, where there is a community of immigrants physically located in a country different from that in which they were born, and having to perform roles within the country of settlement, while at the same time retaining links with their homeland, these immigrants are likely to have problems of 'identity'. By the term 'identity' as we use it here, we refer to the fact that they answer the questions 'Who am I?' or 'What kind of person am I?' in particular ways. Common sense also suggests that the identity commitment of the children of immigrants might not be the same as that of the immigrants themselves and that these children might be cross-pressured, having, on the one hand, to live up to the expectations of their parents and, on the other, to fit in with their peers in the receiving society.

Unfortunately when setting out to do empirical research on the 'identity' of immigrants or their children, these rather loose definitions prove inadequate for the formulation of research questions. In particular, it is necessary to know whether the primary object of the enquiry is sociological or political, on the one hand, or psychological, on the other. The main psychological questions would be 'How far do these individuals succeed in incorporating in their personality systems their feeling of belonging to groups of different sorts?' and 'What kinds of problem arise on the personality level as a result of these feelings of belonging?' The main sociological or political question on the other hand is 'To what national or sub-national society do these individuals belong?'

Our own emphasis has been on the sociological and political questions. But even though it is, the distinction is not an absolute one. For what, after all, does the term 'belong' mean? Clearly 'belonging to' or even 'membership of' a group implies some concept of a psychological state. What has to be done in the first place is to distinguish between a number of different types of social structure and relationship which may involve differing degrees of psychological commitment. It is with this in mind, as well as the need to achieve clarity of definition, that it is necessary to define more precisely the terms 'social networks', 'society', 'social system', 'cultural system', 'personality system', 'association' and 'community'.

The term 'network', as it is used here of course, refers to relationships which arise between individuals in the course of meaningful action. Radcliffe-Brown, in defining 'structure' as a sociological term, uses it to refer to social relations of this kind. Participation in a network of social relations, however, does not, of itself, have immediate implications for the 'identity' of the participants. It may involve no more than 'responding to the demands of' or 'taking account of the behaviour of' another and thus, while it may mean altering a plan of action or the action-orientation of the individual involved, it does not necessarily have any implications for his or her identity. In more systematically organized social relations, on the other hand, the individual may come to be thought of as playing a role, which means acting in ways which are required by the whole group of participants or by the normative order governing their behaviour. In this case obligations are involved and these might have significance for the personality system. None the less it is implicit in the very notion of role, which involves the metaphor of acting in a play, that actions involved relate only to the particular constrained circumstance of that performance and cannot, of themselves, determine the identity of the subject. It is an individual's whole complex of different roles deriving from situations and their relationship to drives, interests and so on which is thought of as making up the personality system, including the notion of the self of which the individual is aware, which is normally thought of as constituting his other identity. Important though the concepts of network and role are, therefore, they cannot be expected by themselves to tell us very much about a central psychological concept like identity.

The term 'society' is the most comprehensive term used in sociology and refers to a complex network of social relations thought of as a bounded system. Of itself it has no implications for 'identity', although it must be assumed that where a society exists there must be some numerical compatibility between the roles that are required of individuals by the whole society or social system and those that well-integrated and functioning personality systems require. The work of Talcott Parsons (1952) is especially interesting in that it seeks to outline systematically the socialization processes through which individuals are thought of as coming to want those basic things which are necessary for social order. Even in the Parsonian scheme, however, it is not suggested that the well-integrated personality is completely the product of the needs of the social system, and a radical variant of the Parsonian scheme would go further and allow for a situation in which a well-integrated personality might actually be at odds with the demands of the social system. The study of societies and total social systems, therefore, will not of itself tell us much about the personality systems of individuals or about their sense of identity.

It is worth while at this point to consider the relationship not merely of society and personality, but the complex three-fold relationship between society, culture and personality. Here again Talcott Parsons is a useful guide (Parsons and Shils 1951). So far as the term 'culture' is concerned, I am happy to go on using E.B. Tyler's definition, 'that complex whole which includes art, knowledge, beliefs, morals, law and any other set of capabilities acquired by man as a member of society'. Such a complex whole may be thought of as having an existence independent of any particular context of interaction. It also has its own independent dynamic. Just as there are tensions between the systematic demands of the social system and the personality system, so the cultural system may be seen as related to, but in tension with, both the social system and the personality system. Interaction in a social system is obviously affected by the kind of culture and cultural system which the social actors inherit. It is not, however, determined by it. Similarly, the personality system of individuals is to some extent affected but is not wholly determined by culture. In studying 'identity', therefore, it should be taken into account what knowledge is available about the whole society and its inherited culture, but it should not be possible to extrapolate from knowledge of society or culture to knowledge about the personality system.

If, therefore, we are concerned with the relationship between sociological and cultural concepts and personality system concepts like 'identity' we clearly have to look at more limited and specific social structures than are suggested by generalized concepts like 'society' and 'social network'. It is in this context that the role of associations should be considered, which the terms of reference of our study suggest should have some implications for identity. Here, I would suggest, the sociological tradition is somewhat negative about the effect of associations on personality and personal identity, and it is necessary, therefore, to note that when speaking of associations as having this effect the term may be being used in a somewhat special sense.

The main tradition of the study of associations in sociology is that which derives from the work of Tonnies (1955) who holds that the concept of association involves precisely an absence of the kind of commitment suggested by the concept of identity. It is, for him, in 'community' where 'the real will' is involved that the individual has a sense of belonging, or when he may feel that his group membership defines his self. By contrast associations rest upon the adoption and pursuit of specialized purposes or, as Tonnies puts it, they rest upon 'artificial will'.

Tonnies's conception of social evolution was either tragic or romantic. Either modern man was to be thought of as doomed to loss of selfhood because of his loss of community or ways had to be found of returning to the golden age of *gemeinschaft*. Durkheim (1973) took a more realistic and, perhaps, a more optimistic view. The contractual ties of modern society were thought of as nevertheless involving a kind of solidarity, both between individuals and between the individual and the group. Commitment to separate and specialized social groups was for him a way of belonging to the wider social system and in his *Division of Labour in Society* (1973) he envisaged the possibility that occupational groups should have a central role in the socialization and moral education of the individual. More fundamentally in his study *Suicide* (1952), he discussed as the background of 'egoistic' suicide a kind of society in which the individual *without group support* was required to develop an individual conscience which would enable him to function effectively in society. In this kind of society, group membership of any kind is of as little relevance as the Catholic confessional.

It is important to the study of immigrant associations that we should be clear about the contrasts which can be drawn first between Tonnies and the Durkheim of the *Division of Labour in Society* and then between Tonnies and the more radically individualistic Durkheim of *Suicide*. The first of these contrasts is of very great importance for the study of immigrant associations, but the second, too, may be of some importance in relation to the identity problems of the second generation in a secular and individualistic society.

For Tonnies, commitment of the individual to the group of a kind which involves the self or 'the real will' is only possible to community, and the trend of history is away from community to 'society' or 'association'. For Durkheim a special role is assigned to smaller and more immediate groups than a relatively amorphous community. These smaller groups may socialize the individual to perform a specialized role, but this specialized role itself has moral significance within a larger pattern of social solidarity. It is only in an undifferentiated society that the individual belongs directly to the whole and this form of belonging, called 'mechanical solidarity', involves the undeniable condition that all individuals have to be the same. The smaller and more intimate grouping to which individuals belong, and through which they were socialized and received their identity, was first provided by the extended kinship group, but since such groups have declined in significance in advanced societies, their role would have to be undertaken by occupational groups.

The immigrant associations which we are concerned with studying may perhaps be thought of as playing for immigrant populations something like the role which Durkheim assigned to occupational groups. Clearly they do play some role in the socialization of the individual and offer him some kind of answer to the question 'Who am I?' At first sight they may perhaps be distinguished from occupational groups, as there is not necessarily any complementarity between immigrant associations and groups within the society of settlement. They may indeed be in conflict. But it is also possible to conceive of immigrant groups in a complex society as united with that society in terms of a cultural division of labour rather than merely being in conflict with it. *Per contra*, Durkheim would have argued that, although the complementarity and integration of minority groups was an ideal, as a matter of empirical fact they were often in conflict with one another. It does make some sense then to see the immigrant associations and community structure as forming the intimate small-scale group which has moral influence over the individual and which yet integrates him with a larger society.

More troubling is the alternative suggested by the more radically individualistic Durkheim in *Suicide*. It should be noted that the individual who is posited there is not thought of as being without moral regulation. It is for the individual in that state that Durkheim reserves the term 'anomie'. The individual in the egoistic society is subject to the dictates of his own conscience which has itself been moulded by society. He has no priest or occupational group to turn to, but is in continual conversation with his own socially-installed conscience. David Riesman (1950) once nicely described this state when he suggested an 'inner-directed individual' who was guided by a kind of internal gyroscope.

Many people in modern secularized societies are in fact like this. They do not need interaction with a group on a continuing basis because some kind of group, some kind of social control has been installed in their heads. Such a state may be difficult to sustain. It produces a lonely life. But it is possible, and it is the ideal which Christian Protestant culture has diffused very widely. It also has to be distinguished sharply from 'anomie' or living in a state of normlessness.

These contrasts are of considerable importance for the young generation in immigrant populations, because they are to be thought of not only as moving from the moral influence of immigrant groups to the influence of groups within the host society. They are also becoming more individualized and secularized and to rely more on their own individual consciences. There is also, of course, the possibility that they may lose contact with norms altogether and slip into a state of anomie.

Before these questions are considered further on the psychological level, however, further consideration should be given to the actual structure of immigrant associations. The first thing to notice about them is that they are not simply associations in the Tonnies sense. They are much more like what he calls communities or at least like the occupational groups in the earlier Durkheim. They are not simply a social instrument. They do actually exert moral authority over the individual and help to define his identity for him. Perhaps, then, it is as well that before proceeding further the meaning of the terms 'community' and 'primary community' are considered.

Robert MacIver (1939) once sought to define a community as a group within which the individual could live his whole life and in which members had a subjective feeling of a shared territory and a shared history. He also thought of it as very much tied to place. Such a definition works in relation to villages and nations which have not been disturbed by population movements. What seems to be characteristic of immigrant populations, however, is that their sense of history and of place is one in which they see themselves as having a different history and a different loyalty to place than the majority around them.

We must now ask, however, how far MacIver's notion that the individual lives his whole life within the community applies to the minority group. Clearly it cannot. The immigrant must work in an impersonal and alien society. He is subject to the government and its law. These are features of his 'whole life'. What then constitutes the special nature of the minority community?

Clearly the central point is that the individual feels a sense of moral obligation to the group. Fulfilment of duties in a wider context rests upon the fact that they are in accordance with interests, or they are backed by impersonal sanctions. This is the public domain within which the individual must live for instrumental purposes. The immigrant minority community, on the other hand, is a group to which the individual feels he is morally bound. To deny its claims would be to deny his own ideal self. In Parsons's terms (Parsons, Shils and Bales 1953) whereas the wider pattern of social interaction may be concerned with 'goal-attainment', 'adaptation' and 'integration', interaction within the immigrant community has to do with 'pattern maintenance and tension management'.

This is true, of course, not only in relation to the immigrant community, but of all primary communities. MacIver is, in fact, wrong in his suggestion that an individual's whole life can be lived within 'community'. But it is through community that the individual receives emotional and social support and through which he is socialized into acceptance of the values of his society as a whole.

In fact, however, the boundaries of the private communal domain have been pushed further and further back in individualist and secular societies so that very often the isolated conjugal family constitutes the sole remnant of *gemeinschaft*. Durkheim groped after the idea of finding some group beyond this which would have such a character. What is found in the immigrant community is that it does still play this role. However much its limitations in this respect in relation to the young generations may be emphasized, it is still true that the springs of *gemeinschaft* are far more evident amongst ethnic minority immigrants in industrial society than they are in the host community.

The points we are making here are made in a far stronger form about colonial society by J.S. Furnivall. For him it is characteristic of these societies that relations in the market place are entirely impersonal, if not actually 'nasty, brutish and short', but that this only serves to emphasize the warmth and the moralizing influence of the separate communities. What is being said here is that something similar is the case amongst immigrant communities when they first settle in industrial societies.

A more detached analysis of 'community', however, must involve the recognition that it is not simply an undifferentiated whole. It develops its own special agencies for dealing with the problems of its members and their relationship to the larger society (both the society of settlement and the society of origin).

In a somewhat functionalist analysis of these special agencies or associations (Rex 1973) I once suggested that they fulfilled four main functions. These were overcoming social isolation, helping individuals in the solution of personal and material problems, combining to defend the group's interests in conflict and bargaining with the wider society, and maintaining and developing shared patterns of meaning. In a later study (Rex and Tomlinson 1974) in which I was more inclined to emphasize conflict with and alienation from the host society I saw these associations as much more concerned with the third of these functions, that is with organizing defensive and offensive conflict with the society of settlement, but also as maintaining and strengthening links with the society of the homeland.

So far as the more adaptive functions are concerned in most societies these are accomplished in part by kinship groups. This would certainly have been the case for many of the immigrant groups before their migration. When, however, as in the process of immigration, kinship ties are fractured, the task may be performed by organizations set up specially as well as by other more informal networks and it is this kind of structure subordinate to the 'moral community' which is usually referred to as the associational life of the immigrants.

We have not, in the British project, confined ourselves to formal organizations in our study of associations. Indeed there are no formal organizations in the sense of organizations registered with and approved by the government. When one has this type of freedom of association, moreover, it is very difficult to draw a line between those forms of collective activity which merit the title of association and those which do not. We should be prepared to apply our mode of analysis not merely to churches, workers' associations or welfare associations, but also to more ephemeral groups such as the clientele of public houses, groups which meet for house parties, or football teams.

The formal mode of analysis which we have had in mind on looking at these associations is that suggested by Malinowski (1944) as a mode of analysing what he calls 'institutions'. For each one of the groups or forms of collective activity we should seek to discover the group's charter (that is its formally declared purpose), its personnel (the division of labour between office holders and the relation of these to the members and clientele), its norms (the rules under which the collective action is pursued and duties distributed amongst the personnel), its material apparatus (the physical means of action and the property system governing it), the actual activities performed, and, finally and crucially the 'function'.

Malinowski uses the term function to draw attention to the fact that the objectives actually realized by groups and collective activities are not necessarily those which are emphasized in the charter. As researchers, therefore, we often have to exercise our judgment as to what function a group is actually performing. But this is not merely a matter of the charter making hypocritical assertions. Quite commonly a group does attain the ends of its charter, but achieves other ends as well. Thus, though, in terms of the adaptive functions which was suggested above, a church might have as its main charter-purpose the affirmation of values and beliefs, one may also act as a welfare organization or an immigrants' trade union. Again a sports club might also be a means of affirming beliefs and values or it may be a welfare organization.

There is no doubt that a set of studies concerned with the identity and affiliations of members of the second generation amongst minority or immigrant groups should study the structure and dynamics of these associations and the way in which they express the spirit of the community in all their complexity. But perhaps the most important aspect of all is that which I have referred to as involving the affirmation of values, meanings and beliefs.

What is involved here is something wide-ranging and complex. In fact it includes almost everything referred to as culture. Within that culture, however, there are many different aspects. The one that most concerns us is that the value system which is being affirmed gives answers to the questions 'What kind of a man/woman am I and how do I differ from other men and women?' and 'What are the ideal standards of conduct which should govern the behaviour of people of my sort?' In so far as the developing group culture of the immigrant community answers these questions it may be said to be offering the individual 'identity options'. Obviously one of the prime concerns of our study should be to discover what these identity options are. They may involve saying 'You are a Kashmiri', 'You are a Muslim', 'You are from a respectable religious family', 'You belong to an oppressed and exploited group' and so on.

The study of associations, their belief systems, ideologies and behaviour is obviously a useful way of studying 'identity options'. It would be wrong, however, to suppose that it was the only way. We emphasized above that 'associations' become important for immigrants because, to some extent, extended kinship ties were fractured. But they are not for all families, and whether they are or not, there remain large numbers of individuals who are neither members nor clients of associations. In their case we have to study their kinship groups and more informal community ties.

For many, too, the cultural interpretation of their life experiences may not be expressed in purely verbal form at all. They may get their sense of identity from the cultural symbols which they take for granted in their everyday life. These symbols are physically visible to the fieldworker who must record them and also perform the hermeneutic task of interpreting their cultural meaning. Anyone who has walked down the main street of Kreuzberg, the Turkish Quarter of West Berlin, or the Ladypool Road in Sparkbrook, Birmingham, will understand what is meant here. Grocers' shops, cafés, photocopying shops, video centres, tailors' shops, Muslim instruction centres, welfare offices, all serve to tell the story of what it is to be a Muslim immigrant, not merely to the sociological observer, but to the immigrants themselves.

We should see then that any serious attempt to follow the socio-institutional approach suggested by our French colleagues and to study associations inevitably becomes merged in a more general anthropological study. We would say that in our study of the Pakistani and Kashmiri and the Greek Cypriot communities in Britain we have not so much made a study of associations but have carried out an anthropological study focusing especially on associations. Thus Dr Joly's study (Chapter 4) which is centred around an actual questionnaire to associations is supplemented by prolonged and sensitive interviews and case studies, while Dr Josephides, though proceeding in

21

the style of an anthropologist interviewing families in depth, none the less does include the study of Greek Cypriot associations in her overall study (see Chapter 3).

So far we have spoken about identity options on offer in the immigrant communities. To say that the meaning system within an immigrant community offers identity options, however, is by no means to say that any individual's sense of identity is automatically determined by them.

Firstly, it has to be noted that the options on offer may differ sharply from one another or even contradict one another. Secondly, the individual may make a very partial and ambiguous response to the options offered. Thirdly, he or she may be torn between taking up the options offered in the immigrant community and those offered outside. Fourthly, he or she may have moved along the path of secularization towards a state in which individual conscience rather than group norms govern his or her behaviour. All of these elements have to be taken into account in the study of immigrant identity, and still more in the study of so-called second-generation identity.

To carry out a study of the responses of youth to available identity options, two strategies were envisaged by the British team. One was that the fieldworkers in the Pakistani/Kashmiri study and the Greek Cypriot study should develop a questionnaire to be submitted to samples of youth drawn from these communities and to control groups of English young people as well as conducting informal interviews and group discussions with them. The other was the use of a highly-developed formal technique called Identity Structure Analysis.

Identity Structure Analysis was developed in the Social Science Research Council's Research Unit on Ethnic Relations in Bristol by Dr Peter Weinreich (Weinreich 1980). It has now been widely used in a number of countries and several of the teams in the present European Science Foundation (ESF) activity will have used it. (The ESF studies using Identity Structure Analysis and other similar techniques will be reported in a separate volume to be edited for the ESF by Dr Karmela Liebkind of the University of Helsinki. Here we are only concerned to indicate its role in the present study.)

Identity Structure Analysis is a flexible but well-structured technique for gathering information about the identity responses of individuals. It is flexible in that the 'entities' which it asks individuals to 'construe' may very well include items to which the identity options mentioned above refer. That is to say that, when it is known what these options and appropriate entities are, they may be included in the schedule submitted to an individual and it would then be possible to discover how he or she construes them. The instrument used then also collects a great deal of information about identification, identity conflicts and so on and can produce for that individual a number of precise indices of his or her identity structure. A complete programme is available to work out these indices from the data collected.

Identity Structure Analysis has been used for both social psychological and clinical purposes. It cannot be said that we are not interested in the clinically interesting conclusions which it produces. It would in fact be interesting to know whether a percentage of individuals had high indices of identity diffusion or foreclosure (which individuals are for Weinreich 'vulnerable'). None the less, our main concern would be with those who were not vulnerable, yet showed a range of responses to the identity options on offer. This is why some considerable time has been spent by the team's social psychologist in working with the two other fieldworkers to find out what are the main identity options on offer in their communities. This enables him to include, in this study, entities which are known to be important to the comments and not just those which the youth subjects might think of or which were introduced a priori. The specific use of Identity Structure Analysis here would be to see how Pakistani/Kashmiri youth and Greek Cypriots were responding to the cultural symbols and identity signals emerging from the study of these communities.

It is now possible to summarize what is involved in the British study as a whole. Our conclusions as to how the work should be conducted are as follows:

1   The study of associations of a formal kind divorced from the notion of a more inclusive community cannot be particularly relevant to the study of identity.

2   Associations in an immigrant community context should be studied as one of the means through which the culture and meaning system of the immigrant community is expressed. Other such means are kinship, friendship and neighbourhood groups.

3   The study of associations, though central, needs to be supplemented by regular anthropological studies of kinship, social networks and cultural symbols.

4   The special significance of both the study of associations and surrounding anthropological work is that they are directed to discovering the identity options which are on offer.

5   The existence of such identity options is thought to be an important factor in shaping the personality and identity of individuals. The extent to which they are so shaped, however, is seen as depending on the social situation and the interests of the individuals concerned as well as on the constraints of their personality processes. The actual extent to which the behaviour of

individuals, and particularly second-generation individuals, is affected by identity options has therefore to be studied independently. This may include questionnaires of a fairly informal kind, specific to the communities involved, but, in the British study, it also includes Identity Structure Analysis, modified to take account of the kind of entities which emerge in the two community studies.

The final object of a study such as that envisaged here is to make a contribution to political sociology. What we are seeking to do is to discover the extent to which both the first and the second generation in immigrant communities are likely to be assimilated into the mainstream culture and society, to withdraw from it in a permanent cultural enclave maintaining its connections with another country, or to fight for its own interests by mobilizing and maintaining ethnic solidarity.

We do not believe that these objectives are very different from those of our colleagues in the French teams or those studying Finns in Sweden or Turks in Berlin. Their studies have occurred in different circumstances and have enjoyed certain advantages and also suffered from restrictions and limitations which we have not. This account of our theoretical approach and the papers which follow are offered in the hope that they may be of use to our colleagues in the ESF teams, and more widely. We too will learn from the different approaches reflected in their papers. But there can be no doubt that the problem which brought the various European teams together is an important one, and that the various studies described in this book as a whole will provide a valuable first venture in a field of study which is likely to be of increasing interest to social scientists in the future.

Before reporting on the study of associations in the Pakistani and Greek Cypriot communities, some of the general problems facing south Asian and Greek Cypriot immigrants to Britain must now be indicated.

The sociological background to Asian and Greek Cypriot settlement
*The Asians**
South Asian immigrants to Great Britain may be divided by nationality, religion and language. They may come from India, Pakistan, Bangladesh or Kashmir. They may be Hindus, Sikhs or Muslims. They may speak Punjabi, Gujarati, Urdu, Bengali, Pashto or one of a number of other minority languages. This may well mean that patterns of adjustment, adaptation and acculturation may be significantly different according to the nationality, religion and language of

* by John Rex

24

the individual or the group concerned. Before we refer to these differences, however, there are a great many features common to all these groups, which constitute their 'Asian-ness' or 'Indian-ness' with which we must be concerned.

The first point to notice is that there is no fatalistic acceptance amongst these immigrants that their forms of communal organization and culture will collapse in the face of a 'superior' or more 'modern' form of social organization and culture. Their culture is rooted in world religions, which it must be assumed are as unlikely to die out as Christianity itself. If it does not fit easily into the pattern of social organization of secular western societies, it is none the less relevant in the event of return to the sub-continent or, and, perhaps even more important, to living in the diaspora. There is therefore no reason to suppose that the various forms of 'Indian' culture and social organization will die out in three generations as has often been the case with the emigration of southern Europeans to the northern European countries or of Europeans to the United States.

The maintenance of this culture and the attendant forms of social organization is not of course incompatible with participation in the society of settlement. Such participation is essential if men (and, to a lesser extent, women) are to earn their living and to protect their right to earn that living. This means that in all these south Asian groups there is likely to be active participation in trade unions and business organizations and in political parties, and a strongly instrumental attitude towards education so that children may be able to achieve the maximum by way of employment opportunities.

All these groups have participated very actively in the life of trade unions. Particularly amongst Punjabi immigrants, those who have arrived have come with strong traditions of workers' organizations behind them. Very often this is based upon some type of Indian Marxism. This had led naturally to the formation of Marxist-led Indian workers' associations (IWAs), which, though they have other purposes than purely trade union ones, and though they are concerned with Indian as well as British problems, are the main means whereby Indian workers relate to their fellow workers and their employers. The IWAs often function as unions within unions, seeking to ensure that Indian workers are adequately represented in the union's committees and amongst shop stewards, and that the union adequately represents and protects the special interests of immigrants. There is always the possibility that Indian workers may be concentrated in particular low-grade jobs and on particular shifts and that the union will tolerate low standards there. The IWA seeks to ensure through its activity in the union that this does not happen.

This pattern of organization is particularly evident amongst Punjabis and perhaps especially amongst Sikhs, whose religion and ethnicity may not be seen as incompatible with Marxism. On the other hand, many may be allied with the Sikh party, the Akali Dal. Very similar patterns of organization have also arisen amongst Gujaratis, Pakistanis, the Mirpuris whose home district is in Azad (liberated) Kashmir, and Bangladeshis.

The IWAs and their equivalents amongst the other religious and national communities are not, however, simply trade unions. They are community organizations which deal with a wider range of welfare issues, organize the symbolic expression of a sense of community and negotiate with the political parties of British society (especially with the Labour Party). In some areas, elections to the governing bodies of the IWA may be more strongly contested than elections to British local councils and the British parliament, even though the IWA encourages a high degree of participation in these.

At the same time, of course, the workers' associations play a part in the politics of the sub-continent. Extremist Kashmiri workers recently assassinated the Indian deputy high commissioner in Britain and British Sikhs have been to the forefront in supporting Sikh movements in the Punjab, particularly during the Indian government's attack on the temple at Amritsar and in Sikh resistance after the assassination of Mrs Gandhi. Even when involvement in Indian politics does not take this dramatic form, however, it nevertheless exists. Thus, when Mrs Gandhi sought to gain re-election to parliament in India and a subsequent return to the premiership, she actively sought the support of the IWAs in Britain, who were deeply divided on whether or not they should receive her.

There is, then, a balance in the activities of the workers' associations. They are a mass means of facilitating entry into British society on just terms, but they are also a means of sustaining a continuing interest in the politics of the sub-continent. Assimilation or acculturation would be signalled by a switch in emphasis from sub-continental to British themes and some of the younger leaders of the IWAs have claimed that this is what they are advocating. None the less, the balance is precarious and the dramatic events surrounding the assassination of Mrs Gandhi have undoubtedly served to re-emphasize commitment to India.

Not all south Asians, of course, support workers' associations. It is true that these organizations do sometimes include small businessmen and there are many workers who also have an interest in shopkeeping. But there have also been other larger businessmen and there are increasing numbers of newly successful businessmen who have little interest in promoting the workers' association, which they see as interfering with their own exploitation of labour. These businessmen tend to be organized in industrial and trade associations and in local Indian chambers of commerce. They often also have links with the Indian Overseas Congress, which is linked with the Indian Congress Party. So far, not many of these businessmen have in fact allied themselves with the Conservative Party, because there is a tendency amongst Indians, as amongst Jewish immigrants before them, for even businessmen to retain socialist and anti-imperialist beliefs, but a process is beginning and the conservative Indian associations are beginning to win support on class grounds.

In fact it must always be remembered that the British society which Asian immigrants are entering is a capitalist society in which class struggle is an important theme, if not the overriding theme, of politics. A sign of Indian acculturation, therefore, would be the growth of divisions within the community along class lines. Such divisions do exist. On the other hand, the divisions are checked by a number of other factors which make for ethnic solidarity and which prevent easy assimilation into British political life.

One such factor is the tendency of Asian immigrant businesses to form a separate 'pyramid' within the main economy. At first, at least, Asian businesses are promoted to serve Asian needs or to fill niches as in the restaurant trade which are open to outsiders, and business can and does grow on this basis. The basic commercial outlets need to be supported by manufacturing, wholesaling, import–export businesses, banking and travel organizations and serviced by professionals like accountants, lawyers and estate agents. Thus the immigrant economy might well grow even if there were very little interaction between it and the economic mainstream and, even when there is such interaction, the basis of the operation might be in the separate community.

All that has been said so far refers to the first adult generation of immigrants. But, of course, some of the most crucial cultural issues are those which arise from the attitudes of this generation towards the education, both instrumental and moral, of their children.

It is useful to distinguish between social interaction in the public domain, which manifestly includes economic, political and legal matters, and the private domain, which refers to such matters as marriage and the family, religion and moral socialization. For many immigrant groups, their goal will be full and equal participation in society of settlement institutions in the public domain and, at the same time, the maintenance of their own culture in the private domain. Asian immigrants to Britain certainly belong in this category. One important problem, however, remains unresolved. This is whether education belongs in the public or the private sphere and whether what the minority community demands is full and equal participation in it or their own separately controlled educational system.

The striking point about Asian immigrants in Britain, unlike perhaps Turks in Germany, is that they all demand full and equal participation in what the British educational system has to offer. They see the education system as a selective system which ensures material advantages in the job market, and they want their children to be successful. They are not particularly interested in any form of ideal education based upon the precept: 'Certificates don't matter, what matters is the education of the whole child.' They are profoundly aware that certificates *do* matter, especially for those who do not have the advantages of social connections. The subjects that matter most, therefore, are subjects like mathematics and the natural sciences, and sometimes subjects like Latin which give access to professional careers. In addition to this, improved skill in English, and perhaps other European languages, may be seen as having commercial value.

For these reasons, that is to say because of their belief in the instrumental value of education, there is rarely any problem in the schools in persuading Asian parents to take an interest in their children's education. They constantly reinforce the teachers' disciplinary demands and are anxious to know what they themselves can do by way of providing additional discipline or resources. They do not, on the whole, expect the school to be responsible for teaching Asian cultures or to be primarily responsible for the moral education of their children.

All of this assumes a division of labour between the school, which is responsible for training in high-grade survival skills, and the home, which is responsible for training in social duties, morality and religion. Herein, however, lies the basis of conflict. The school does have a moral mission, and, though part of this involves a puritanical ethic of hard work and individualism which the immigrants share, it does also imply training in matters which relate to 'social duties, morality and religion'. In these matters the likelihood is that, if the school intervenes, its teachers will be insensitive to the community's values and will teach them in a stereotyped or vulgarized form. At the same time it might well inculcate values such as individual freedom in general, and the freedom of women in particular, which are antithetical to their own value system. Hence, one is likely to find a surprisingly negative attitude towards plans for 'multi-cultural education' and a high degree of suspicion towards the liberal British values which are being inculcated.

These problems seem to be more acute for Muslims who were of special concern to us in our study of Pakistani associations. Their food habits and their attitudes to personal and sexual relations are very rarely understood by British people, and the educational system makes little allowance for them. Here and there, halal meat may be provided by the school meals service and sometimes girls are allowed to have separate lessons in or wear special clothes for swimming and athletics. But there is a lot of British hostility on both of these matters. Animal rights organizations combine with racist and Fascist organizations to campaign against the alleged cruelty of the methods of killing involved in producing halal meat, and feminist groups see the separation and covering of women as demeaning. By way of contrast, Muslim parents are apt to see the attack on halal meat as being an attack on their culture and the 'emancipated' attitudes to sex, which the schools and the feminists advocate, as opening the door to the whole world of commercialized sex which they see as being characteristic of the west.

Sikhs and Hindus have, on the whole, been prepared to compromise on these matters, because of the instrumental value of education. Muslims find it more difficult, and the failure of the schools to meet their needs has led to demands for separate Muslim schools. This could mean, of course, that such schools, under Muslim governors and Muslim teachers, could both sustain Muslim customs and prepare children for success in the individualistic and competitive public domain, but it could also mean a radical withdrawal of education from the public domain, so that it actually disabled children in the occupational sphere.

To say that this problem is an acute one for Muslims is by no means to say that it does not exist at all for the other Asian communities. Even those who most willingly give up their children for seven or eight hours each day to the public educational system may be concerned that the rest of the day should be spent by their children, and particularly their daughters, within the protected environment of the home. Here the central question is that of arranged marriage, which is now discussed.

The whole success of the immigrant enterprise is based upon the maintenance of strong extended kinship ties. This is not only important for maintaining the social system and the culture of the minority community. It may well also be highly functional for capital mobilization and economic success. If, therefore, the randomized mating processes based upon 'falling in love' are allowed to operate, not merely do parents lose control of their children in moral matters, but the whole community structure and the gains which that brings will be threatened.

Even girls who resist 'being arranged' can see this. They know that if they accept their parents' guidance they will make real gains, which come through the dowry system and which are expressed in the form of financial help towards buying and furnishing a home or buying a motor car. The young Romeos and Juliets of modern British society who fall in love at discos cannot expect such benefits with any degree of certainty. Apart from the question of marriage, moreover, the extended kinship system implies that the earnings of wives, sons and daughters should be handed to the head of the group. While this might appear to be to the disadvantage of the wives and children in terms of individual freedom, it may also be to their advantage in that capital may be mobilized in this way so that, amongst other things, it can be used to meet their own needs.

Together with the control of social relations within the family the other main form of social control is the control of ideas. One of the features of south Asian immigrant communities is the appearance of numerous temples, particularly Sikh temples and mosques. Birmingham, for example, has no less than thirty-eight mosques after twenty-five years of Pakistani immigration. These mosques and temples, particularly the mosques, are centres of religious instruction, and their work is supplemented by other teaching centres which are often attached to video and cassette libraries and which have a considerable influence over the young. We have been particularly impressed in our research with the emergence of groups of young men in their early twenties who have an almost missionary zeal about the propagation of Islam amongst their peers.

There are then many reasons to suppose that, at least in the private sphere of family life, moral socialization and religion, Asian minority cultures are being reproduced, while in the public domain minority organizations exist which serve to defend the interests of minority members in the impersonal world of the economy and the polity. It must be said, moreover, that it is precisely the strength of the socialization process in the private sphere which makes the solidarity necessary for collective action in the public sphere possible. Our own research leads us to the view that these mechanisms amongst south Asians are strong enough to prevent the occurrence of what has happened to European migrants to other European countries and to America, namely the virtual disappearance of minority culture after three generations. What should be expected is something far more like what has happened to Jews, where the Orthodox continue to propagate their culture in a strong form, and even those who on the surface appear to have become absorbed none the less have a strong sense of kinship and of ethnic identity and still continue to practise their religion in some form.

However, all these points have been made about the strength and adaptiveness of immigrant culture not in order to deny that change and acculturation occur, because they certainly do. The point is, simply, that the nature of this acculturation process can only be fully understood when it is recognized how strong and adaptive the culture of these immigrant minorities is. Against this background the cultural situation of the second generation can now be looked at.

The first thing to notice, perhaps, is that the dualism of cultural commitment of Asian families, involving, on the one hand, participation in the individualistic and universalistic world of the public domain together with an acceptance of the instrumental value of education and, on the other, the maintenance of ethnic community through the institutions of religion and the family, does contain an internal contradiction. In the last analysis, participation in the public domain must have some corrosive influence in the communal ethnic culture. Sooner or later, the cult of individual success is likely to make the maintenance of communal obligations and cultural forms difficult, and individuals who succeed will be attracted to the cultural forms associated with individualism. Many successful ethnics will therefore become 'bourgeois'. To some extent, too, those who participate in organizations like the IWAs will begin to share in working-class culture and solidarity.

How quickly this corrosive process begins to operate may depend on the extent to which the Asian minority are proof against the attractions of the consumer society. Most English people have long ago become tied to consumerist values. This means that success is measured by the extent to which it can be cashed in terms of houses, motor cars, furniture, holidays and consumer durables. It is therefore important to notice (and it is certainly a worthwhile topic for research) that many Asian immigrants in Britain at least have not accepted these goals at all. They work hard and live meagrely (so much so that it is sometimes said that the only followers of the Protestant ethic in Britain today are, Weber notwithstanding, the Hindus!). But this doesn't mean that competitive success is not judged by another standard. What it and its monetary rewards may be used for is to increase family honour (*izzat*) and to do this by the deliberate adoption of, or even return to, traditional culture. This has been especially true amongst the Sikhs. In the first tough days of their immigration, when they worked for low wages in factories, they often abandoned their symbols, cut their hair and ceased to wear turbans. Economic success, however, meant for many that they returned to the symbols, both for themselves and for their children. However, there are successful Sikhs who cut their hair and behave like other citizens and there are adaptations amongst other groups which are no less important despite them not being visible.

Most important are the adaptations which occur amongst the young. Obviously, despite all the controls on marriage and leisure-time activities which may occur, there are some who will include within their patterns of life elements derived from peer-group cultures. The most obvious areas of investigation here are those which relate to participating in and watching and following sport and popular music and dancing. The situation here, however, is not a simple one. There is not simply a peer-group culture by affiliation, through which the children of immigrants enter British society and acquire its culture. On the immigrant community side, those parents who cannot actually prevent participation in this culture try to ensure that it is contained within the school-day so that, even though a boy may be an ardent follower of a football team or a girl very well informed about and interested in popular music and musicians, this will be only a small part of leisure life, the bulk of which will still go on in and under the control of the home.

On the British side, it must be recognized that the youth cultures which flourish are not simply part of British culture. They are an escape from it as well as sometimes the centre of resistance to it. To a very large extent they are concerned with asserting, contrary to the competitive credentialling culture of the school, that an ordinary working-class child can succeed and gain fame and money by an alternative route which does not involve the sort of competitive test required by the system. These are ideas which also have some communication with adult working-class culture, which also has a strong fantasy element.

There is also, however, another element in the youth cultures, not of fantasy, but of resistance. Very often the particular sub-cultural forms which have flourished in Britain (Teddy boys, mods, rockers, skinheads, punks and so on) are in fact asserting value alternatives both to mainstream society and to the culture of parents. One point which is common to the majority of them is an openness to the ideas of minorities and an opposition to racism, although it also has to be noticed that there are one or two of the sub-cultures which go in the opposite direction and which actually foster racism in its most virulent forms.

Some immigrant minorities, particularly those from the Caribbean, have responded by asserting their own version of youth culture, involving not merely opposition to mainstream and parents social values, but also the values of white society as such. This has not yet happened to any great extent amongst Asian youth, but it may well be expected to occur.

One particularly interesting point to note, however, is that, while Asians have only been partly attracted to the fantasy elements of youth culture and hardly at all to youth culture as resistance, they have participated in some of the more serious aspects both of leisure-time activities and in serious adult forms of resistance. The first of these is exemplified by participation in the more approved sports.

Asian boys often play rugby football, which is part of the old public school and grammar school culture and are encouraged to do so by their parents, who see it as part of the achievement-oriented school culture, a symbolization of the values of the public domain, rather than soccer which stands opposed to those values. At an adult level, too, young Asians are serious about their politics. They will support many of the struggles of the workers' associations, but often regard the attitudes of their parents as insufficiently militant and turn to an alliance with various far left and Trotskyist groups to pursue both working-class and anti-racist causes.

It should be possible then, for sociologists to map some of the ways in which Asian youth participates in aspects of British youth and adult culture for their own reasons. Much of this participation, however, will be compatible with the maintenance of a cultural base in their own community. There remains, however, a more serious problem which affects a small but increasing minority. This is the problem of what happens to those who drop out of their Asian culture altogether.

The problem is exemplified especially by the case of Asian runaway girls. In extreme cases, these girls will break all ties with their homes and earn money outside the community. That final radical step, however, is rarely taken. More frequently the girl is not resisting marrying in her community or even being 'arranged'. All she is doing is resisting a forced choice imposed on her by her parents. What therefore happens is that Asian friends or Asian social workers might intervene to set up negotiations so that within the context of an Asian arrangement, the girls' needs are respected.

What is perhaps most striking about the Asian communities in Britain is that in the second and third generation as immigrants, they have not yet accepted the pattern of randomized mating which is so central to an individualistic society, but have maintained in a modified way the forms of marriage, mating and thinking about these matters which support extended kinship and collective communal action.

The Greek Cypriots*

Greek Cypriots are possibly a more homogeneous group and certainly less numerous than Asians—more homogeneous in the sense that they share a language (a dialect of Greek), a religion (Greek Orthodox) and that they all come from the same small island in the Mediterranean. Because both the island and the population are small, most Greek Cypriots either know one another or, when they

* by Sasha Josephides

33

meet, can trace relatives or acquaintances whom they have in common. Nevertheless, to think of Greek Cypriots as coming to Britain with a well-bounded common culture and then encountering a different well-bounded common culture which they either adopt, resist, or part adopt and part resist, is simplistic to the point of being false.

To begin with, although it has been said that there is a certain amount of homogeneity, the differences among Greek Cypriots should also be stressed. These include class differences, regional differences, differences between villagers and townspeople, variations in political philosophy and degrees of religious commitment. Secondly, all Greek Cypriots come from Cyprus but they are not the only inhabitants of that island. Greek Cypriots are the largest group but there is also a sizeable population of Turkish Cypriots and significant numbers of Armenians and Maronites. Greek Cypriots have therefore not lived in some sort of cultural exclusivity prior to migration. Finally, although Cyprus is a small island, Greek Cypriots have a relationship with Greece, and for many Greek Cypriots there is some kind of cultural continuity between Greece and Cyprus. Given the variation among Greek Cypriots and the kinds of constant interaction with other groups it is neither possible to see Greek Cypriots as having a 'common culture' nor to see this culture as well bounded.

However Greek Cypriot culture is seen, it has always been on the move and there have always been outside influences. The point has already been made that colonialism has meant that the countries that Britain's immigrants have come from are often violently-created plural societies. In the case of Cyprus, because of its strategic position in the Mediterranean, it has been colonized by every power in the area—in fact Cyprus has apparently always belonged to some outside power—and has even been immortalized in English literature (*Othello*) as a colony of the Venetians. The British, as well as colonizing Cyprus for a period, have remained since independence, predominantly in their own base, but many English people also have retirement homes all over Cyprus.

Besides outside powers coming into Cyprus to rule, there has always been movement among Cypriot populations themselves. For example in the 1920s, at the time of the exchange of populations between Greece and Turkey, many people came into Cyprus from Asia Minor as refugees. There has also always been movement between Cyprus and Greece and between Cyprus and Turkey. Armenians who escaped the holocaust also came to Cyprus when they lost their country. More recently Lebanese are setting up homes and businesses in Cyprus.

An important aspect of this constant movement as regards the present study is that although many Greek Cypriots like to believe that despite all these influences they have always been 'Greek', the evidence suggests that Greek Cypiot culture, even taking its most objectively distinguishing features, that is language and religion, has always been in a state of flux. For example although now people talk of the main populations of Cyprus as being either Turks or Greeks this has not always been the case. There are past accounts of villages where the population spoke a common language but which included both Muslims and Christians. There is also evidence of conversion from Islam to Christianity and vice versa. In terms of language, although the languages of Cyprus are now rigidifying into Greek and Turkish, there was a time, according to a number of sources, when something called the Cypriot language could be spoken of and a Cypriot dictionary existed as late as the 1930s. At the present time it is difficult to envisage what such a dictionary could have looked like and it is taken for granted that the dialects spoken in Cyprus are variations of standard Greek and standard Turkish.

One final point to be taken into account in any discussion which concentrates on the differences between the sending society and the receiving society in processes of migration and on the kinds of adjustments that migrants might have to make in commuting between the two is that the sending society itself does not fossilize after certain people have emigrated. Neither is the society, and therefore the culture, static before migration; nor does it become static after the migrants have gone. It is a common idea among Cypriots in London that the kinds of attitudes and forms of behaviour which London Cypriots are trying to maintain are ones which have now changed in Cyprus. For example, it is said that Cypriot girls in Cyprus now have considerably more freedom than Cypriot girls in London, because Cyprus has changed in the way that every living society changes, while London Cypriots, the ones that insist on maintaining traditions, are trying to maintain a fossilized set of customs and values that may have been current when they left Cyprus some thirty years ago but which have now altered. Besides this idea that values have been changing in Cyprus there is the fact that many objective changes have taken place in Cyprus and many new influences have come to bear on the island. It has already been mentioned that there is now a sizeable Lebanese population living and working in the country; the tourist industry has also slightly changed in recent years, the island now attracting large numbers of Scandinavians; there has been a coup, an occupation and a war in Cyprus. Changes in communication, including air travel and television have meant that Cyprus, like every other country, is receiving ideas from all over the world. In terms of language and the importance of mainland Greece for Greek

Cypriots, television has been a most powerful influence. Because many Greek programmes are being broadcast in Cyprus, Cypriot dialect is becoming closer and closer to standard Greek and Greek life-styles more and more familiar to Cypriots.

Given that Cypriot history has never stood still, and given the fluidity of what we call culture and the fact that it is always changing and accommodating new influences, the picture of one cultural group (Greek Cypriots) coming to England and suddenly coming up against a different cultural group (the English) with dramatic consequences is obviously a false one. However, questions can still be asked regarding the degree to which Cypriots adapt to English life-styles both in the sense of participation and in the sense of how they see the dominant values in British society.

In fact the issues of participating in British society, what is 'good' and what is 'bad' in English life-styles, whether Cypriots who become anglicized fare better in this society than those who stick to their Cypriot ways, what combination of 'Cypriotness' and 'Englishness' parents should try and instil in their children to make them well balanced and successful, are questions constantly being debated among Cypriots with strong views being expressed on every side. Since these are all live issues it is not possible to give a Cypriot position on them but the main issues can be identified and discussed. Both older Cypriots (those who migrated) and the generation born in this country are taking part in this debate.

The major questions being discussed can be grouped together under two headings: those to do with culture and life-style, and those to do with country and political commitment. With regard to the first heading, some background information on Cypriot culture and social values is necessary here.

Key terms when talking about these issues are reputation, virginity, *proxenia* and dowry, all of which are related to the family and marriage. The family is considered very important in Cypriot life and marriage is crucial since, particularly for women, not to be married carries a social stigma and there are very few roles available to women other than that of wife and mother. Furthermore, gender roles are rigid in Cypriot society and it is difficult for anyone to step outside these. Obviously none of this is unique to Cypriots but it is considerably more pronounced among Cypriots than among, for example, English people.

Because the family is considered to be the most important social grouping and marriage more or less essential, the terms listed above are of the utmost importance to Cypriots. It is important that a family should have a good reputation for people to want to marry into it. A number of things can affect the reputation of a family, but without a doubt the most important concerns sexual behaviour and particularly the sexual behaviour of women. It is important that women should not be seen as 'loose' in any sense, which means not only that unmarried girls should be virgins but that married women should be faithful and widows irreproachable. However, the important thing is not simply that they should be these things but that they should be seen to be these things by other people. It is therefore not tolerated for a girl to go out with non-family members (particularly with other girls who have a 'bad' reputation), not necessarily because there is a fear that she would sleep with someone, but because other people might think that she would. Also, for a girl to be seen out with a boy other than someone she is engaged to is unacceptable, because, even if her parents know that she is not sleeping with the boy, other people might think that she is, and so she would lose her reputation. This in turn would lead to the whole family and particularly the father, losing its reputation since, he would be seen as weak and ineffectual and unable to control his daughter's sexuality. A man whose wife is suspected of having an affair loses all credibility as both his ability to control her and his sexual prowess come into question. The converse is not true, however, as it is culturally acceptable for a man to have both a wife and a girl-friend, and it does no harm to anybody's reputation.

Proxenia is a form of arranged marriage which entails introducing two young people to one another. Prior to any introduction a discreet investigation takes place to ensure that the person in question is suitable, that is that they come from a respectable family and are economically acceptable. *Proxenia* can take a number of forms from inviting the boy and some of his people to the house and then sending the girl into the room to hand around coffee so that she can be seen (and see), to discreetly inviting a couple of young people to a restaurant as part of a bigger party to give them the opportunity to meet. A number of different categories of people can initiate *proxenia*. The negotiations after the young people meet can also vary but have usually included discussions of the dowry. Customarily in Cyprus a girl needed a house as a dowry in order to get married (but see Loizos 1975) though there are countless examples of marriages where such a dowry could not be provided.

These values and practices are currently in operation both in Cyprus and in Britain but are continually changing, and ideas regarding the position of women which they give rise to are being challenged. In Britain all these practices are important and indeed, according to some people, dowry is becoming increasingly important. However, as has already been pointed out, these issues are constantly being debated, particularly the question of allowing girls more freedom. As might be expected, it is generally younger people who argue for greater freedom for girls and ridicule *proxenia* and the dowry system, while older people argue that going out every night and mixing with different people would expose a girl to all sorts of dangers (including the risk of not being marriageable afterwards) and that a carefully thought-out marriage where the girl and boy are suitably matched will have more chances of success. However, there are also both older people who are extremely liberal and younger people who are not totally against these practices and often accept the logic behind them. Also, many successful marriages are being made in Britain in the customary way, and trusting to their parents and relatives to find them a suitable spouse does take a certain burden off young people.

The concern with culture and life-style leads on to a final point, that of education. Unlike some Asians, many Cypriot parents do not want separate schooling for their children but they do want to continue with community schools, run by Greek Cypriot groups, for the teaching of Greek language and culture, and they do not want these subjects taken over by the mainstream school curriculum. The reason for this is that they consider the community school (which operates on Saturdays and in the evenings) to be teaching children a whole life-style and this is not something they would entrust to the British education system (see Chapter 3).

We turn now to the issue of country and political commitment. A major question for many people is whether their loyalty, particularly their political loyalty, should primarily go to Britain or to Cyprus.

The first point to be made in this context is that one can't talk of a *myth* of return in terms of Cypriots (because many of them *do* return) and many of the people who migrated feel that Cyprus is their real home and Britain just the place where they work. Come the summer they go 'home' for holidays and one day, when they are economically able and when the political climate in Cyprus has changed, they hope that they will go back for good.

Although this attitude is still strong among Cypriots, it has been challenged in the last decade from two directions. For many people the partition of the island has meant that there is no longer a 'home' or a home village to which they can one day return. For the displaced persons who came here after 1974 their reason for coming to this country was that they no longer had a home (and many of those sent back by the British government are still living in refugee camps). The political climate would have to change very radically indeed before these people could conceivably return.

The other direction from which the dream of returning is being challenged is from the generation born here. Many young Cypriots express an interest in trying to make a life in Cyprus but it is generally recognized that such a move would be extremely difficult and Cypriot parents are coming to terms with the unlikelihood of their British born and bred children going back to Cyprus for good. Many people feel that if they did go back it would be without their children—an option they are unlikely to contemplate.

There is therefore a mixture of feelings regarding whether what is important for the future is Britain or Cyprus. This dilemma is reflected in the form of political activity that London Cypriots have taken on.

To sketch in some of the background, Cypriots, like Asians, have had a long tradition of political activity on both the left and the right and a number of the people who came to London during the early years of migration were exiles forced to leave Cyprus by the British because of their political involvement. Some of these people later went back to Cyprus, in some cases taking up political office, but others remained in London and devoted or are devoting their lives to finding a solution to 'the Cyprus problem'.

This applies to activists of all political persuasions, but it is likely that members of the Communist party are in the majority. The present situation is that active members of the Communist and Democratic parties (a centrist party at present in power in Cyprus) are very well represented in London and are attempting to dominate the political life of London Cypriots. Members of the far right party, and of the Socialist party are also in evidence, but only on the margins. All these politically motivated people have strong links with their parties in Cyprus.

As to how all this relates to politics in Britain, the first point to be made is that for many Cypriots there is only an interest in British politics in as far as it can be seen to affect the situation in Cyprus or the relationship between the superpowers and other countries with a sphere of influence in Cyprus. This is so because of the idea held by many Cypriots that 'home' is Cyprus and because the most politically active Cypriots in London are here, as already discussed, to fight for a solution to the Cyprus problem. These kinds of attitude are now being challenged however. For example, during the last general election it was being suggested that a list should be drawn up of all the MPs who have an acceptable policy on Cyprus and that Cypriots should be urged to vote for those candidates irrespective of which party they represent. A motion to this effect was debated at an ESEKA meeting (see Chapter 3) but was finally defeated by a small margin. Many people on the left, particularly students, argued that although the issue of Cyprus was close to their hearts, there were other issues, such as nuclear disarmament, which were even more important to them and they could not ask their membership to vote for a candidate whose position was unacceptable in other respects simply because he or she had the right policies concerning Cyprus.

The other challenge to the view that what is primary is the Cyprus problem comes from people who are saying that London Cypriots must start improving their lot in Britain because that is their home, and that they should have a higher profile in British political life. This view is mostly being voiced by the increasing number of council workers, community development officers, etc. These people are becoming increasingly involved in council politics and there are two Cypriot (Labour) councillors at present. However, these people take pains to point out that by becoming involved in British politics (mostly in the race relations contexts) they are not abandoning Cyprus. They argue that they may even be able to help Cyprus more by being more powerful within British politics.

Other than this relatively small set of people Cypriots are not actively involved in British politics or concerned with British political parties. There is some Cypriot membership of the Labour Party and of the British Communist Party and a potential Cypriot SDP parliamentary candidate, but in general Cypriot participation in British politics is confined to voting (and when they vote most Cypriots vote Labour although there is some interest in the SDP and limited support for certain Tory MPs who are seen as having favourable views on Cyprus).

For the most part, Cypriots' real party interest is in the Cypriot parties listed above. AKEL, the Cypriot Communist Party is particularly strong and powerful with a large membership in London. However, although it is supposed to be a class party it is difficult to see it as operating in that way in Britain (Anthias 1982) although in Cyprus it does, and its concerns, unlike the IWA, are less to do with union issues and so on, than with keeping the ethnic group together and with struggling over the partition of Cyprus. Membership of the Cypriot Communist Party is therefore less a matter of joining with people of the same class and putting class interests first than with joining with people of the same ethnic group.

To conclude this chapter, the picture that I want to highlight in this overview is not one of a group of people taken unawares by the vast differences they found on migrating and having to make sudden and drastic adjustments, but one of a group of people negotiating the new situation and introducing an ongoing debate on everything that seems problematic. It also emerges that changes come about in any case and some of the debates, particularly those discussed under the culture and life-style heading, are also taking place in Cyprus. In terms of political commitment it is only when Cypriots start to see

Britain as their home that they take an interest in British politics and this is only just beginning to happen in a very small way.

References

Anthias, Floya (1982) *Ethnicity and class among Greek-Cypriot migrants*, PhD thesis, Bedford College, University of London.

Anthias, Floya (1983) 'Ethnicity and class in Cyprus', *Race and Class*, vol. XXV, no. 1, pp. 59–74, Institute of Race Relations, London.

Durkheim, Emile (1973) *The division of labour in society*, Free Press, Glenton, Ill.

Durkheim, Emile (1952) *Suicide*, Routledge & Kegan Paul, London.

Furnivall, J.S. (1939) *Netherlands India. A study of Plural Economy*, Cambridge University Press, Cambridge.

Glucksmann, Miriam (1974) *Structuralist analysis in contemporary thought*, Routledge & Kegan Paul, London.

Levi-Strauss, Claude (1966) *The savage mind*, Weidenfeld & Nicolson, London.

Loizos, Peter (1975) 'Changes in property transfers amongst Greek-Cypriot villagers' *Man*, vol. 10, no. 4, pp. 503–23, Royal Anthropological Institute, London.

Lundberg, George (1939) *The foundations of sociology*, MacMillan, New York.

MacIver, Robert (1939) *Society*, Macmillan, New York.

Malinowski, Bronislaw (1944) *A scientific theory of culture*, University of N. Carolina Press, Chapel Hill.

Parsons, Talcott (1952) *The social system*, Tavistock, London.

Parsons, Talcott and Shils, Edward (1951) *Towards a general theory of action*, Harvard University Press, Cambridge, Mass.

Parsons, Talcott, Shils, Edward and Bales, Robert (1953) *Working papers in the theory of action*, Free Press, New York.

Radcliffe-Brown (1952) *Structure and function in primitive society*, Cohen and West, London.

Rex, John (1961) *Key problems of sociological theory*, Routledge & Kegan Paul, London.

Rex, John (1973) *Race, colonialism and the city*, Routledge & Kegan Paul, London.

Rex, John (1977) *Race, colonialism and the city*, Routledge & Kegan Paul, London.

Rex, John and Tomlinson, Sally (1974) *Colonial immigrants in a British city*, Routledge & Kegan Paul, London.

Riesman, David (1950) *The lonely crowd*, Yale University Press, Newhaven, Conn.

Tonnies, Ferdinand (1955) *Community and association*, translated by Charles P. Loomis, Routledge & Kegan Paul, London.

Weber, Max (1968) *Economy and society*, vol. I, Bedminster Press, New York.

Weinreich, Peter (1980) *Manual for identity exploration using personal constructs*, SSRC Research Unit on Ethnic Relations, Birmingham.

3 Associations amongst the Greek Cypriot Population in Britain[1]

Sasha Josephides

The largest settlement of Cypriots outside Cyprus is the community in London, known by its inhabitants as 'our colony' (*paroikia* in Greek) which has managed to maintain a high degree of cohesiveness and a distinct ethnic character and lifestyle.

A number of factors serve to keep the community together, including the existence of a vast number of ethnic associations, many of which have as a specific aim the maintenance of the ethnic group and the preservation of Cypriot culture.

The question of the role of ethnic associations in relation to ethnicity and ethnic identity has been posed in a number of ways and associations have been seen both as helping immigrants to assimilate through providing a community for them within the host society, and as creating an anti-assimilationist or separatist environment. Neither of these arguments are specifically discussed in this chapter because, as will become apparent, Cypriot associations have both tendencies, with different emphases at different periods. Also, although associations are specialized forms of organization in the sense that, by forming ethnic associations, Cypriots are self-consciously organizing along ethnic lines, they are nevertheless part of the ethnic group and have to be seen as part of the community structure.

This chapter looks at the growth and significance of associations in a community which is, in any case, bound together in a variety of ways. It attempts to see the associations contextually and to assess their role within the community as well as in terms of ethnicity. Although a theoretical discussion of ethnicity is not within the scope of this chapter it is necessary to say something about the use of terms. Throughout, 'ethnic' and 'ethnicity' are used to refer to a social category based on an ideology of common origin and common culture. I have found it useful to distinguish between ethnic affiliation and ethnic identity, reserving 'affiliation' for referring to concrete, measurable group membership,[2] and identity for talking about the subjective view of self *vis-à-vis* the group. However, for most of this chapter the discussion is too general for this distinction to be made, so the less specific term 'ethnicity' is used.

The data on associations were gathered by talking to the organizers, attending meetings and other activities, and reading the material put out by the associations and the ethnic press. In addition, informal interviews with members of the community who are not active in associations have enabled me to form an impression of the relevance of ethnic associations to their lives.

The Cypriot settlement in London

Migration and settling in[3]

The Cypriot[4] migration to Britain started before the First World War and by 1939 it was officially estimated that there were some 8000 Cypriots living in London. These early settlers were nearly all Greek Cypriots and there was a predominance of single males. In the years between the Second World War and 1966 a further 75,000 people, both Greek and Turkish Cypriots, left Cyprus for Britain. The migration reached a peak in 1960 and 1961, with over 12,000 people entering Britain in each of those years. In 1966 there were 100,000 Cypriots in Britain, three-quarters of them settled in London. Since 1966 the migration of Cypriots has continued, but at a very low level, with the exception of the year 1974–5 when the upheaval in Cyprus and the subsequent displacement of many people brought several thousands of Cypriots to Britain as refugees.[5]

Cypriots migrated for economic reasons, and they chose Britain because of work opportunities and their colonial connection. Despite this connection, migration to Britain was subject to controls. From 1937 the colonial government in Cyprus imposed a system of affidavits, thereby preventing would-be migrants from coming to Britain unless they had sponsors already established there who could guarantee their support. After 1962, with the implementation of the Commonwealth Immigration Act, Cypriot entry into Britain, like that of all other Commonwealth citizens, was controlled by the British government through the voucher system. Only in the years between 1959 and 1962 were there no controls. The status of most Cypriots, once in Britain, has been that of British subjects and, with the exception of the displaced persons who entered this country after 1974, their position as regards residence has been stable. Nevertheless, until recently the desire to return to Cyprus has been a strong element in the Cypriot community, and many people bought plots of land in Cyprus in the hope that one day they would go back there for good.

The process of moving to Britain, especially in the post-war years, took the form of chain migration along kinship and patronage lines. This can be explained in terms of traditional Cypriot cultural patterns but it was also promoted by a government regulation which made it necessary to have sponsorship in order to migrate. It is therefore a case of government regulations and tradition coinciding. Another feature of the post-war migration is that whole families moved. This meant that the primary unit in Cypriot life, the nuclear family, was not seriously undermined. Usually the man travelled first and the woman and children followed, but in the majority of cases the separation was only a matter of a year or so. This is another instance of a traditional value being underpinned by government policy, since affidavits were not issued to men travelling on their own who had not made adequate provision for their family (Oakley 1979: 33). The outcome of this form of migration is that family and other ties were never broken (if anything they were strengthened) and a cohesive Cypriot community developed in London.

The first migrants to London got work as waiters in the restaurants and hotels of the West End of London and lived in lodging houses in Upper Soho. This was the area where the first Cypriot cafés and other businesses were started. Later migrants found employment in clothes manufacturing, the industry which eventually absorbed nearly all Cypriot female labour. For a variety of reasons many Cypriots were economically successful, both in catering and in clothes manufacturing, and from being employees a number of men (with the help of their wives' labour) became self-employed or even employers. They achieved this by either starting up shops and other services for fellow Cypriots or by setting up on their own in the clothing and catering industries. Thus they developed a specific ethnic economy with both internally and externally oriented components (Oakley 1970).

As well as moving economically Cypriots moved geographically within London in a predominantly northerly direction. In the 1950s and early 1960s Camden and Islington were the areas with the largest numbers of Cypriots. By 1971 Haringey, the borough to the north of Camden and Islington, had the highest Cypriot concentration. This is still the case today, but there are signs that the movement is continuing as the boroughs north of Haringey have sizeable Cypriot populations.

This movement from the centre involves moving out of rented accommodation and into smaller owner/occupier homes and is therefore probably part of a process of upward mobility. However, in this case, decentralization does not appear to mean dispersal (although there is some dispersal) but concentration in another area. Furthermore, as the Cypriots move they take most of the ethnic economy with them.

The present community

From its early beginnings the Cypriot community in London has been a vital one and it has continued to function as a community in many ways. Spatially the Cypriot community is still concentrated in Haringey and the boroughs around it. Out of some 90,000 Greek Cypriots in London 30,000 live in the borough of Haringey. Moreover, within Haringey certain wards have a greater concentration of Cypriots than others while in certain streets it is estimated that every other house is occupied by Greek Cypriots. The area reflects this concentration through the presence of large numbers of Cypriot shops, cafés, restaurants, dress factories, and offices of various kinds.

The occupational concentration of Cypriots also continues and so does the tendency towards self-employment. There are some signs that changes will come about in the ethnic economic niche (the clothing industry). For example, Cypriot-owned firms are now more likely to employ non-Cypriots (partly because fewer Cypriots are now willing to work unofficially) while more Cypriots, particularly younger people, are finding work outside this sector. However, at present the Cypriot section of the industry is surviving and it is still maintaining its ethnic character.

The other facet of the ethnic economy, providing a service for fellow Cypriots, has grown in its scope. Most services and specializations can be performed by Cypriots and many members of the community use Cypriot hairdressers, shoemakers, accountants, lawyers and, under certain circumstances, even doctors (although this usually means costly private consultations). There is even a directory and telephone catalogue of Cypriot businesses and there is very little in the way of goods and services for which a Cypriot living in London would have to go outside the ethnic group.[6] Some people consciously use the services of fellow Cypriots on the basis that Cypriots must stick together and by a system of personal recommendations. Others find themselves dealing with Cypriots because of their connections and requirements.

One other way in which Cypriots stick together is in their personal and social relations. Most leisure time is spent with the family and socializing takes place within the extended family and the circle of distant and fictive kin. Weddings, baptisms and other celebrations involve a still wider circle and are a regular and frequent part of most Cypriots' lives. Men also go to the *kafeneion* which is like an informal club, and both sexes use shops, churches and schools as social arenas. There is little socializing with English people. This is not due to any reluctance on the part of Cypriots to mix, but rather because they and the English move in different spheres. Young Cypriots have English friends while at school, but the friendships are often allowed to lapse at the end of their school career. The incidence of marriage outside the group is relatively low and there is pressure on young people to allow their elders to arrange marriages[7] for them, either with London Cypriots or with people from their own village in Cyprus. The links between Cyprus and London are extremely strong and most Cypriots go for regular holidays to Cyprus.

This is the background and context within which formal associations can be looked at.

Formal associations

As well as being tightly bound with informal ties of many kinds the Cypriot community is a place of formal association. At present there are about seven Greek Orthodox churches and over seventy associations in north London alone, as well as two Greek Cypriot newspapers published in London and two pirate radio stations. The associations have been growing in number since the early 1970s. A brief look at the history and development of associations in London is necessary before the present situation can be assessed.

Historical developments

In the early days of migration, Cypriot associations were linked with either the church or the Communist party as this brief overview will show.

One of the first associations was set up in 1934 in the Soho area of London by the Greek Orthodox church and the colonial government of Cyprus. This was the Greek Cypriot Brotherhood and its aim was to act as a meeting place for the early immigrants who were seen as isolated. In 1950 the Brotherhood was still active in Soho and had a student association, EFEKA, attached to it, and still had strong links with the church. The first Greek Orthodox church for Cypriots opened in Camden Town in 1948 (up to this time Cypriots had been using the Greek cathedral in Bayswater) and two years later it started a school. These various connected bodies made up the right-wing camp of early Cypriot associations and are all still in existence, although they have changed in their aims and character.[8]

To turn now to the left wing, the Cypriot Communist Party of Great Britain was founded in 1931 and has existed under a number of different names to the present day (Adams 1971: 72). The first left-wing social-welfare association to be set up at this time was the Union of Cypriots in England. These two organizations, along with the first Cypriot newspaper, *Vema*, shared a building in Camden Town, part of which they maintained as a social centre. The next development was the setting up of a school by some activists from these groups who eventually also formed a students' group and the Cypriot Women's League. There have also been theatre groups associated with the left-wing camp. Most of these associations and groups still exist in some form or other.

In the 1950s and 1960s other groups, less obviously partisan, were set up to organize teaching children Greek, and over the years the numbers of churches and schools of every kind (often with youth clubs attached) grew in pace with the community. The community therefore had a small number of associations which catered for its needs.

This picture changed in the early 1970s when a large number of new associations were formed, many of which are broadly based, and others of which have a well-defined and limited scope. A majority of the new associations fall into one of two groups: general social organizations (such as village, local and cultural associations), and very specialized ones (pressure groups and unions). Another development is that community activists have succeeded in securing government funds and setting up community centres. These centres offer a number of services to Cypriots and have permanent staff. Each centre has its own character and objectives.

The broad trends which emerge in the history of associations in the community are the following: the first associations were inspired by the church or the CP and they met the needs of the early, single male migrants. In the 1950s and 1960s the population grew, church facilities were extended and associations started to provide schooling in Greek and a few other facilities. In the 1970s and early 1980s advisory and community centres have been sprouting up, as well as more associations of all the other types. There have clearly been different phases in the development of Cypriot associations which correspond to the development of the ethnic group, and it is unlikely that associations have the same type of relevance at every stage. Because of this it would be a gross oversimplification to regard associations as promoting either integration or secession.

The range of Greek Cypriot associations[9]
At present there is a wide range of Greek Cypriot associations in London. What follows is a summary of the different types of groupings.

Community centres   The community centres offer a variety of facilities, but all deal with the welfare needs of Cypriots and have various groups attached to them and/or hold meetings in their premises. They all receive some public funding. The Haringey centre is considerably larger than any of the others and has many more facilities and activities. It is the only centre with its own bar and café and is open as a social centre every evening of the week with billiards, table tennis and other games, and offers keep-fit classes, dancing, language classes, etc., as well as special events put on by the various associations which use the premises. It also houses a number of groups run by the social services including a women's health group, and an elderly and handicapped group.

Educational/youth associations   These are the most active associations and are responsible for running various schools or classes in schools. Only the church schools have their own premises, which they decorate with religious and patriotic symbols. The schools receive assistance in the form of teachers and teaching materials from the Cyprus high commission, as well as teaching materials from Greece. Many of the educational associations belong to a federation.

There are also a number of youth clubs, and an association has recently been formed to unite them. The church and certain other establishments organize their own youth clubs. The youth clubs concentrate on dancing, music and sport, and some of them run football clubs. A limited number of teachers and youth workers do the round of all the schools and clubs.

As well as administering the schools and clubs, the educational associations arrange concerts and other social events which are very well attended.

Churches   There are seven Greek Orthodox churches for Cypriots in north London and several others in the rest of London. There are a number of church committees and a structure for administering the church schools.

Village associations   The village associations are a growing phenomenon, and seven new ones were formed in 1984 alone. They give their functions as social and charitable/welfare and mainly organize social functions. The proceeds from these functions are often used for such purposes as contributing to the building of clinics in their home villages and helping their own old-age pensioners in this country.

Local/cultural associations   These organize talks and cultural events as well as social functions. A majority give as two of their aims the cultural welfare of young people and the forging of links with other ethnic groups. They also get involved in other groups and one of the cultural groups is now backing an education advisory centre for parents.

Political parties and groups   With the exception of one or two of the socialist groups, which are student-inspired and have not had much impact on the community, the parties operating here are branches of the parties in Cyprus. The Communist party, AKEL, has a very large following, with thousands of people attending its public meetings, and its own centre and restaurant. The parties all sponsor socials and arrange dinners and other entertainments for visiting politicians from Cyprus.

Unions and professional associations   The majority of these hold cultural/social events and lectures and seminars. They also get involved in political activity and, in the case of unions, organize on behalf of their members.

Action groups   These pursue the fairly narrow and specific aims for which they were formed, but many of them also put on socials for fund-raising purposes, and they disband or lie dormant when the particular issue they have been campaigning around is resolved. The existing action groups are either concerned with particular problems to do with the aftermath of the war in Cyprus, such as campaigns against the deportations of refugees and the struggle to find out what has happened to the many people who have been missing since the Turkish occupation; or with issues involving Cypriots in London. The Homeworkers' Working Party and several groups pushing for provisions for the elderly are examples of the latter.

Women's groups   At present there are four women's groups: one of long standing which organizes talks on issues of relevance to women, and excursions to places such as Greenham Common, as well as holding socials; a newly formed women's action group, which has not yet got off the ground; the two ladies' branches of some of the other organizations which hold lunches to raise money for philanthropic causes. One of them has recently raised money for the family of a murdered policeman in Cyprus, while the other sent a donation to Ethiopia.

Miscellaneous

The Thallassaemia Society   This society is solely concerned with people suffering from the disease (a fatal form of hereditary anaemia) and their families, and organizes many fund-raising functions which are extremely well attended. As well as acting as a support group the society raises money for research into the disease and sponsors new forms of treatment.

ESEKA   This group was set up to co-ordinate the other associations, especially in their campaigns on the Cyprus issue. It chiefly concerns itself with organizing the annual demonstration to mark the day Turkish troops entered Cyprus. The important associations are all members of ESEKA and their representatives make up the committee of the group.

Theatron Technis The theatre group has been established for a long time and as well as putting on plays, poetry readings and the like, runs an advisory/community centre.

Relationship between associations and community

Many associations meet at the Haringey Community Centre while a few meet at the other community centres. Others either have their own premises or no regular meeting place at all. Nearly all the associations have a large executive (four to eight people) and many executive members are on more than one committee. There also appears to be a concentration of members of the same family on committees. The picture is therefore one of a small interconnected set heading most of the associations. These people are all first-generation migrants and they are mostly over forty years old. The membership numbers of the associations cannot be estimated but there is agreement among executive members that active participation is low.

However, although the associations probably do not have many active members, large numbers do get involved in their fund-raising activities and celebrations. Most associations have regular dinner-dances which are attended by hundreds of people. Also, the associations which provide a service involve many people in that they use that service. The clearest examples of this are the schools, the youth clubs and the churches. About half of all Cypriot children are sent to Greek school on Saturdays or in the evenings and many of them use the youth clubs. The church involves still more people, since a majority of people go to church, especially at Easter, and they use the church for weddings, christenings and other celebrations.

Although I have characterized associations as specialist forms of organization, it is worth noting here that using the services of an association is closer to informal association and has similarities with the kinds of link which are created through using the services produced by the ethnic economy. In one sense using a Greek church or sending a child to a Greek school is not very different from going to the *kafeneion* or buying imported Cypriot food. In both cases Cypriots are showing that they have common special requirements through being Cypriot, whether it is to eat particular types of food or learn a particular language. They are therefore demonstrating a 'community' of needs. In more concrete terms, using the same church or the same shop are both ways in which Cypriots meet and maintain links with one another.

This section is not intended to imply that the associations do not play a significant role in the community, but to stress two points: first, that there is a difference between active involvement in the running of an association and in using the services it provides (and as it happens most people's involvement is as service users or 'clients'); secondly, that the kind of association that is created in this way for the clients is not unlike that created through using the commercial services of the Cypriot community.

Explaining associations

There are many ways of analysing and classifying associations and of assessing their role and their functions. To discuss Cypriot associations I have found it useful to consider them from three perspectives and under the following headings: associations and community needs; associations, ethnicity and identity; and associations and power relations.

Associations and community needs

Naturally every existing association sees itself as meeting some need and every new one points to a particular need as the reason for its formation. In some cases the needs in question explicitly refer to the situation in Cyprus while in others they are general concerns regarding keeping the community in London together. However, the bulk of the work of the associations involves looking after the welfare and educational needs of Cypriots in London. This raises questions regarding why it is necessary for Cypriots to make their own provisions in Britain—a country which is still considered to be a welfare state. There are a number of answers to this question. To begin with, until the last decade the British state did not recognize the needs of ethnic minorities or make any provision for them, so they had to provide for themselves whether they wanted to or not. Now needs are recognized, but this does not lead to automatic provision, nor is the provision, when it is forthcoming, without adverse effects. Ethnic associations are therefore involved in both pushing for resources and in trying to have some control over how they are provided.

At present most Cypriots want and expect state provision but there are two ways in which resources and services can be made available: the first possibility is for provision to be made directly by the relevant department or statutory body; the second is for funds to be given to the ethnic associations to provide for the community themselves. Both systems are currently in operation but there is an ongoing battle regarding how each new demand for resources and services should be dealt with. In general, especially where social services are concerned, local authorities are in favour of providing directly and appear to feel that it would be an attack on the welfare state if they allowed ethnic associations to cater for the needs of their own communities. For example, at a recent meeting of the Islington Race Relations Committee when it was suggested that a proposed centre for the Cypriot elderly should be run by an ethnic organization, the leader of the council said that this would be a form of privatization and opposed it on those grounds. (It is relevant here that it is only when funding is required that the work of the ethnic associations is seen in this light.) Most Cypriots working within the social services are generally also in favour of projects being directly run by the local authority. The reason they give for this is that the service would be more professional and standardized and would also have a higher degree of permanency, as it would be on mainstream funding. People active in ethnic associations, on the other hand, while not opposed to every project which entails taking control of community needs out of their hands, worry that in many cases this can lead to disadvantages for two reasons. First, the provision might not be in a form that is acceptable to Cypriots since, even if the workers on the projects are Cypriots themselves they are likely to be 'anglicized' Cypriots and, still more importantly, they would be under the control of the relevant department whose ideas about how this sort of service should be provided might have little to do with how Cypriots themselves would like it to happen. The second problem is that many people fear that the shift from community to state provision might be the first step to community collapse.

The most hotly debated issue at the moment is youth provision and especially the question of teaching the mother tongue in mainstream school. The arguments in favour of incorporating mother-tongue teaching into the school system are, once again, that it would be more professional and the teaching would be of a higher standard. There is also an argument that children should not be handicapped by being made to stay behind after school or go to Saturday school in order to learn Greek. This is seen as more likely to induce a hatred of their mother tongue rather than a love of it, and also since it is something 'extra' which is taught outside of normal school hours, children are likely to feel that it is less important than the rest of their schooling.

Those who are sceptical about making any changes point out that Greek learning *should* be 'special' and not just another language on the curriculum. They also argue that there is a risk that the teaching may not be more competent, as a new diploma has just been introduced for the teaching of the mother tongue, and the only language requirement to get on to the course is an A-level in Greek. This means that if the diploma becomes a requirement for teaching the mother tongue, people who barely speak Greek might be able to teach it while the present teachers, who were raised and educated in Cyprus, will not have this diploma and will not be able to. However, the main objection is that the advantages of the community school will be lost, which will mean two things: the children will only be taught a language and not a whole culture and an identity which is what the community schools aim to do, and the community spirit which has been built up around the schools with parents actively participating will evaporate. In fact the education attaché from the Cypriot high commission came dangerously close to saying that the main point of the community schools is to keep the community together, since people have to have a common cause that they are working towards in order to maintain unity. These remarks, made at a public meeting, were greeted by a certain degree of anger from some quarters, especially from teachers who felt that what they were doing was teaching children, not keeping parents together; however, there was also a great deal of support for his views. So the issue of providing for the needs of the community is very closely bound up with the question of maintaining the ethnic group and preserving ethnic identity in the young. These issues will be taken up again in the next section.

To get back to the relationship between organization versus local authority provision, the fact that there is now recognition and some provision for ethnic minorities has not meant that the organizations or their concern with community needs are in any way becoming less significant but simply that they are coming increasingly into contact with the local state. The old style associations are making their welfare provisions more explicit and asking for funding, while new groups are forming specifically to look at community needs and campaign for provision (these new groups are often called 'action groups' or 'working parties'). Also the issue of representation has become a major one and community activists feel they have to be in associations for their views to have added weight and in order to be co-opted on to race relations committees and other bodies. Therefore, far from a decline in associations caused by the local authorities having taken over some community provisions people feel they need to organize in order to be heard by local authorities.

A certain cleavage is now beginning to make itself apparent between the sorts of general association which have always taken everything on board and the new working parties which are less concerned with the maintenance of the ethnic group than with getting provision for Cypriots. It is also interesting, and possibly significant, that while a majority of the people active in the old-style associations are first-generation men, many of the people involved in the working parties are young women. This obviously has something to do with the fact that more women than men go in for the caring professions so from that point of view it is an accident, but it is likely to have consequences for the future development of the community.

Whether the provision of needs will be divorced from the struggle to maintain the ethnic group through the agency of these Cypriot professionals is yet to be seen. At present, however, the issue of needs and the maintenance of the ethnic group are very intimately connected. This leads to the second perspective on the associations which is the way they relate to ethnicity.

Associations, ethnicity and identity

As well as many associations being explicitly concerned with ethnicity and working for the preservation of Cypriot culture, all ethnic associations implicitly stress ethnicity by organizing along ethnic lines. According to many informants the reason why there was such a sudden increase in the number of associations after 1974 is that events in Cyprus had made people more patriotic and so they wanted to display their ethnicity. What was important was to belong to a group called 'Greek Cypriot Parents of North London' and so on. Whether it is seen within the context of recent events in Cyprus or not, the relationship between associations and ethnic consciousness obviously needs looking into.

The question of Greek Cypriot ethnicity and ethnic labelling is a complex one and involves a number of different inclusions and exclusions. Greek Cypriots can identify with Turkish Cypriots as 'Cypriots' (although few do) or with mainland Greeks. It is therefore not a simple matter of their relationship with the host community. On the level of the associations, the public ethnic character can be looked at by considering their names and their membership.

The only associations that do not have an ethnic element in their names are the Dressmakers' Association, the Thallassaemia Society and the Academy Club. In terms of membership, the Dressmakers' Association has a number of mainland Greek members and may have people of other ethnic groups, as it is open to everyone. The Thallassaemia Society includes Asians and some Turkish Cypriots, but the bulk of the membership is Greek Cypriot. The Academy Club is very much a Greek Cypriot association.

One other exception is Theatron Technis (originally Greek Theatron Technis). This is the only association within which Greek and Turkish Cypriots are successfully mixing and working together.

They also hold various workshops which attract non-Cypriots. Theatron Technis is committed to uniting all Cypriots and appears to support groups which organize on a class rather than on an ethnic basis.

The names of the rest of the associations each include the words 'Cypriot', 'Greek', 'Greek Cypriot' or the names of specific villages in Cyprus or some other specifically Greek Cypriot element. Most of the ones with only 'Cypriot' in their names claim to welcome Turkish Cypriots, but do not actually have any as members. The representatives of some of these associations said that they used to have Turkish Cypriot members but that they withdrew in 1974. The community centres are used by both Greek and Turkish Cypriots but there is not necessarily much contact between the two groups. From the Greek side, many associations encourage links with Greece and actively welcome Greek members. However, with the exception of certain professional associations which are Greek-backed, Greek membership is minimal.

This brief look at the names and the membership composition of associations indicates that although there is added complexity because of the relationship with Turkish Cypriots and mainland Greeks, the associations are nevertheless clearly displaying their ethnicity. Some might stress Cypriotness and others Greekness; but nearly all announce themselves as ethnic associations both through their names and their membership.

Another aspect of the public face of associations is that of the campaigns in which they involve themselves. Most Cypriot associations mobilize almost exclusively around the Cyprus issue. They have come together in ESEKA to plan their campaigns and every year they stage a demonstration. What this means is that the only time the associations show themselves publicly and *en masse* is to stress their identity with their place of origin.

One other way in which the associations literally 'display' ethnicity is in the concerts, dances and lectures which they arrange, all of which celebrate Greekness or Cypriotness.

Without a doubt the majority of Cypriot associations are separatist in the sense that they organize as Cypriots and want to maintain their own culture and their links with Cyprus. However, this is not inconsistent with their other claim, which is that they want to forge good relationships with other communities. The extent to which they succeed in doing either is an open question.

One final point is that although the associations canvass ethnicity at every opportunity, as we already discussed, the Cypriot ethnic group exists as a community without reference to ethnic associations.

This suggests that the associations are the public face of the group but that the set of conditions perpetuating ethnicity are to be found within the ethnic community as a whole. However, a special case has to be made for the *services* of the associations which are aiming to be considerably more instrumental in arousing and maintaining ethnic awareness, especially where the second generation are concerned. This goes back to the issue regarding community needs.

A large number of associations are concerned with the second generation. The form this concern takes ranges from a fear that youngsters will be assimilated and the group 'lost', to a desire to help young people resolve what are seen as identity problems. The various schools and clubs which have been set up by the associations are an attempt to deal with these problems and are therefore directly concerning themselves with the issue of identity.

Whether the schools are interested in making children into 'good Greeks' or simply in helping them gain self-confidence through an understanding of their ethnic background, what they offer is Greek language tuition, dance and music classes and occasional courses on Cypriot history and culture. Naturally, there are differences in the way these subjects are approached, depending on the politics and philosophy of the school. Some 50 per cent of Cypriot children pass through schools and clubs and there is a certain amount of parental pressure to attend classes, especially Greek language classes. Most of these associations are made up of parents, some of whom are active organizers.

What can be seen happening here in terms of the associations and ethnicity suggests that many older Cypriots are themselves underoing some sort of problem to do with 'ethnic identity'. On the one hand, they are losing Cyprus, their roots, because of the occupation, and on the other hand they feel they are losing their children, who, they fear, are becoming assimilated into a British life-style. Their main struggles around ethnicity are therefore connected with the Cyprus issue and with the preservation of ethnic identity in their children.

The question of whether they are succeeding in forming their children's identity is even difficult to pose in a meaningful manner and certainly cannot be answered in such terms. What has become clear in this study is that young Cypriots are very concerned with the issue of identity, frequently volunteering ethnic identity statements such as 'I'm not a Greek Cypriot, I'm a *Cypriot*', 'I'm not from Cyprus, I'm from north London and that's that', 'I suppose we're Grenglish really', and so on. Many young people are also aware that they are believed to have problems to do with their identity while others 'know' that they have identity conflicts and start off interviews by explaining the whole of the 'between two cultures' thesis. Whether they would be talking in this way if they had not been exposed to these ideas through their parents, the associations, the Cypriot press and various youth and community workers is hard to tell.

Other issues connected with identity are easier to deal with. Language, for example, is considered important by young people, most of whom like the idea of speaking their 'own' language, even if they get angry and frustrated when they are teased by older Cypriots for making mistakes and speaking with an odd accent. This can reach such a pitch of defensiveness that they refuse to speak any Greek at all or exaggerate their lack of fluency. Cypriot dances and music are also popular and although young people sometimes moan about 'having' to do certain things they appear to enjoy them and to think of them as 'our' ways. Church is attended on special occasions because, according to the young people themselves, it's an opportunity to meet their friends.

As to how they feel about the Cypriot community in London, most of the young people I have spoken to make disparaging remarks about the community as a whole and yet their close friends and the people they mix with are mostly other Cypriots. All the engagements and marriages that took place among people I had contact with during my research period were between Cypriots (and in at least three of these cases at least one partner was a professional person).

A final issue concerns the effect of British racism and ethnocentrism on young Cypriots' identity. What is happening here is that although young Cypriots reject what they see as the illiberal and authoritarian style of older Cypriots who are pushing Cypriot culture and identity on to them, in the face of British attitudes they reaffirm this identity and culture (a form of reactive ethnicity). This tendency means that on many issues they are often on the same side as the traditionalist older Cypriots. In terms of associations this ties in with the discussion of the differences between the new working parties (with younger professional Cypriot members) and the old-style associations, since a struggle which may become more important in the future is the struggle for some kind of autonomy and control *vis-à-vis* the dominant group in this country. This is probably the area where the concerns of the old-style associations and the working parties and action groups can come together.

Associations and power relations

Party influence   Cypriots have always had strong left/right divisions. In villages there have tended to be 'left' and 'right' coffee shops with constant power struggles between the two. In London a great deal of the history of the associations has to do with this struggle. The history of the Greek schools, which has already been touched on, is a good example. First some left-wing intellectuals opened a Greek school in London under the auspices of the CP. Shortly afterwards the church (right wing) opened a Greek school. In the decades that followed several other associations formed themselves to organize schools. The next development was the formation of a federation of the schools. After a while the federation was seen to be under left-wing control and the right-wing elements felt they were being swallowed up. They therefore pulled out of the federation and formed their own school which they claimed would stay independent. By this they meant that it would not be party-dominated. Other members of the community are amused at the indignation of the secessionists and point out that at least one of the people behind this move is a leading member of the (centrist) Democratic party. And so it goes on.

The pattern of a party taking over from above, that is, of forming federations in order to get control of various groups, appears to be a common one in Cypriot associational life. Another common pattern is for the left and the right to try and come together, but in the past this kind of unity has been short-lived. At present, however, left and right have come together in ESEKA, a group which organizes solely on the Cyprus issue. It has already kept going longer than any other group of that kind.

What the parties (and the church) can achieve in concrete terms by controlling associations is hard to assess, but that they have control is considered to be a fact by many people in the community and when discussing an association, informants often start off by commenting on whether it is left-wing or right-wing. On the issue of schools and party influence, some parents suggested that the schools are not really to do with teaching children but with controlling parents by keeping tabs on them. An explanation of the proliferation of associations in terms of party manoeuvring and political splits was given by several people.

Personal power Another significance attached to associations, which also explains their increase in numbers, is that they serve as 'windows' for successful entrepreneurs. This fits in with the classic studies of voluntary associations where rank and prestige are conferred through office. In the case of immigrants, since they rarely have access to the wider prestige system of the country in which they live, they need to be acknowledged as important and respected people within their own community. With Cypriots, the holding of office is also used to increase status outside the community. For example, a businessman will try to impress his bank manager (often English) by taking him to a dinner given by his association and at which he is presiding.

This kind of prestige involves personal power and leaders of associations make full use of this power. Since these entrepreneurs are often factory owners, the relationship between ethnic associations and ethnic business could be an interesting area of investigation.[10]

This dimension of associations suggests that although they are *ethnic* associations their significance is not confined to the relationship between ethnic groups and the host community. On the contrary, they appear to play a crucial part in the *internal* workings of the ethnic group. This means that associations can only be adequately understood by looking at them in the context of the community.

Conclusion

Ethnic associations are multi-dimensional and they can change in character over time. Clearly, these changes are related to the stages of development of the ethnic group. A main explicit reason for the existence of ethnic associations is that the community has certain needs to which they cater. Implicitly, if not always explicitly, the associations also seek to maintain ethnicity by stressing divisions along ethnic lines and by pushing the idea that the ethnic group has common interests.

The associations also provide a framework for the display of ethnicity. As far as second-generation ethnic identity is concerned, once again the associations have an indirect effect, both through their role in the community and because they organize schools and clubs. Another of the dimensions of present-day Cypriot associations is the political one. They can be seen as the political wing of the ethnic group, providing an arena for power and prestige struggles. This means that the associations play an important role in the internal organization of the ethnic group, thereby helping to perpetuate the ethnic group and indirectly perpetuating ethnicity.

Notes

1   This chapter was written in 1984 and it should be noted that some changes have taken place since then (for example one of the newspapers has closed down, the Brotherhood has been evicted from its premises by the church).

2   Examples of membership include involvement in the ethnic economy and Cypriot social life. This is outlined on pp. 45-6.

3   The data for this section and the next come from Oakley (1970, 1979 and unpublished), from *Cypriots in Haringey*, and from my own Cypriot informants.

4   This chapter is about Greek Cypriots (although there are many similarities with Turkish Cypriots' experiences) but the general data and statistics take into account all Cypriots unless otherwise stated. Where clarity does not require otherwise, the term 'Cypriot' and not 'Greek Cypriot' is used. For ethnographic accounts of Cypriots in London see Anthias (1982) and Constantinides (1977)—Greek Cypriots, and Ladbury (1977)—Turkish Cypriots.
5   Of the unofficial refugees that stayed on in Britain many have been deported and those remaining are under constant threat of deportation.
6   This does not imply that the Cypriot community is either self-sufficient or outside the state system. Even the Cypriot share of the clothing industry connects at every stage with people outside the group, since most Cypriot factories take work on contract from larger firms. In terms of the state, Cypriots live by British law, pay taxes, etc. and make use of state services and benefits. However, in their day-to-day life, many sections of the community do not have to deal with non-Cypriots if they do not choose to do so. The one exception to this is school (and it is during the school years that Cypriots have most contact with non-Cypriots).
7   *Proxenia*, the Cypriot form of arranged marriage, is more a matter of introducing two young people to one another than of forcing them to marry.
8   For example, the Brotherhood now sees itself as more of a cultural and less of a social centre, while EFEKA has become ultra right-wing and is out of step with its former allies.
9   For ease of presentation the main associations have been set out under different categories but in fact they are not so discrete. For example, one of the community centres is run by a village association, another by a political party and a third, as already indicated, by a theatre group. Also, some of the action groups are offshoots or sub-groups of the other, more permanent, associations.
10   Anthias (1982: 337) analyses the relationship between ethnicity and class and devotes a chapter to ethnic organizations in which she makes the point that for London Cypriots, organizing on an ethnic basis is an alternative to class organization.

References

Adams, T.W. (1971) *Akel: the Communist party of Cyprus*, Hoover Institution Press.
Anthias, Floya (1982) *Ethnicity and class among Greek-Cypriot migrants*, PhD thesis, Bedford College, University of London.
Anthias, Floya (1983) 'Ethnicity and class in Cyprus', *Race and Class*, vol. XXV, no. 1, pp. 59–74, Institute of Race Relations, London.
Anthias, Floya (1983) 'Sexual divisions and ethnic adaptation: The case of Greek-Cypriot women', in A. Phizacklea (ed.), *One Way Ticket*, Routledge & Kegan Paul, London.
Barth, F. (1969) *Ethnic groups and boundaries*, Allen & Unwin, London, 1969.
Cohen, A. (1969) *Custom and politics*, Routledge & Kegan Paul, London.
Cohen, A. (ed.) (1974) *Urban ethnicity*, Tavistock, London.
Constantinides, P. (1977) 'Factors in the maintenance of ethnic identity', in J.L. Watson (ed.), *Between two cultures*, Oxford University Press, London.
Cypriots in Haringey, Haringey Borough handbook prepared by Fuat Alkan and Suzie Constantinides.
Epstein, W. (1978) *Ethos and identity*, Tavistock, London.
Khan, V.S. (ed.) (1979) *Minority families in Britain*, Macmillan, London.
Ladbury, S. (1977) 'The Turkish Cypriots: ethnic relations in London and Cyprus', in J.L. Watson (ed.), *Between two cultures*, Oxford University Press, London.
Leavenbury, J. (1979) *The Cypriot in Haringey*, research report no. 1, School of Librarianship, Polytechnic of North London.
Miles, R. (1982) *Racism and migrant labour*, Routledge & Kegan Paul, London.

Oakley, R. (1970) 'The Cypriots in Britain', in *Race Today 2*, vol. 2, April, pp. 99–102, Race Today Publications, London.

Oakley, R. (1979) 'Family kinship and patronage: the Cypriot migration to Britain', in V.S. Khan (ed.), *Minority families in Britain*, Macmillan, London.

Oakley, R. (unpublished) 'Changing patterns of distribution of Cypriot settlements'.

Rex, J. and Moore, R. (1969) *Race, community and conflict*, Oxford University Press, London.

Wallman, S. (1979) *Ethnicity at work*, Macmillan, London.

Watson, J.L. (ed.) (1977) *Between two cultures*, Oxford University Press, London.

4 Associations amongst the Pakistani Population in Britain

Daniele Joly

Britain's post-war economic expansion brought about the shipment of a labour force from colonies or ex-colonies. It was not envisaged that this process would entail the establishment of 'alien' communities on the national soil, but it has become evident that immigrant groups have settled, and one can already dispute the use of the term 'immigrant' as applied to the second generation. Immigrants have become an object of concern to governments and politicians, who consider them at least a potential problem, at worst as threatening to swamp the British character and way of life. They are often used as political pawns and bear the brunt of prejudices.

Pakistani settlement in Britain
The first Pakistani settlers were former seamen who had joined the merchant navy or the British army. They settled in the early 1940s or at the end of the Second World War, when post-war expansion led to recruitment of labour from colonies and former colonies.

By 1951 there were 5000 Pakistanis in Britain.[1] The number of incoming immigrants from Pakistan continued to rise steadily, reaching a first peak in the early 1960s (see Table 4.1) and a second peak in the 1970s, (see Table 4.2).

Table 4.1   *Pakistani annual immigration into the UK, 1959–66*

1959	850
1960	2,500
1961	25,100
1962	24,843
1963	16,336
1964	10,980
1965	7,427
1966	8,008

Source: D.L. Milner (1970) *Ethnic identity and preference in minority group children*, PhD thesis, University of Bristol, p. 43.

Table 4.2   Pakistani annual immigration into the UK, 1976–81 (000s)

	in	out	net
1976	12	2	+10
1977	12	2	+10
1978	19	1	+18
1979	14	2	+12
1980	11	2	+9
1981	9	1	+8

Source: CRE memorandum, from Muhammed Anwar to all principals and section heads, 19 November 1982, Table 44.

According to the 1981 census the Pakistani population reached 283,000, of which 103,000 were born in the UK.[2] For a combination of reasons[3] the majority of the Pakistani population in Britain originated from two main areas: Punjab and the Mirpur district in Azad Kashmir. They form two groups of equal strength, each of them accounting for 37 per cent of the Pakistani population in Britain.[4] The vast majority of these migrants are of rural origin (95 per cent).[5]

The motivation for this migration was economic, and initially men came on their own with the intention of returning home once they had accumulated sufficient savings to expand their land-holding and property back home; the idea was that they might then be replaced by a male relative. They also sponsored kin and fellow villagers to come over, producing a chain migration. As a consequence almost entire villages from Punjab or Mirpur migrated to Britain.[6] This process was reinforced by the fact that after the restrictive legislation of 1962 and 1968 immigration was almost entirely confined to dependants. In 1966, twice as many women as men came into Britain and over six times as many children as men.[7] But the bulk of wives and children arrived in the 1970s. While there were 206 men per hundred women in 1971,[8] there were 112 men per hundred women in 1981.[9]

The age structure of the Pakistani population is also considerably different from what it used to be in the early stages of migration or even ten years ago. While 61.9 per cent were between twenty-five and forty-four in 1961,[10] in 1981 45 per cent were under sixteen, that is of school age,[11] and the British born component of this population amounted to 36 per cent.[12]

Pakistani 'immigrants' now constitute a stable settled population and represent a substantial and visible group in some areas of Britain.

The economic character of the migration determined the patterns of settlement in four main industrial areas: London and south east

63

152,000; West Midlands 54,000; West Yorkshire 43,000; Greater Manchester 34,000.[13] In Birmingham there are 45,000 persons of Pakistani origin, which means 2.5 per cent of the total population.[14] This percentage is much higher in a few wards, as immigrants have formed settlement clusters in the inner-city zone. About 50 per cent reside in two areas: the Small Heath/Sparkbrook district and the Saltley/Alum Rock district.[15] In the corresponding wards slightly less than one person in five is of Pakistani origin. In addition, people of the same regional origin have gathered in the same neighbourhoods. Saltley is known to be mostly populated by people from Mirpur/Azad Kashmir. In Birmingham as a whole 60 per cent of Pakistanis originate from Azad Kashmir.[16]

The structural circumstances of migration and settlement combine with the numbers and characters of the migrants to create the conditions for the reconstitution of ethnic entities in the country of settlement. Pakistani immigrants have sought to reproduce in the British context the social characteristics which used to shape their way of life. This has been supported by a network of services, businesses and institutions in the field of food,[17] banking,[18] cultural distribution[19] and religious observances. The establishment of ethnic and social/kin networks has been accentuated by the continuing reunification of the *biraderi* through the practice of arranged marriages, which mostly take place amongst kin.

They do not, however, constitute a separate socio-economic system. The Pakistani population is becoming more and more a section of British society. In the first place, through work; most of them form a part of the unskilled working class.[20] Moreover, whereas in the early period of migration it was possible for Pakistanis (single male workers) to limit their interaction with British society, this is not the case today. The establishment of the Pakistani settlement in Britain and the presence of families occurred at a time of major changes in the economic climate, when the period of recession replaced the boom of the 1950s and early 1960s. This has meant that they have found a place within the housing system and, because Pakistani residents have been badly affected by unemployment,[21] they have also become claimants of the welfare state. As a corollary, Britain in turn is increasingly having to take into account the existence of a substantial Pakistani minority.

Research methods
After this brief presentation of the population of Pakistani origin in Britain, it is now appropriate to broach the subject which is our main concern: that of the associations which arise within this population in Birmingham.

This study presents a number of methodological difficulties: in the first place, there is no legal requirement that associations should register[22] and there exists no such register. The first task therefore consisted of a compilation exercise to gather the names and addresses of associations. This information was drawn from a variety of sources:

—the list of officially registered charities
—the directory of ethnic minority organizations (Midlands and Wales)
—the Pakistani consulate in Birmingham
—the *Birmingham Post* year book.

This was complemented by a careful reading of grants applications submitted to the Birmingham inner city partnership programme. Taken by itself this would be misleading as a comprehensive list of associations, but it is a useful supplement to other sources of information.

Apart from the associations which have closed down or moved, there are also many one-man or two-men ventures, which involve the setting up of a paper organization only. In addition, a main organization often forms sub-associations (a cultural group, a youth group, etc.), so that they may appear to be several organizations, whereas in reality they ought to be treated as one single organization.[23] It could also be the case that an organization launched by a 'mother' association takes on a life of its own. Finally, it was only possible to obtain a satisfactory register of associations through methodical fieldwork, obtaining names and addresses by word of mouth and then checking them personally.

Taking all types of association there were approximately seventy Pakistani organizations in Birmingham, which were studied by means of a questionnaire submitted to all associations of which two-thirds replied.[24] Crude quantitative data, however, need to be supplemented by detailed qualitative studies.

A few associations were submitted to a closer study.[25] An attempt was made to select a sample including a range of different sexes, ages, goals, roles, activities, size and dynamism. This study was based on:

—interviews with leaders and some members of the associations
—documents published by the association
—videos used and produced by the association
—participation in the activities of the association.

Inevitably there must be some doubt about the accuracy of some of the information given in replies to questionnaires,[26] and it was therefore desirable to check such information during personal interviews and through participant observation.[27]

One group of associations was excluded from this study. This was the group of associations with political goals concerned with events in the Indian sub-continent. Specifically it proved impossible to interview leaders of associations concerned with the future of Kashmir, because of their possible involvement in the death of an Indian diplomat.[28]

General characteristics of associations

An overview of the associations reveals a number of general characteristics. The geographical distribution of the associations shows that all but 5 per cent of them are situated in inner-city areas populated by a high concentration of Pakistani people, and 50 per cent of them own their premises.[29] This may be partly explained by the religious character of 70 per cent of the associations; as the first duty of a Muslim is 'to establish prayers',[30] the initial *raison d'être* of a mosque is to provide praying facilities. The premises are almost never purpose-built (except for the Central Mosque and the Saddham Hussein mosque in Aston, which was left unfinished) and frequently consist of a private house which may have been donated by a pious individual or a family as a prayer hall. About 15 per cent of all the associations use rented accommodation and the same percentage do not have any premises at all, but use those of other associations or the home of a member.

Almost all the associations arise from local initiatives and are only based in Birmingham. Naturally, Islamic associations, in principle, partake of an international religious *umma*,[31] but in practice only a few of them belong to a structured organization, which may be British-wide or international.

The formation of associations does not derive from the pattern of social relations which Pakistani people experienced prior to migration; formal associations are not part of the homeland culture of the majority of Pakistanis in Britain[32] who come from rural areas[33] where kinship and village networks provide a sufficient basis for social organization.

Associations came about to cope with various aspects of the British situation and to represent interests which ethnic networks could not meet. In that respect they are a departure from traditions. They also denote an adaptation to and an understanding of the British system which responds more to formal corporate and organized pressure groups than to individuals. And yet the character of the leadership and membership of the associations are stamped by the patron–client pattern of social relations brought over from a Pakistani set-up, which is then reproduced within the association.

66

Membership

In the majority of cases the association does not have a formal membership.[34] Only an active core of members truly participate; the rest is composed of 'passive' members, attending the social functions organized for them, and using services provided by the association (premises, advice etc.).

The great majority of 'members' are men; only 13 per cent are women. This is very much in keeping with a way of life where the traditional focus of activities is the home and the family.[35] Mosques in theory welcome women for the Friday afternoon prayer, but in practice very few attend. There are three women-only organizations; two of them are branches of an organization with its headquarters in Pakistan;[36] the other one is a project for Asian ladies, initiated by Birmingham local authority.[37]

The bulk of members of associations work in manual employment (46 per cent) and many are now unemployed. Eight per cent of them own a business and 3 per cent are professionals. Naturally, professional associations do not follow this pattern; nor does the Pakistani women's association, which comprises mostly middle-class educated ladies.

The ethnic origin of the members corresponds roughly to the general structure of the Pakistani population in Birmingham; about 53 per cent come from Mirpur/Azad Kashmir.[38] Most associations tend to have a majority of members who share the same ethnic origin and a few group people from the same village.[39]

This feature is emphasized by the structure of settlement which brings together people who originate from the same area. However, it is not true of a number of associations: the Asian women's project, the parents' associations and some of the religious associations, where varying degrees of mixing can be found. In any case, questions of ethnic origin have become slightly sensitive as a result of the kidnapping and death of an Indian diplomat. Some leaders of associations refused to identify the ethnic origin of their members. There may be several possible explanations for this attitude: it may stem from a cautious mind or a political stance reaffirming the unity of Pakistan against the claims of Kashmiris. Assessments on ethnic origin are therefore mostly based on the researcher's own observations.

As for age distribution, the largest number of members ranges between twenty-five and forty-five (48 per cent) and 30 per cent are between forty-five and sixty. Altogether these percentages are representative of a young population but do not reflect the Birmingham average which shows 45 per cent of the population of Pakistani origin below sixteen. This membership is also well settled in Britain and 70 per cent have lived in Britain for more than fifteen years.

In addition, the numerous *madrasa*[40] attached to Islamic associations bring a substantial number of children[41] under the influence of associations.

Leadership

The 'passive' character of most associations' membership tends to enhance the importance of leaders in decision-making. Leaders of associations and leadership of the communities are changing in accordance with the circumstances of migration and settlement. The leadership reflects the interests and level of consciousness of the Pakistani population in Britain.

The initial group of Pakistani immigrants who came to Birmingham intended to return home to their families as soon as they had made enough money. Their whole orientation of life was directed towards Pakistan. Essentially in their eyes there was nothing more to Britain than a source of work and earnings, for themselves and for male relatives (for example a younger brother or cousin) whom they would bring over. Most of them were not accustomed to city life, knew little about Britain and spoke no English. In this set-up, the leaders who arose were people capable of facilitating the achievement of those goals. They were the individuals who, by their class background and level of education or length of experience in Britain, could play the role of intermediaries between the Pakistani workers and the British system; as they spoke English they could give some help in matters of immigration and administrative formalities. Most of these leaders were of urban petty bourgeois origin, as these were generally prerequisites for obtaining a good level of education in Pakistan.[42] (Many were of Punjabi origin since Azad Kashmir was much less urbanized.)

In Britain they may have been working in a factory but often later set up a business or became landlords; and they also played a role as money-lenders.[43] Their position became strengthened by British authorities and institutions which, in search of interlocutors, turned to these 'leaders'. The prestige accorded to them by the British establishment enhanced their status in the eyes of their own people, and for that reason they often sought this recognition even more.[44] This type of leadership is highly personalized; it relies on a network of duties and debts, kinship and village allegiances informed by a tradition of *clientelisme*.[45]

Frequently the same individuals were also active in the organization of British branches of Pakistani parties.[46] Another group held the deference of the early population who do not fit into the same category: these were the religious men who served as imams in the early mosques, and who may have gained respect through their piety.[47]

The configuration of associations and leadership today reveals that they have undergone and are still undergoing major changes. The date of formation of associations still in existence indicates that many have been formed recently: 38 per cent of them were founded between 1979 and 1984, only 8 per cent were formed before 1960, and 22 per cent between 1960 and 1969. A closer study of the associations shows that the change is not only quantitative but also qualitative.

The Pakistan-based political parties and leaders have had little influence for several reasons: they have concentrated almost solely on issues related to Pakistan, whereas the emphasis of Pakistani residents in Britain has shifted to Britain, as they have become permanently settled; moreover, developments in Pakistan were unable to stimulate a sustained or renewed interest.[48]

The team of leaders and the associations which now emerge as the more successful and developing ones are those which address themselves to the present interests and outlook of the Pakistani population. Unlike the earlier leaders, who were concerned with immigration issues and return to Pakistan, these leaders have taken on the task of ensuring the basis for the maintenance and reproduction of the community. The one single element which has been retained is that of Islamic identity and the prime concern of parents and leaders is the preservation of Islam among the 'second' generation. Some of them belong to international Islamic movements and organizations which form a part of the recent Islamic revival. One stream is related to the Pakistani Jamaati Islami. Another group draws its inspiration from the Saudi Arabian school of Islam. In those cases, ideology and programme are intimately linked to their spiritual and/or organizational centre. A third current does not profess allegiance to a defined international movement. They are perhaps more flexible as they arose from local conditions and focus on local conditions, being intent on adapting Islam to them.

Not only do they all share the firm intention of securing a place for Muslims and Islam in Britain, outside the *Dar el Islam*,[49] they have also given themselves the tools to achieve their goals by:

—framing the organizational structures necessary to sustain that effort
—adopting new approaches to the young generation: teaching methods, medium of communication and range of activities (the old traditional imams are being challenged)
—taking active steps to secure alliance and support from British institutions and society.

This leadership is expressed through leaders 'old' and 'new'. The ones who have already been on the scene many years retain a lot of the characteristics described above,[50] in particular the personalized aspect of leadership. The new ones comprise young people of varied ethnic and socio-economic backgrounds, who have received part of their education in Britain. Many of them work in action centres or in posts related to community work (having benefited from the Section 11 provisions of the Local Government Act 1966 which enables local authorities to obtain additional finance for tasks resulting from the presence of large numbers of immigrants). In addition, a few English converts seem to have assumed a more intellectual than organizational leadership through their theological knowledge.[51]

The other new development among the leadership of the Pakistani and Muslim population is an intervention into British mainstream politics, largely through the Labour party. Three Labour councillors were elected in 1983 who illustrate different types of leadership:

—the first one to be elected (for Aston) is a mature person of Punjabi origin, who owns a business and is involved in the work of the Central Mosque[52]

—another one elected for Sparkhill comes from Mirpur/Azad Kashmir; he came to Britain as a teenager and worked in a factory[53]

—the third one, who represents the suburban ward of Fox Hollies, is a young professional woman who also received her education in Britain.[54]

Prior to this a Yemeni, Councillor Abdi, active in Muslim affairs, had been elected in the Handsworth ward.

Specific characteristics of associations
Associations could be classified and analysed in a variety of ways, all of which contain advantages and shortcomings because of the complexities of the reality under study. Associations overlap and interlock whether one is concerned with their goals, roles, activities, composition or size.

The basis of our classification is the concrete situation of the Pakistani population settled in Britain: a transplanted minority with a different socio-economic, cultural and religious background to that of the majority of the population, but also a minority which is now settled and stabilized and in the process of contributing a patch to the fabric of British society. The different categories of association will then derive from the diverse interests of the population which has not yet broken all relations with Pakistan, but is set to establish its position firmly and survive in one form or another in the country of adoption. Evidently, different sections of the population will not necessarily emphasize the same range of interests.

Links with Pakistan

One of these interests is the continuing concern to maintain links with Pakistan. This is manifested by the existence of Pakistani banks which handle the transactions to send remittances back home,[55] by the numerous travel agencies for the toing and froing between Britain and Pakistan. This is also the case for associations. One of the women's organizations illustrates this link, as a branch of a Pakistani organization: it is limited in scope and activities, gathering a small number of educated ladies who meet socially to celebrate Pakistan Day,[56] for instance.

The Ex-Servicemen's Society is a good example of an association servicing a section of the population which has a concrete interest in pursuing its relationship with the country of origin. The association plays both an advice and pressure group role in helping its members to solve problems to do with pension rights which they are eligible to enjoy as ex-members of the army. In addition to this main concern, the association calls upon the Pakistani government to look after its people: it pleaded for the improvement of educational facilities in Pakistan;[57] and requested that the Pakistani authorities protest against the racial discrimination exercised against its nationals in Britain.[58] The clientele of this association is doomed to decrease and perhaps disappear altogether, as the limited flow of immigration does not allow for a great number of ex-servicemen to come over. The association now tries to cater for ex-servicemen's children.[59]

The third type of organization which corresponds to this category of interests is that of 'death committees' or 'funeral associations'. These are numerous and about a third of Pakistani men belong to this type of association. These associations are funds which assist the relatives of a deceased person so that they can send the body back to Pakistan to be buried in the ancestral soil. This constitutes a departure from traditional patterns and even initially met the resistance of some members of the community, who felt that it was a shame and a stigma on the family not to cater for the burial of their near ones.[60] But the financial difficulties incurred by the high cost of sending bodies by plane prompted the formation and multiplication of death funds. Most of them are *biraderi* or village-based as regards the origin of its members, except for people of urban origin who do not necessarily form a 'death committee' in this manner.[61] They are locally based in Britain but do not have a structured organization, save two or three officers, one of whom is the treasurer.

These associations are likely to subsist for a time while first-generation migrants grow old and wish to be buried in the *Dar el Islam*. Increased unemployment makes it difficult for most families to bear the financial burden on their own. As the second generation grows older and as burial grounds are granted for Muslims in this country, the need for death funds is likely to diminish.

A variety of other associations has taken up tasks which deal with the servicing of links between Britain and Pakistan, in particular dealing with immigration problems which still figure as an important priority. Advice centres and Islamic associations also handle such cases, although their prime concern often focuses on other issues. These associations and the particular service they provide are still a vigorous reality today, although they may be less important in the future.

Insertion in British society
As a counterpoint to its continued attachment to its homeland, the Pakistani population tries to make the best of its situation in Britain.

Associations have grown to deal with different aspects of Pakistani people's everyday life in Britain. A few advice centres have been created or expanded to handle such matters. The Azad Kashmir Welfare Association states in its constitution its intention to 'work for their social welfare'.[62] A closer examination of its work shows the range of problems it deals with.

Whereas when immigration first started, very few Pakistanis would have drawn the benefit of their tax contributions, they are now increasingly behaving like white natives. The shift from economic expansion to depression and unemployment has increased people's awareness of the necessity to work within the welfare state. The presence of reunited families creates the demand for child benefit, and for adequate advice towards successful claims, as is shown by the 105 cases dealt with by the Azad Kashmir Welfare Association advice centre.[63]

The staying over or the arrival of older people who no longer spend their retirement 'back home' explains the need to enquire about old age pensions (231 cases).

The greatest number of enquiries, however, relates to supplementary benefits (608 cases).[64] Matters connected with nationality also constitute a strong object of concern (382 cases).[65] These cases demonstrate a departure from traditional patterns, whereby financial help would have fallen solely upon the family.

This report on advice supplied by the Azad Kashmir Welfare Society tends to confirm the association's claim that it works to 'help Kashmiris to integrate into British society',[66] at least on an economic plane.

The 'integration' of Pakistani people or their taking part in life in Britain is also exemplified through other associations which include Pakistanis together with other members of minority groups and English natives.

As Pakistani families endeavoured to improve their standard of accommodation in Birmingham rather than concentrate on buying a plot of land back home to build a *pakka*[67] house, housing or residents' associations took on more importance. Most of them have a mixed membership; in the inner-city areas where many Pakistanis live, and which are reputed for sub-standard accommodation,[68] these associations often enjoy the active participation of Pakistanis.

Saltley News mentions several housing associations for the Saltley area alone in 1975.[69] These associations provide advice on obtaining improvement grants and act as pressure groups: a case in point is the Durham Road Residents' Association which, after organizing a survey on the environmental conditions of residents,[70] presented its case at a Labour Party meeting, attended by city and county councillors. About ninety people attended the meeting, and numerous residents came forward to voice their grievances and give support to the representatives of the association.

Other associations deal with other areas of concern, such as the Nechells school committee, which launched a militant and sustained campaign to keep the school open. A third of the committee members were Pakistani and Pakistani parents actively participated in the fund-raising effort to keep the campaign going.[71]

The Pakistani associations themselves follow the trend towards 'integration':

—more and more mosques are now applying for planning permission to comply with the law of the land. One of the leaders of the Central Mosque vouched that no new mosque would be created without planning permission[72]

—the video shop owners' association sought advice from local authorities so that they could better ensure the implementation of the legislation against video 'piracy', and thus preserve their trade

—the main associations have taken the initiative to be represented on police liaison committees

—the grants made available through the urban partnership programme attracted numerous applications for funding,[73] the applicants thereby, to an extent, becoming more a part of the British institutions.

Associations of this type and the issues they concern themselves with are likely to endure as their relevance to Pakistani people's lives continues.

The maintenance of culture and religion

The associations which deserve more attention from this study's point of view[74] are also the ones which have become noticeable by their size and growth over the last few years. They have addressed themselves to one of the most essential features of Pakistani culture: Islam. Islam is the one single element which provided a basis for the foundation of Pakistan in 1947. People originating from rural Pakistan and Azad Kashmir in particular are known to be very pious. Since General Zia's coming to power in 1978, there has been a sharp turn towards increased Islamization of the state. And this has coincided with international revivalist movements in Islam. Last but not least the specificity of Islam as a *din*[75] makes it an all-embracing project governing all aspects of the life and conduct of its followers. All these elements contribute to explain why attempts to secure the preservation of a Pakistani 'community' have focused on Islam in a predominantly Christian British society.

The first religious associations to be created were *zaouia* (centres of prayer and Islamic instruction) and mosques,[76] and they soon multiplied.[77] Jorgen Nielsen suggests the figure of 450 mosques in England and Wales in 1983.[78] In Birmingham there are over forty mosques and new ones keep being created. Their first function is to provide facilities for the practice of Islam; most of them publish a calendar of prayer times in Birmingham.

The more dynamic Islamic associations propose a clear ideological programme, and a specific Islamic world outlook. They challenge the dominating ideology in Britain: they oppose the corruption and decadence of a 'materialist capitalist' society which has lost its moral values,[79] and point to the spiritual crisis of Europe and Christianity.

The success of these associations conveys the aspiration of Pakistanis in Britain to safeguard their religion. The associations here take on a vanguard role as they stress the need to be vigilant and remind the population of its duties to Allah and Islam, not only for itself but more importantly for its children. The Jamiat Ahl-e-Hadith even published a special booklet informing and instructing parents on the rights of their children in schools.[80]

These associations deplore the fact that 'the only people who attend mosques and Islamic centres are the older people or the very young'.[81] As one association leader commented: 'We realise that we have already lost one generation'.[82] These associations have become well aware of the need to concentrate on the youth because: 'The younger generation is the link which will convey Islam to future generations and people'.[83]

For that reason, numerous *madrasa* have been formed alongside mosques, and the better organized centres are deploying large resources to recapture the interest of the youth.[84] They set up libraries and bookshops with a varied literature on Islam, in English, Arabic and Urdu, some of which have been specially designed for the youth. The Muslim Educational Trust specializes in publications on Islam. It organizes lessons not only for the study of Qur'an (which could simply consist of a reading of the holy book in Arabic without the slightest hint of comprehension on the part of children), but includes other subjects, Islamyat, Fiqr, history, with the aim of raising the standard to a comprehensive Islamic education. In the bigger centres which we are now considering, between 300 and 400 children attend weekly classes.

Particular attention is given to the education of girls because 'the girls of today are the mothers of tomorrow'[85] and on them will largely depend the raising of children in an Islamic way of life. Classes are organized for girls on a par with boys, and this concern is exemplified through the numerous articles on wives and mothers in the journal *The Straight Path*.[86]

A few associations have realized the need to adopt new modern approaches to the teaching of Islam. Some are campaigning against the traditional 'ignorant *ulema*',[87] who teach Qur'an in the majority of the mosques. The other 'vanguard' associations just concentrate on developing and promoting the new methods: they emphasize the necessity to explain and bring about understanding rather than compel the children to learn by rote.[88] In these associations the use of the stick is rare. One of the girls' classes attended by the researcher is a marvellous demonstration of this new approach. The teacher was both firm and gentle, she displayed great resources of patience and was prepared to repeat explanations until the students fully grasped their lesson; at the same time she expected and obtained participation from the class. All this skill was put at the service of furthering a most 'orthodox' purist doctrinal line in Islam.[89]

The medium of communication stands high on the agenda. As most children are more conversant and certainly better at ease in English than many other languages, the use of Urdu (different again from their mother tongue, which in most cases is Punjabi) is detrimental to an optimal efficiency in teaching. The more forward-looking associations hold classes either solely in English or combine the use of English and Urdu (in addition to teaching Arabic, which is the language of the Qur'an). English is the language which probably will be widely used in the future for the teaching of Islam, if associations want to avoid a total loss of influence on the younger generation

The language issue is even more important where publishing is concerned, since very few youngsters are capable of reading Urdu; three publications aimed specifically at a young readership have appeared in English.[90] Another publication, from the Sparkbrook

Islamic Centre, was in Urdu until 1983 when it began to include a page in English for young readers. One of these publications, *The Straight Path*, appears to calculate its layout and the formulation of its material to make it more attractive to the youth.

The same forward-looking associations have begun to organize recreational and sports activities for the youth. This has the double advantage of keeping them away from community centres which are seen as unpropitious to Islamic customs[91] and of attracting them to Islamic centres. The use of modern equipment, such as videos, is very common. A popular activity is camping, where recreation is combined with careful observance and learning of Islam in practice.[92] However, the message taken up by the youngster is not necessarily the exact one intended by the leadership. Ideological questions are resolved in practice through the participation and acceptance or non-acceptance of the members.[93]

Although the major interest developed by these associations is that of Islam, one regular feature of their work includes the teaching of Urdu (as a subject *per se*, but not necessarily a medium of communication to teach Islam). This is one feature through which Islamic associations differentiate themselves from one another. Not only are there several of them, because of territorial dispersion which necessitates at least one mosque per area of high Pakistani concentration in Birmingham, but also because of the different branches of Islam, and because of differentiation on a national basis. Bengalis and Yemenis have their separate mosques, and even among Pakistanis one can find a 'regional specialization', so that one association will include a majority of members originating from Azad Kashmir,[94] another will be Punjabi-based[95] and a third will have a good number of members from the North-West Frontier.[96] Pakistan tends to be more pronounced if the membership and leadership are mostly Punjabi-based.

The category of associations analysed above has to be further investigated, as they appear to represent a lasting interest among most of the Pakistani population, which wants to retain its Islamic character.

Changing Britain
The associations which organize the preservation of Islam for Pakistanis in Britain generally do not plan for the constitution of an isolated enclave. They have recognized the need to find a place for Islam and Muslims within the fabric of British society.[97] Most of them work actively to achieve that goal. In this respect, the associations truly contribute to the elaboration of a 'multi-cultural and multi-faith society'. This process meets resistance both from government authorities and

sometimes the English people themselves[98] as the dominant ideology is being challenged.[99]

Some of the associations reiterate their wish to act in a 'constructive co-operative manner'.[100] They say that they do not wish to seek 'confrontation'.[101]

Their declared intention is in the first place to dispel misunderstanding and ignorance about Islam. They want to change the 'wrong image' given of Muslims. They intervene to correct the 'misconceptions' spread by the press.[102] They attempt to explain their case to the neighbouring white population and its churches.[103] Courses are organized on Islam for non-Muslims.[104] Advisers on Islam are made available to health authorities, schools and hospitals.[105] Some of the literature published by Muslim organizations is designed for a non-Muslim readership.

A public-relations exercise is directed to different sections of society, as is exemplified by the *Id* parties organized for non-Muslims by the Sparkbrook Islamic Centre or the list of invitees at a yearly prize distribution of the Jamiat Ahl-e-Hadith. The list of visitors to the Sparkbrook Islamic Centre reveals that an ever-increasing emphasis is placed on opening the centre to visits from and the scrutiny of different non-Muslim institutions (schools, churches).[106]

The associations have elaborated a policy of exchanges and discussion with sections of British society, in particular the churches: regular monthly meetings are held with churches in the neighbourhood[107] and ecumenical ceremonies are held to celebrate religious festivals.[108]

The Central Mosque is in the process of negotiating the prerogative of celebrating marriages that would be legally recognized.

As their prime object of concern is the younger generation, the schools have become a priority area for initiatives. The Muslim Education Co-ordinating Committee has put forward a series of demands covering the teaching of and respect for Islamic customs, and the teaching of Urdu in schools.

The Muslim Liaison Committee comprises about fifty Muslim organizations and negotiates with the Birmingham education authorities on the basis of a thirteen-point memorandum. The East Birmingham Parents' Association acts on a local basis and discusses directly with head teachers.[109] Its members are governors of schools. Some of them have arranged to take responsibility for Muslim assemblies in schools. Adjustments have been made with the co-operation of head teachers.[110]

In some cases churches and schools are used for the activities of associations such as religious celebrations and sports activities.[111]

Political parties have been approached to lend their support. On a national level, the Union of Muslim Organizations made representations to the Conservative Party conference on the question of single-sex schools. More often, it is the Labour Party which is contacted by Pakistani organizations—in Birmingham through Pakistani and Muslim councillors.[112] These developments are significant. The growth and continuation of the associations will partly depend on their success.

Associations and ethnic identity

The identity options put forward by the associations to an extent reflect the variety of identity facets which exist and govern the life of Pakistanis in Britain.

The initial purveyors of identity are the primary group, the family and kinship networks. Among Pakistani people the family and *biraderi* play an important role in the socialization of children, much more so than among their English counterparts. But the Pakistani family does not propose a homogeneous single image of identity. And different sets of allegiances are formulated: to the caste, the village of origin, the area or region (Mirpur/Azad Kashmir, Punjab or other), to Pakistan, to Islam. As a result of staying in Britain, some would perhaps develop allegiances to Britain or to being Asian or black. Class position and consciousness must also be taken into account.

All associations convey a certain identity message whether explicit or implicit. Pakistanis who belong to a trade union, or to a mixed residents' association, will necessarily partake of some of the values and interests put forward by the association, and this has an impact on ethnic cohesiveness and identity. The young people who belong to anti-racist or anti-deportation groups tend to identify themselves as Asians or black, but do not necessarily eliminate other aspects of their identity, related to ethnic origin. An association such as the Azad Kashmir Welfare Association, as its name suggests, appeals to a Kashmiri sense of belonging, but in practice helps to meet the interest of people settled in Britain, and objectively works towards a modification of traditional patterns (such as the transfer of family responsibilities on to the welfare state).

The ex-servicemen's associations make a definite 'economic' commitment to people's Pakistani origin, as this is a source of sustenance. Death committees similarly reaffirm attachment to one's land and home village or town. By their very existence, these associations make concrete an affirmation of identity. However, it will remain limited in depth and future perspective unless the associations considerably change their character and the nature of their influence.

The associations which merit more consideration are the ones which specifically address themselves to culture and identity, or put forward an ideological programme. No 'cultural' association *per se* exists (except on paper). The only associations which have taken on this task are Islamic associations.

The notion of Muslim identity is mentioned repeatedly, verbally and in writing, as one moves amongst Islamic associations, whether they address themselves to Muslims or non-Muslims.[113] The general message on Muslim identity concerns all the community, but the associations' main goal is the preservation of this identity which leads them to show particular concern for the youth.

The *ideological* programme clearly places itself in the context of a non-Muslim country and in opposition to a hostile environment—hostile in so far as it is considered to be diametrically opposed to Islamic values. Islam is

> a more dynamic, moral and ideological force which sweeps ahead in the form of a flood against any element of evils and vices, injustices and corruptions, mental and moral indignity. In the case of Westernism, which is making man an object of lust and desires, it is being continuously challenged and threatened by Islamic revolutionaries' hard work to liberate man from the clutches of materialism.[114]

It is a widespread view among Pakistani people that Islam is morally superior and that the looseness of western society (drinking, 'revealing' clothes, the mixing of boys and girls, etc.) creates a threat to the morality and good conduct of their children. The associations are therefore bound to find an echo among first-generation settlers.

Because of the nature of Islam, Muslim identity is an all-embracing project which concerns everyday customs (eating and clothing habits for instance), religious practices, social relations (placing a high emphasis on sex roles and on the family). It is bound to strengthen further some of the established patterns such as the already prevailing allegiance to the family.

In the sphere of international politics, Islamic associations lend their support to the PLO against Jews and Israel and to the Afghan Mujahideen against the Soviet Union and communism. Support for the Islamic Republic of Iran is widespread, but General Zia Ul Haque's government comes under a certain amount of criticism.

It remains to be seen if the programme and options proposed by these associations have any influence or simply ricochet on the youth. They act through several channels to achieve their messianic task:

—they attempt to reinforce, clarify or modify the parents' observance of Islam

—they provide Qur'anic lessons, *Islamyat*, Arabic and related lessons to children sent to study after school hours

—they agitate for modifications in the state school syllabuses so that all the children for whom school is compulsory until the age of sixteen will be able to 'preserve their identity'

—they organize recreational and sports activities which are attractive to the young people, all the more so as parents' permission to attend will be achieved more easily.

Already the more enterprising associations have realized that old methods of teaching have proved to be a failure. Their new 'progressive' approach, combined with the general despondency of the youth who have no real prospect of reward from 'materialist' Britain, may lead to a positive response from the young people. Islam offers a sense of collectivity, solidarity and an ideal to strive for in the context of a British recession.

And yet despite declarations on the unity of Islam, Islamic identity options are diversified. Different centres propose different schools of Islam. In addition to the Shiab/Sunni divide, there are a lot of different streams among the Sunni. Here the 'fundamentalists' oppose the orders of syncretic Islam.

One of the main points of the fundamentalists' programme is precisely the fight against the cultural and ethnic practices of Islam, 'which are not truly Islamic',[115] such as the worship of shrines and the influence of Sufis. In practice, it tends to oppose many of the practices of 'popular' Islam, such as the worship of *Pirs* (holy men) and also everyday customs which are specific to the Indian sub-continent (for example, some of the practices in marriage ceremonies are identical to those of the Sikhs or Hindus, for example the tying of a knot on the arm of the bride and bridegroom and the dowry tradition).

Another association follows a different line; it wants to ensure that its members can participate fully in British society and remain Muslim at the same time. It emphasizes the need for Islam to be 'articulate' and taught in English.

Islam proclaims that it has no national boundary: this is the official message put across. In parallel to this message there exists a reality which must have an influence on the people's ethnic identity.

The faithful gather on a regional basis. One particular mosque in practice is a focus for Kashmiri identity. In the first place, the majority of its members is of Kashmiri origin, and their gathering together through the association reinforces their natural bonds. But, more importantly, the leaders of the association stimulate and inform a debate on Kashmir. Another association linked with the Jamaati Islami of Pakistan will convey more of a Pakistani identity message through its guests of honour and through its celebration of Pakistan Day. Generally it incorporates mostly Punjabi members.

The majority of the associations, however, teach Urdu which is the official language in Pakistan, and one of its strong demands for changes in the school curriculum is the teaching of Urdu at certificate level.

The question of language is an important one for identity and the young people are given a series of choices in this matter: for Punjabis and Azad/Kashmiris the mother tongue is Punjabi or a dialect of Punjabi; Urdu is not only the national language but also the written and literary language; Arabic is the language *par excellence* of Islam, as the language of the Qur'an. The last two are taught by a number of Islamic associations. Punjabi and English are the more common media of communication; the older people speak Punjabi, the younger ones English. In a girls' camp, when the organizer addressed himself to them in Punjabi, they answered in English (and sometimes found it difficult to understand him). In one of the associations where lessons were taught in Urdu, the students answered questions in English. The associations which are more flexible and dynamic will adapt to this developing trend; the others will fail to retain the children's interest.

The membership therefore does have some influence on the shaping of identity options offered to them, not only in the field of language, but in the implementation of Islam (as is shown in the Muslim girls' camp).

The question remains unresolved; the schools, the media, the concrete reality of living in Britain are potent factors contributing to the identity of the second generation. They are agents or recipients of a youth culture which is expressed through cricket teams (the Pakstars), or in teenagers' gangs (the Lynx, the Dragons). These would be fruitful areas for investigation and future research.

Notes

1   Jorgen S. Nielsen (1984) 'Muslim immigration and settlement in Britain', *Research Papers, Muslims in Europe*, no. 21, March, p.3, Centre for the Study of Christian-Muslim Relations, Selly Oak Colleges, Birmingham.
2   Office of Population Censuses and Surveys (1983) *Labour Force Survey 1981*, p.3, HMSO, London.
3   The recruitment of Punjabis and Mirpuris (Azad Kashmir) into the army; the displacement of populations across Punjab and Kashmir at the time of partition between India and Pakistan (1947), which turned many of their inhabitants into *mujaheers* (refugees); the construction of the Mangla Dam in Mirpur in the early 1960s flooded many villages.
4   Jorgen S. Nielsen (1984) p. 4, see note 1.
5   Badr Dahya (1972–3) 'Pakistanis in England', *New Community*, Winter, vol. 2, p. 25, London.

6   It is not unusual to see, in a wedding ceremony, 1000 guests almost all members of the same *biraderi* (extended family).

7   1966 10 per cent sample census (London, General Registry Office, 1967).

8   1971 Population Census of Great Britain and 70 per cent of these women had come after 1967. Verity Saifullah Khan (1975) 'Asian migrant women in Britain', in Alfred de Souza (ed.), *Women in Contemporary India*, p. 174, Minohar, Delhi.

9   *Labour Force Survey 1981* (1983) p.30.

10   1961 census.

11   *Labour Force Survey 1981* (1983) p.3.

12   *Labour Force Survey 1981* (1983) p.3.

13   *Labour Force Survey 1981* (1983) p.4.

14   1981 census.

15   *Ibid.*

16   Mark Johnson (1985) '"Race", religion and ethnicity: religious observance in the West Midlands', *Ethnic and Racial Studies*, vol. 8, no. 3, July, p.429, London.

17   According to the *Evening Mail*, 11 November 1972, there were fifty-two private slaughter-houses in Birmingham to service consumers who wish to buy halal meat (meat from animals killed in accordance with Islamic rules). There are also numerous grocery shops supplying all the relevant vegetables and spices.

18   There are five Pakistani banks in Birmingham: United Bank of Pakistan, National Bank of Pakistan, Muslim Commercial Bank, Habib Bank, Allied Bank of Pakistan.

19   Mostly videos of Indian films. Videos are a thriving business among Pakistanis in Britain.

20   Mark Johnson (1985) Table 3, p. 433, see note 16.

21   In Saltley (Birmingham) there are up to 27 per cent Pakistanis unemployed, Daniele Joly, 'The opinions of Mirpuri parents in Saltley, Birmingham, about their children's schooling', Research papers, *Muslims in Europe*, no. 23, September 1984, p.7, Centre for the Study of Islam and Christian–Muslim Relations, Selly Oak Colleges, Birmingham. In Birmingham as a whole, there are 15.8 per cent unemployed, *Employment Gazette*, August 1983, Table 2.4.

22   As in France (Loi 1901).

23   Such as Sparkbrook Islamic Centre and its sub-sections such as the Muslim Youth Association.

24   If one discounts the associations which are now defunct.

25   List of associations: Asian Ladies Group, Norton Hall, East Birmingham Parents' Association, Sparkbrook Islamic Centre, Markazi Jamiat Ahl-e-Hadith, Islamic Resource Centre, Central Mosque, Naseby Youth Club.

26   The vast majority of associations does not keep a register of members; figures regarding membership are only approximate.

27   In some cases the answers could be verified by the researcher herself. A prior classification of the associations according to size and activity had been arrived at through discussions with members of the Pakistani community. The answers provided did not contradict it.

28   On 3 and 4 February 1984, an Indian diplomat was kidnapped and killed by an organization which called itself the Kashmir Liberation Army. As a consequence the Pakistani population was submitted to intense questioning from the police. This incident held back the distribution of the questionnaire that was about to begin. It made it virtually impossible to pursue research on political organizations.

29   Answers to questionnaire.

30   Safdar Butt (1983) 'The concept of religion in Islam', *Al Tawhid*, The Journal of Muslim Youth in Birmingham, monthly, vol. 1, no. 1, March–April, p. 17.

31   *Umma* means community.

32   Mosques do exist in Pakistan, but do not fulfil the same function as an Islamic association in Britain.

33 Dahya Badr (1972–3) 'Pakistanis in England', *New Community*, 2, Winter, p.25, London.
34 See Chapter 1 in this volume. Also John Rex (1973) *Race Colonialism and the City*, Routledge & Kegan Paul, London.
35 A characteristic of the Pakistani rural Muslim population.
36 The All Pakistan Women's Association.
37 The Asian Ladies Project, Norton Hall Community Centre, Ralph Road, Saltley, Birmingham 8.
38 Mark Johnson (1985) p.3, see note 16.
39 This mostly applies to 'death committees'.
40 Qur'anic schools.
41 Around 3500 children, according to the results of the questionnaire.
42 'Good' schools where English is taught can be found mostly in cities, and in all cases is not free.
43 John Rex and Robert Moore (1967) *Race, Community and Conflict: A Study of Sparkbrook*, pp.167–78, Oxford University Press, London.
44 One of the early leaders whom we interviewed proudly showed a file containing all the official letters and invitations he received from local and national authorities, including the Queen. (Private interview, 2 March 1984.)
45 John Rex and Robert Moore (1967), p.117, see note 43.
46 This is rendered evident by the identical addresses given in connection with early associations and Pakistani political parties.
47 But they did not assume any real leadership role.
48 Punctual interest is manifested when major events occur in the Indian sub-continent, e.g. the East–West Pakistan armed conflict (*Birmingham Post*, 13 December 1971), Ex-Prime Minister Buttho's execution, M. Buttho's execution in Indian Kashmir February 1984.
49 Muslim land.
50 Educated business or professional men, of urban origin and a personalized style of leadership.
51 For example, Dr Yaqub Zaqi, who was originally a Scotsman who changed his name.
52 Councillor Afzil.
53 Councillor Khan.
54 Councillor Hafeez.
55 According to *Akhbar e Watan* London (23 February 1972) £5 million a month are remitted through official channels.
56 Celebration of Pakistan Day, APWA, *Birmingham Post*, 12 May 1983.
57 Letter from the Pakistan Ex-Servicemen's Association (UK) to General Muha.nmad Zia-Ul-Haque, dated 10 September 1978.
58 Interview with the president of the association, Birmingham, 21 June 1984.
59 Letter from the Pakistan Ex-Servicemen's Association (UK) to Brigadier Ayaz Ahmed, Embassy of Pakistan, 35 Lownden Square, London, SW3X 9JN, dated 18 January 1983.
60 Interview, Birmingham, 1 July 1983.
61 Interviews: Birmingham, 21 July 1983; Birmingham, 17 May 1983.
62 Constitution of the Azad Kashmir Welfare Association (AKWA), p.1.
63 AKWA. Report for the year 1983–84.
64 Ibid.
65 Ibid.
66 *Constitution*, AKWA, p.1
67 A concrete house.
68 John Rex and Robert Moore (1967), see note 43. This has been confirmed by my own empirical research.
69 *Saltley News*, 14, January–February 1976.
70 The association circulated 159 questionnaires investigating problems related to rubbish collection, rats, heating, accidents of children in the street, etc. The

association made five recommendations:
—that information on grants entitlement be circulated in several languages
—that the environmental health authorities intervene to clear out rats
—that the council looks after its property
—that information and assistance be given for better roof insulation
—that the area be declared a housing action area.
Meeting held in Birmingham, 28 July 1983.

71 For example, Nechells Parents' Action Committee meeting 4 July 1983 in preparation for a jumble sale, disco and fete. Lobby in the Council Chamber 19 July 1983.

72 *Evening Mail*, 19 July 1976.

73 For 1982 there were twenty-three applications from Muslim organizations.

74 The ones which are more related to the preservation or affirmation of 'identity'.

75 Something which governs all aspects of one's life. Safdar Butt (1983) *Al Tawhid*, vol. 1, no. 1, March–April.

76 Muhammad Mashuq Ally (1979) 'The growth and organisation of the Muslim Community in Britain', *Christian–Muslim Relations*, research papers, March.

77 The *Evening Mail* kept printing the notice of newly created mosques. 'Mosques are beginning to spring up in Birmingham like mushrooms', 10 October 1972.

78 Nielsen (1984: 10).

79 *Constitution*, Markazi Jamiat Ahl-e-Hadith, Birmingham, p.6.

80 Imtiaz Karim *Muslim children in British schools, their rights and duties*, Birmingham, 20 Green Lane, Birmingham B9 5QB.

81 Markazi Jamiat Ahl-e-Hadith UK, *A Brief Introduction*, Birmingham, p.7.

82 Interview, Treasurer of Sparkbrook Islamic Centre, Birmingham, 16 May 1983.

83 *A Brief Introduction*, p.7, see note 81.

84 Markazi Jamiat Ahl-e-Hadith, UK, Sparkbrook Islamic Centre, Islamic resource centre.

85 *A brief introduction*, p.7, see note 81.

86 *The Straight Path*, vol. 3, Rajab 1402, Markazi Jamiat Ahl-e-Hadith, Birmingham.

87 MECC *Inauguration of teaching programme in Birmingham*, 19 November 1980, p.2.

88 Interview, Birmingham, 7 June 1984.

89 Lessons held every Sunday between 11.30 a.m. and 12.30 p.m., 20 Green Lane.

90 *The Straight Path*, *Al Tawhid*, *The Young Muslim* (publication now interrupted).

91 *Al Tawhid*, January–February 1983, Islamic Resource Centre Newsletter no. 1, p.2.

92 Muslim girls' camp, Alvechurch, organized by the Islamic Resource Centre 20–22 April 1984.

93 *Ibid*. The issue was raised whether men and women should pray together or not, and should have activities together.

94 Markazi Jamiat Ahl-e-Hadith, 20 Green Lane, Birmingham 9.

95 Sparkbrook Islamic Centre, 179–187 Anderton Road, Birmingham 11.

96 Anjuman Khuddamuddin, 15 Woodstock Road, Birmingham 13.

97 Some of them do not make any ideological compromise, but all build political alliances within British society.

98 The *Leicester Mercury* (3 June 1981) reports that the residents of Wigston protested against the construction of an Islamic Research Centre as 'it would seriously damage the character of the area'.

99 The ideology that can be summarily defined as that of a 'white Christian capitalist Britain'.

100 Interview, Birmingham, 26 July 1984.

101 Interview, Birmingham, 9 June 1984.

102 Interview, Birmingham, 3 August 1984.

103 For example, representatives of the Central Mosque held meetings with priests in the area, prior to its construction and continue to do so today.
104 Islamic Resource Centre.
105 *Ibid.*
106 Sparkbrook Islamic Centre, *Annual Report 1983–1984*, pp.14–15. Invitees at the prize giving ceremony, 20 Green Lane, 24 July 1983 included the Lord Mayor.
107 Interview, Birmingham, 16 May 1983.
108 St Francis Hall, Birmingham University, 27 November 1983.
109 Interview with A. Majid, Birmingham, 28 April 1983.
110 On the question of swimming and uniform for girls in particular.
111 For example, by the Islamic Resource Centre.
112 Public meeting on problems of Muslim parents regarding their children, specially the girls, Sunday 18 March 1984, 2 p.m., Sparkhill Centre, Stratford Road, Birmingham 11.
113 Sparkbrook Islamic Centre, *An Introduction*, p.16. Markazi Jamiat Ahl-e-Hadith UK, *A Brief Introduction*, p.3. MECC *Islam and education in Britain. Report on the day conference*, Muslim Education Consultative Committee, Birmingham, 12 July 1980, p.2.
114 *Al Tawhid*, vol. 1, no. 1, March/April 1983, 'Towards the death of westernism', p.3.
115 Markazi Jamiat Ahl-e-Hadith UK, *A Brief Introduction*, p.3.

References

Anwar, Muhammad (1979) *The myth of return: Pakistanis in Britain*, Heinemann, London.
Bentley, Stuart (1970) *The structure of leadership among Indians, Pakistanis and West Indians in Britain: a structural approach with special reference to Bradford*, MSc thesis, University of Bradford.
Dahya, Badr (1972–3) 'Pakistanis in England', *New Community*, 2, Winter.
De Souza, Alfred, (ed.) (1975). *Women in contemporary India*, Minohar, Delhi.
Khan, Verity Saifullah (1977) 'The Pakistanis: Mirpuri villagers at home and in Bradford', in James Watson (ed.), *Between two cultures*, Basil Blackwell, Oxford.
Nielsen, Jorgen (1984) 'Muslim immigration and settlement in Britain', Centre for the Study of Christian Muslim Relations, *Muslims in Europe*, research papers, no. 21, March, Selly Oak Colleges.
Rex, John and Moore, Robert (1967) *Race, community and conflict: a study of Sparkbrook*, Oxford University Press, London.
Wallis, Sue (1974–5) 'Pakistanis in Britain', *New Community*, vol. 4, no. 1.

5 A Micro-Society or an Ethnic Community? Social Organization and Ethnicity amongst Turkish Migrants in Berlin

Ali Gitmez and Czarina Wilpert

Since the 1970s Kreuzberg, with its turn-of-the-century working-class tenements, has become known as Berlin's 'Little Istanbul'. The settlements of Turkish families also exist in several other districts, usually following the pockets of the city designed for urban renewal in the 1960s. These enclaves of Turks in German cities often appear to the outsider as a cohesive Muslim community, united by their conservative Islamic beliefs and Anatolian customs.

The Turkish way of life in Berlin is, of course, more than the exotic odours and colourful dress seen on the streets and in the shop windows of Kreuzberg. A great deal of attention has recently been given to the growing organizational presence and the increasing visibility of the Turks in German society. Since the size of the Turkish population in Berlin began to expand in the late 1960s, so has the number of associations and businesses run by Turkish nationals. About one hundred formal associations of varying size and importance have been established, and over 4000 shops and small businesses have mushroomed, especially in the decade between 1975 and 1985. This is not an unusual development, when one considers that more than 100,000 Turks of all ages are resident in Berlin.

The types of formal association and economic activity among Turks in Germany indicate much about the nature of their articulation with German and Turkish society. However, the meaning they hold for the ethnicity and social identity options for the second and third generation of Turks may not easily be deduced from this analysis. Their meaning can only be approached if the parameters of the Turkish migration to Germany, and informal social factors such as the family, as the most important institution for the transmission of values from one generation to another, are taken into account.

Ethnic organizations are often seen as institutions contributing to integration into or further segregation from the receiving society. An approach based on the experience of classical immigration countries assumes that the extent of the institutional completeness (Breton 1964) found among the immigrant community in the setting will influence their ability, willingness and likelihood to assimilate into the majority society or to develop an ethnic subculture. When this approach is pursued in a comparative perspective, studying several immigrant groups at a certain period in history in one receiving country, it may be a useful concept. Then the question might be raised as to why some nationalities are more institutionally complete than others.

This evaluation is not within the scope of this chapter. Instead, our argument is that the configuration of Turkish society in Germany and its articulation with the majority society evolves as an interactive process influenced, on the one hand, by the parameters set by the conditions of the treaty-regulated guestworker policy and, on the other hand, by the nature of Turkish society itself.

We are writing during a period of transition, about the settlement of people who for the most part are neither candidates for citizenship nor express this desire. This, of course, has to do with the difference between contemporary 'guestworker' migration and 'classical' immigration, which will briefly be elaborated. Moreover, the historical period of this migration is short, and not documented in a comprehensive way. Therefore, we face the dilemma of trying adequately to present the complexity of data often for the first time, and their interpretation.

For a number of Turkish migrants to Germany, chain migration has played a major role in the incorporation of kin and fellow villagers into the migration stream. Certain natural social networks initially useful for finding work and housing continue to operate in other spheres. Moreover, because of the negative reception of Turks in Germany and the stigma attached to being Turkish, the 'myth of return' is reinforced for the majority of the first generation and many of their offspring.

But the stagnant social and economic situation in Turkey does not hold out a real prospect of return for the majority of the offspring of migrants. In the meantime, enclaves of Turks concentrated in urban areas tend to foster an economy of small tradesmen. They form a micro-society with distinct social networks and, at times, conflicting ideological orientations. The basis for this micro-society is the Turkish nationality, which includes some minority identities.

Despite this diversity of backgrounds, Turkish migrants in the Federal Republic of Germany are relegated to a common structural position. Ethnic/national subordination is an element essential to the guestworker system. Nonetheless, formal organization which would mobilize workers to make claims for legal rights and demand a voice in their own destiny has not taken place on a large scale.

This chapter sets out to investigate the relationship of these factors to the forms of social organization and the nature of ethnicity as an expression of collective identity within the Turkish population in Berlin. Several levels of social organization, which address different dimensions of ethnicity, will be examined.

In the study of informal social networks among Turks we focus on the role of chain migration in strengthening the position of rural Turks in Berlin and creating a diversity of specific and possibly closed social networks among, at times, conflicting groups. The informal networks illustrate how patterns of social interaction may carry over from experiences in Turkey, and how first-generation parents attempt to preserve these ties through family, village or ethno-religious group endogamy. The study also provides an indication of the strength of informal networks among groups which may be less represented in formal associations.

Alongside the extensive informal social networks and institutions operating among the migrants other forms of social organization exist. The establishment of a complex infrastructure of goods and services provides an economic basis for a Turkish way of life in Germany which meets new and traditional cultural and social needs. Finally, the formal associations represent still another level of identity options. Their ideologies reflect unresolved conflicts with respect to the achievement of a secular and mono-cultural society within Turkish society. This also poses some problems about acceptable and legitimate symbols of Turkishness.

More questions will be raised than can be answered. The analysis is based on research in progress, and takes place before the majority of the offspring of guestworkers born in Germany have reached full maturity. The primary data have been gathered through participant observation and numerous narrative interviews collected by the first author between 1982 and 1983 in Berlin. In addition, some fifty interviews have been conducted with Turkish workers who have been involved in chain migration and who come from a variety of backgrounds and areas.[1]

The context: the conditions of the Turkish migration to Germany
Three essential conditions characterize the Turkish migration to Germany:
- —the guestworker policy which has institutionalized an ideology of temporariness and a special legal status of resident non-citizens into the second and third generations;
- —the rapid growth of the Turkish population in Germany in a short period of time;

—the social and ethnic diversity of the Turkish groups involved in the migration process.

Guestworker ideology and legal context

At first, we did not realize that our going would be different from a visit or leaving for work. (Aras Ören)

Both the workers and the organizers in the recruiting country initially perceived being a 'guestworker' as limited in time and space. The workers desired to earn money in order to return with status and a secure future at home. From the perspective of the Federal Republic of Germany, German enterprises had labour needs which could not be easily met by natives. The foreign men and women they recruited were seen strictly in their functions as workers. Only in 1973, the year of the official cessation of recruitment, did German politicians begin to sense the human implications of labour migration, and especially what this aspect would cost the German economy.

One factor is of special significance in Germany—that the Federal Republic of Germany does not consider itself a country of immigration. Since migration was never intended to become immigration, naturalization and assimilation were neither the goals of the recruitment country nor of the migrating workers.

Access to citizenship is not a basic right open to foreign workers as a whole. It is always decided on a case-to-case basis. The German concept of citizenship is inseparable from nationality. Nationality, based on *jus sanguis*, is hereditary. As a result, birth on German territory does not guarantee the right to citizenship. Hence, guestworker migration has resulted in a specific form of legal marginality which permits the legitimacy of the institutionalization of the status of a foreigner over two and more generations.

The growth of the Turkish population

The most rapid increase of Turkish workers into Germany took place in a five-year period between 1968 and 1973. Labour migration reached its height in 1973, the year when recruitment ended. Owing to additional migration of family members, the Turks had in 1971 become the largest migrant worker nationality in Germany, when their number first surpassed Yugoslavs and Italians. The net result is that, despite the ending of recruitment in 1973, in the fifteen-year period between 1967 and 1982 the Turkish population in Germany grew from 172,400 to over one and a half million.

The apparent increase in family integration among the Turks suggests a greater stabilization. In fact, however, the Turkish population in Germany, even during this latter period, experienced a continual rotation of a certain percentage of persons between Turkey and Germany. Between 1976 and 1979 about half of those returning to Turkey as well as entering Germany were youths under eighteen years of age (Trommer and Köhler 1981).

Frequently, there were rotations within families. Sometimes the same child was transferred for child-care or education to Turkey, later returned to Germany, education completed or not, because of the strain of separation, homesickness or financial or caretaker problems. Underneath the superficial apparent stability in numbers of Turks, fluctuation continues.

Specifics of the Turkish migration to Berlin   Massive recruitment to Berlin began a little later than to the industrial areas of West Germany. There were less than 3000 Turks in Berlin in 1965. Four years later, the number of Turks had reached 24,000. From the beginning, they constituted the largest fraction of foreign workers and their numbers grew to over 79,000 in 1973.

Peculiar to the Berlin labour market needs was the high demand for women workers. By 1973 over 40 per cent of Turkish nationals employed were women. According to a large-scale survey in 1974 (Kudat *et al.*), at that time over three-quarters of the married Turks had their spouses, but only one-third of their children, with them abroad.

In the majority of families, the children were split between Germany and Turkey. Between 1976 and 1977, there was a slight decrease in the number of Turks living in Berlin, but this was only short-lived. In the following years, other members of the family arrived and the Turkish population in Berlin increased steadily, reaching 100,000 in 1978. The first noticeable decrease in the total number of Turks took place in 1983.[2]

The majority of Turkish workers were recruited for unskilled and semi-skilled jobs.[3] Their first employment in Germany did not, however, reflect the heterogeneity of their educational and occupational backgrounds. According to the 1974 Berlin study, over 15 per cent of the Turks interviewed in Berlin had been employed in some form of civil service before departure (Kudat *et al.* 1974). Many had been primary-school teachers. An above average share, 18 per cent of the men, had more than nine years of schooling. A few were artists, musicians and small shopkeepers before departure. The worker migration stream was accompanied by an increase of Turkish students registered in German universities, and some waves of political refugees.[4]

Housing concentration and the ethnic enclave   The limitations of post-war housing development in German urban areas, and especially in Berlin with its high percentage of nineteenth-century *Mietskaserne* (working-class apartment blocks) earmarked for urban renewal, created conditions which made temporary foreign residents particularly attractive clients.

Even if there had not been discrimination, which there was (Freiburghaus 1974), large families were not candidates for the state-subsidized social housing, since these have high rents and restrict the number of persons to each room. As a result, in Berlin the Turkish population is found concentrated primarily in the five most dense inner-city districts of Kreuzberg, Wedding, Neukölln, Schöneberg and Tiergarten.

There are some city blocks where Turks account for over 60 per cent of the population. Since the families with the largest numbers of children are forced to live in these areas, the population of young persons under fifteen is particularly high. Certain schools, playgrounds, youth centres and street corners are populated primarily by Turkish youth. In some elementary and secondary (*Hauptschule*) schools, the majority of the student body is Turkish nationals. Living in neighbourhoods with traditionally poor social infrastructure has necessarily had a tremendous influence, both on the quality of the educational experience and social interaction with the remaining, also to a large extent socially disadvantaged, German population.

These conditions have set certain parameters for life as a Turkish minority in Germany and the socialization of the following generation. The internal social structure of Turkish migrant society in Berlin presents additional contingencies which contribute to the perception and evaluation of world views and collective, ethnic or national identities. This kind of information has been overlooked in most research, and it is, of course, not easily collected in quantitative studies. The internal structure of the Turkish micro-society in Germany may only be approached in indirect ways. Our fieldwork in Berlin has convinced us that a more detailed history of the Turkish migration to Germany is necessary in order to understand the complexity and the diversity of the migration streams and their impact on the social organization of Turks in this country. This task would take us, however, beyond the limits of Germany. Therefore, in the following sections, we will only be able to scratch the surface and present three levels of social organization, while indicating the implications each may have for ethnicity. However, before informal networks and associations are discussed it will be necessary to have an idea of the origins and migration histories of these families.

The geographical origins of Turkish migrants
Little accurate data exists on the regions of origin of the Turks in

Germany and little attention is generally given to the cultural diversity within the group. Nevertheless, the discussion about the origins of Turkish migrants frequently reflects extreme contradictions. Either the majority of Turks are assumed to be east Anatolian peasants, and a traditional, conservative population, or they are considered to be the most qualified of their class, originating from the western part of the country.

Official statistics support the latter interpretation in the early period; the first Turkish migrants to Germany were the most highly skilled and came primarily from the western sections of Turkey. Only about a quarter of the workers came from the agricultural sector (Abadan-Unat *et al.* 1975). A more detailed analysis for Berlin indicates that recruitment in this early period favoured workers from northern, western and southern Anatolia, with the gradual increase of east Anatolian migrants after 1970 (Kudat 1975: 44). By 1974, however, almost one-third of the Turkish workers in Berlin had been born in the eastern regions of Turkey (Wilpert 1983) and even the majority of those who came from the west, with the exception of the Marmara region, were born either in villages or in small towns. As a result, at least half of the Turkish workers in Berlin originated from basically rural areas of the west or the east.

Chain migration Our research in Berlin illustrates that it is exactly these migrants from villages and rural areas who were the most likely to participate in chain migration, contributing to their growth in numbers after 1973. The increased participation of peasants in the migration stream may be attributed to several factors: German recruitment policy, the intervention of the Turkish government in favour of certain kinds of migrants, the social and economic conditions in Turkey, and the nature of the peasant groups in question.

The German recruitment system tended to recruit Turks on a large scale to work in large firms, which created regional clusters. Until 1973, it was the practice for an individual to request the recruitment of family members or friends. In Berlin, there was an especially high predilection among spouses to join workers after about a year abroad. This was due to the high demand for women workers, and this factor turned the Turkish migration to Berlin very early into a migration of families.[5] By 1974 about 80 per cent of the workers in Berlin had their spouses with them (Kudat *et al.* 1974), and, after the ending of recruitment in 1973, the only legal channel which was open for entry into Germany was for the spouses of workers and their children. Until November 1981 it was possible for the children of workers who reached a marriageable age to bring their spouses from Turkey.[6]

An additional influence on regional chain and rural migration was an exceptional request of the Turkish government to give priority to a selection of persons from these categories: people from areas which had been hit by natural disasters; members of village development-cooperatives. The concern for preferential treatment of people from disaster areas resulted in the high representation in Berlin of people from the Varto/Erzurum and Gediz/Kutahya areas (earthquakes) as well as Konya and Isparta (floods). Also, in an attempt to encourage rural development through investment in co-operatives, about 12,000 people were sent through co-operatives to Germany. Since the above factors all had a geographical base, it was not long before members of one family, village, or region were working in the same firm or living in the same city abroad (Gitmez 1983).

Cultural diversity Geographical origins alone cannot adequately explain the ethno-religious origins of the migrants. There exists a diversity in traditions and potential minority identities within Turkey, which has also come to the fore in international migration. The largely homogeneous structural position of Turkish migrants in German society is not matched by internal cohesion or a unity of world views. The geographical distinctions between east and west or rural and urban origins are considered important because they are assumed to indicate the position of the migrant on the continuum between traditionality and modernism or religiosity and secularism (Kudat 1975). This is justified to the extent that certain regions and rural areas are particularly underprivileged with respect to natural resources, economic development and social infrastructure. Access to educational opportunities is limited in these areas. Beyond this, however, important distinctions exist in the cultural and religious traditions of Turkish migrants, which cannot easily be classified according to geographic origins.

This is particularly true for the eastern part of Turkey, which historically has been the home of a myriad of ethnic, linguistic and religious affiliations (Yalman 1969; Karpat 1976). This is in part explained by its geographical characteristics, rugged mountains, deep valleys and its distance from the centre of national, that is imperial power. According to Yalman (1969) this is also due to its location on the borders of the Persian and Ottoman empires which was the point of the religious division between the Sunni and Shi'a Islamic folds.

Ethnic and religious diversity and antagonism among the Turkish minorities and the majority is further complicated by histories of nomadism, tribal structures, internal labour migration (Karpat 1976) and the forced resettlement of the Kurds into other areas of Turkey (Engelbrektsson 1982). Most important is probably the discrepancy between the aspirations of the young Turkish nation state to a modern, secular and culturally homogeneous society and its achievement.

The Kurds are the largest linguistic and cultural minority in Tur key. Originally at home in central east and south-east Anatolia, a large number of them have been forced for political and economi reasons to resettle in other regions. Where they are resettled the may be linguistically, but not necessarily socially, assimilated (En gelbrektsson 1982). They speak two major distinct dialects and ar primarily either members of the Sunni or the Alevi branches of Islam However, there are also Yezidi[7] and other Kurds who have chai migrated to Germany and Berlin.

Some authors feel that it is the religious distinction which draws th most rigid boundary between the Islamic Turks (Yalman 1969). Th major split occurs between the Sunni and Alevi, and it has signifi cance for ethnic Kurds as well as ethnic Turks.

The Alevi are followers of Ali, usually considered to belong to th Shi'a branch of Islam. Elements of a folk religion make them quit distinct from classical Shiism. Some scholars find their ritual an customs closer to ancient Turkmen traditions (Gokalp 1980). Fo these purposes, their most important features are to be found in thei less rigid practices of Islamic ritual. They neither visit mosques, sen children to Qur'an schools, pray and practise ritual purification fiv times a day, nor fast for a month during Ramadan. They have a ric mystic and folkloric tradition, which has influenced Turkish folklor music and poetry. They consider themselves politically progressive socialist and more liberal than their Sunni fellow-countrymen. Thei women are not veiled, and interact more freely in public sur roundings. Tribal structures and ritual kinship play an important rol in their social organization.

Our interest here is less in the content of the beliefs and values o religious membership and more in the bonds experienced due to a ideology of common origins and solidarity with the group of origin Socio-economic and political conditions in Turkey, in addition to th selection policies of the German and Turkish governments, enhan ced the attractiveness of migration abroad for the Turkish ethnic an religious minorities.

Chain migration and informal social networks Chain migration i one of the major factors in the social organization of at least half o the Turkish population in Berlin. The initiative and support that i necessary for chain migration tend to reinforce mutual obligations The first-generation chain migrants in Berlin socialize primaril within their kin, village, regional and/or religious networks. More over, for some, the experience of ethnic minority status in Turke expresses itself abroad in the prolongation of 'we-they' feeling toward migrants from the other group. These group identities influ ence social interaction in Berlin. Some especially striking cases o chain migration may be observed among the east Anatolian and Kurdish population in Berlin:

— in one case, about thirty-five families, consisting of about 180 people all come from a small region of a few villages of central east Anatolia (Malatya) (this same group has about 200 families in Stuttgart);

— over 100 families are from a single village in the central eastern part of Turkey (Erzincan), with about 550 people;

— some 140 families, about 1050 people, are from about six villages (provinces) close to each other in the south-eastern part of Turkey (Urfa);

— over 250 non-Muslim Kurdish families, of about 1850 members, are from the south-eastern part of Turkey (Siirt);

— over 140 Sunni families of Kurdish, Laz and Circassian origins, come from villages in the Samsun area near the Black Sea coast.

The extended family and friends from the area of origin provide a number of social services. Villagers who have initiated the migration stream are proud of all they have been able to do for relatives and friends. They help one another 'to find jobs, apartments, arrange marriages, settle financial problems and family quarrels'.

Since 1973 many persons entered Germany through marriage transactions. As is often common in Turkey, children's marriages are arranged with cousins from their village of origin. Marriage into a Turkish family in Germany may provide an added attraction for a young man seeking work. It may also raise the bride-price and the bargaining power of the young girl's family.

In some areas, people of the same origin inhabit a large section of a city block or an entire house. Close relationships may be maintained, however, even between more remote locations. Many point out that they don't see anyone else, aside from relatives, and that if it weren't for the presence of the extended family, life in Berlin would not be bearable.

Not only does participation in chain migration permit at least partial reconstruction of family and village networks abroad, but it also ties the migrant and his family into interactions back home. In these cases, the village community, although geographically distant, may continue to exercise a certain social control over its members abroad. A second-generation young man from a Kurdish Alevi village in the Malatya province explains how social pressures from the village may even work among the young in Berlin:

> Social relations are only with people from the same village. . . Everyone is related to everyone else anyway. Even most of the young people primarily have to do with others from the same area.

Everything which happens to us here, every new event, is immediately known back in the village. That's why people are very careful here. If someone here gets off line, doesn't earn any money, separates, gambles, etc.—every bit of news gets at once back to the village. People are afraid of that. When there is fear of gossip in the village, and fear that one can't be looked in the face, then one keeps out of trouble.

Motivation toward social interaction and ethnic boundaries within the Turkish enclave in Berlin

Although most chain migrants come from rural areas and peasant backgrounds, this common attribute is not sufficient to provide the basis for a homogeneous Turkish community with interaction across ethno-religious boundaries. Experience in Turkey influences the interactions of these villagers among themselves in Berlin, their receptiveness to a claim on Turkish identity and to different ideological orientations, and their willingness to intermarry. Although there is no doubt that new kinds of solidarity are also found among Turkish peasants abroad, chain migration, which transplants village networks and neighbour and kin relations to the new setting, is a strong counteracting force. Nevertheless, not only common village, but also common regional, cultural or religious identity may become an additional dimension of social identity in the foreign setting. As one Turkish worker informant from the Black Sea area emphasized about Kurds: 'When the Kurds find a job, they immediately send for their relatives and friends. They don't leave any work for others.' This worker, it turns out, means only certain Kurds, his kind, who are Sunni. He differentiates between helping his fellow countrymen from the Black Sea, whether they are Kurdish, Laz, or Circassian, and the Kurds from the east. He feels he has more in common with the former than with the latter. This Sunni Kurd looks down upon 'eastern' Kurds because of their backwardness, 'they couldn't even speak Turkish'. But, also contrary to the usual image of the division between east and west, because of their quick adaptation to more western behaviour—'They dress like Europeans', 'Their women have discarded their scarves'. These observations, of course, have less to do with Kurdishness than with the Islamic orthodoxy and the less strict attention to the traditional clothing customs for women which may be found among some Alevi. Ethnic and religious affiliation remain important distinguishing features for social interaction among rural Turkish nationals living in Berlin. For some, all eastern Anatolians are Kurds, for others, all Alevi are referred to as Kurds; but neither is strictly the case, and eastern Kurds may be either Alevi or Sunni. Among peasants who migrated to Berlin from the Black Sea area there is some socializing across ethnic groups as expressed in the solidarity patterns of the *Landsmannschafts*-system when looking for work. However, the majority of first-generation village chain migrants prefer to practise endogamy with respect to the marriages of their children.

> These people from the village keep close ties among themselves. They form their own groups. Marriage is only possible within these groups. The Laz, Kurds and Circassians only marry among themselves. Sometimes, a Kurd takes a wife from the Laz. But, they don't give their own daughters to marry outside the group. The Circassians only marry among themselves.

Reluctance to intermarry is also found between those of the same ethnic group but of another religious faith. Endogamy is the rule among the rural Sunni and Alevis, even when both may have a Kurdish background.

A twenty-year-old, second-generation Alevi-Kurd from another village in the east explains how he felt about respecting his father's wish that he should marry within the village:

> We have a custom that the wish of one's father must be followed. And my father did not want someone outside the village . . . I only wanted what my parents desired, so we married. Families do not marry their children outside of their own circles. And marriages are not contracted with Sunni. Among our villagers abroad there is only one woman who came from a Sunni family.

Some rural families will consider marriage with someone from another village, but not with someone of another religion. As another second-generation Alevi-Kurd from a village in the Malatya area observes:

> Marriage with a Sunni is seldom. In general, we think that we understand ourselves better. After a certain point we have difficulties with Sunni. Even if we can get along with one or the other, we cannot get on with their parents or their environment.

Our research in Berlin indicates that to be a Kurd might also influence one's openness toward life in Germany and distance from the Turkish nation (Wilpert 1986). In certain areas, Kurds suffer especially from hardships, poverty and discrimination. Having lived as one of a minority in Turkey, one man explains how his people feel forced to stay in Germany for ever:

> We don't have a good future in Turkey, since we have no chance to share in economic or political power. There is no work . . . no property. To return would be meaningless. . . In the public offices . . . the civil servants cry: 'Go, get a translator'. . . Even in the towns bad things were called after us. . . As a child I couldn't understand this. Isn't [this] our

town, too? I thought, are not we, too, the children of Ataturk, why do they punish us like that?

The pre-migration experiences of the Turkish minorities may vary greatly. Some Turkish minorities in other areas are evidently used to living together side by side with diverse ethnic groups in the towns of Turkey. For others, animosities and old wounds are still too vivid. However their networks operate, in Berlin they may find themselves happy or not living side by side. Here, they may share staircases, parks, playgrounds and schools. Village and kin networks also provide the basis for numerous social gatherings. The most important are the celebrations required for the traditional engagement, wedding and circumcision ceremonies. These events attract relatives from near and far, old and new friends and acquaintances. There are several large halls in the 'Turkish' neighbourhoods, which are rented for three to four thousand Deutsch Marks a day and hold several hundred persons. These do such a thriving business that they are rented almost every weekend and need to be reserved months in advance. These are events which warmly highlight traditional customs, and nurture feelings of solidarity, as well as serving as excellent opportunities to look for a future spouse.

What do these observations about informal social networks mean for ethnicity among Turks in Germany? Informal social networks are, of course, not limited to chain migrants. And not all migrants have been involved in chain migration. There are isolated individuals, and, more often, the migration of individual nuclear families. Since the latter have come alone, their primary interaction may be with neighbours or colleagues from work. In cases of isolated migration, new forms of solidarity have very often been bridged while abroad (Kudat 1975). But even then, a common origin, language, dialect or religious faith becomes a significant symbol of a common social identity. For the first generation, socializing among Germans is rare.

Fieldwork in Turkish urban *gecekondu* areas (Duhetsky 1976; Karpat 1976) illustrates clearly the role that *Landsmannschaften (hemseri)* have, but especially that which religious differentiation has for the social organization of internal migrants living in the shanty towns of Turkish metropolitan areas. It is unlikely that these patterns take exactly the same course here, but they remain important background factors for the distinctive modes of interaction and social differentiation in Berlin. Whenever possible, these characteristics become criteria for selecting with whom one does business, which café, travel agent, hairdresser, or repair shop one decides to use, and, above all, who is qualified as a marriage candidate for one's daughter. There is also an economic significance. It is a sign of solidarity for extended kin and villagers, but also among brothers in the Islamic community, to be willing to put all their money on the table when someone is in need. A number of businesses have been able to start in this way. The interest paid in return is the obligation to do the same when needed.

The development of a business sector among Turks in Berlin
In 1984 there were about 6000, mainly small, firms run by foreigners in Berlin. More than half of these were run by Turks. According to the 1982 mini-census, 5100 foreigners were self-employed that year, which was an increase of 800 foreign ownerships from the previous year (Der Senator für Gesundheit 1985). There are more shops owned by foreigners than are officially registered, since a certain kind of residence permit (*Aufenthaltsberechtigung*) is required to set up in business.[8] In Kreuzberg, the city district where about a quarter of the Berlin Turks live and where half the residents are foreigners, 12 per cent of enterprises are in the hands of Turks. And, as many as 40 per cent of service sector firms are Turkish-owned.[9] The turnover in ownership is, however, very high and more than half of the number of new registrations yearly is matched by a dissolution of business (see Table 5.1).

The first signs of Turkish economic activity in Berlin began in the late 1960s. Before 1965 there were no more than two or three restaurants owned by Turks. The first Turks to establish their businesses in Berlin were usually professionals who did not necessarily come to Berlin as workers. Others were academics who studied in Berlin and realized the opportunities which the rapid immigration of Turkish workers to Berlin after 1967 offered them. They sensed the demand for familiar cultural products. Restaurants were generally too expensive for workers who had to save for return, and German food did not suit their taste. Tradition required meat which was properly slaughtered by the blade of a Muslim. Lamb and the range of green vegetables and fruits common in Turkey were lacking.

From door-to-door sales to neighbourhood grocers
Turkish business in Berlin began with something unknown in Turkey, door-to-door sales and the home delivery of goods. Turkish women sold linen, tablecloths, crockery and pots through their informal networks of relatives and friends, providing a useful service to families where both husband and wife were gainfully employed and did not have time to go out shopping.

In 1966 an enterprising Turkish worker initiated the delivery of packaged foods, to workers' dormitories, and later, as time went on,

Table 5.1 New registrations (R) and liquidations (L) of trade enterprises by foreigners between 1981 and 1985 in Berlin

Economic/Branch	Turks		Italians		Yugoslavs		Greeks		Others	
	R	L	R	L	R	L	R	L	R	L
Gardening/animal husbandry	–	–	–	–	–	–	–	–	12	5
Manufacturing	341	210	28	20	34	26	37	22	296	168
Construction	47	28	7	8	59	25	33	23	97	52
Commerce	1524	1034	146	100	104	57	115	61	1062	629
Transportation/communication	83	39	7	4	15	5	18	13	86	48
Banks/insurances	49	25	3	–	9	–	11	–	44	12
Services	253	109	34	16	99	35	58	21	633	265
Restaurants/hotels	909	607	545	534	381	305	285	192	600	459
Total	3206	2052	770	682	701	453	557	332	2830	1638

Source: Statistisches Landesamt, Berlin.

home delivery became popular. This sort of grocery shop on wheels was especially attractive, because workers felt secure that halal meats were being provided by a fellow Muslim. It was the market for halal meats which helped Turks get a foothold in commerce in Berlin.

The trade with 'legitimate' meat first began outside Berlin, especially in Munich, Stuttgart and Frankfurt. Lamb was considered legitimate, because it was slaughtered and sold by Muslims, and it was distributed from door to door, and transported in the trunks of cars from one area to another. In the beginning the 'legitimate' meat was bought from ordinary slaughter houses and only the distributors were Turkish. This was evidently enough at the time to convince the buyer. Similarly, this was later also the first meat to be sold in Turkish meat markets.

In 1967 the only products from Turkey obtainable in German supermarkets were 'Vatan' canned foods. At the end of 1968 the first Turkish butcher shop opened with meat cut according to Islamic specifications. This was the turning point in Turkish commerce in Berlin. A short time later, trade connections between Turkey and Germany expanded, and a continuous flow of goods from Turkey to Germany began.

Only five Turkish grocery stores existed in Berlin in 1970. For a foreigner, permission to open up a business requires a special residence permit. Only recently have Turks begun to obtain this.[10] Without this residence permit no trade permit could be obtained, so it was necessary to find a German to be the straw boss. The straw boss profited without the need to invest capital or personnel. For this reason the first shops were opened with German trade names which, however, did not stop the success of these first grocers; even with their German names the word spread quickly to the Turkish clientele.

Who are the businessmen?
Going into business for oneself is a common aspiration among Turkish migrants. But these first businessmen had not, for the most part, been farmers or workers in Turkey. As pointed out earlier, at least one-fifth of the worker migrants came from other backgrounds: small tradesmen, primary-school teachers, and lower level civil servants. Some arrived in Germany as students or professionals. Some served as the first company translators for factories with large numbers of Turks. And it appears that these are the people who in the long run have been the most successful in this highly competitive area of small business ventures.

Expansion into other trades
Although the corner grocer is the most apparent area of investment

for Turkish small business in Berlin, the first Turkish investors were quick to enter into the travel agency trade and later charter and air travel business. In the early days, travel agents were multi-functional, providing a number of services to workers who needed help with the German bureaucratic system for the translation of documents, the completion of forms and other mediating services. These were multi-purpose businesses which today have managed to expand to the tourist trade with Germans. The first all-purpose dry-goods shops were in the import–export trade. These first initiated the business of Turkish music and later video-cassettes. The video-cassette trade especially flourishes because of the significance it has as the main tool for the reproduction and extension of the Turkish culture abroad. According to the Berlin government[11] about 60 per cent of Turkish households own video-cassette recorders, and many more people—family and neighbours—congregate as viewers. Stacks of cassettes are borrowed from videotechs for weekend entertainment. The flow of Turkish films into the video business in Germany has had repercussions in both countries; since this custom began abroad, video films have returned for distribution within Turkey. There is much criticism about the 'B' quality of the films and their reification of a heroic past and romantic traditions. Their success and profitability are clearly related to the major role they play as a medium which projects needed symbols of identification. Thus, the video business is an attractive investment for the aspiring shopkeeper and requires only limited capital and few special skills.

Turks also began early to open their own restaurants, cafés and casinos. These were often the meeting places for people from a certain area or a certain political orientation. In the last decade, Turkish 'doner kebab' stands have entered the fast food trade, finding a niche as well in the German market.

Less apparent to the outsider was the expansion of Turks in the area of the mending of clothing (*Änderungsschneiderei*). Many of the workers had been trained as tailors in Turkey and many Turkish women, especially those from the cities, had been recruited to work in the clothing industry in Germany. It was not long before these persons, either dissatisfied with factory work or victims of unemployment in this branch, looked for a way to become their own bosses, as they may have been or aspired to be in Turkey. In hard times this was also the ideal way to unite the resources of the entire family in the goal of achieving a more secure position at home. In a number of cases the men continue to hold down another job while their wives run the shop. It is in this area of family business that migrants appear to be especially adaptable. First-generation migrants have traditionally been the backbone of small business, mustering energy together no longer found among families whose wives and children may have other ambitions for themselves. In fact, family business provides a small loophole to the highly regulated German working conditions, since minimum wages, social security, child labour, even taxes and the overtime required to make economic gains are less controlled. These family tailors and repair shops have filled a gap in the Berlin service sector, reaching into almost every residential area in the city. Turks have become essential, not only as factory workers and cleaning personnel, but also in the area of food and clothing in Berlin. Turkish pita bread can be found in almost every grocery shop, produced by Turkish and now even German bakers.

The development of the wholesale trade
The success of the first shops and the future potential for Turkish goods became immediately apparent. This was especially true in the produce business, where grocers began to transform their shops into relatively large wholesale companies, which would supply all necessary goods to the 'dependent' retailer. This initiative began in 1971 when the first Turkish grocer transformed his business into a small wholesale company. 'Istanbul Bazaar' set an example for others, and the Gel-Tat group appeared in Kreuzberg. And since the majority of Turks did not have the necessary legal status to be granted a permit for opening their own business, the first wholesalers also obtained the necessary permits including the German 'straw bosses' and paid off the German who lent his name to the venture.

What happened as a result was to become a particular pattern of development in Berlin: Turkish wholesalers established a number of dependent retail shops in German names and delegated these to Turkish shopkeepers, as well as providing all of the supplies for their stores. Thus, 'Istanbul Bazaar' had about twenty and Gel-Tat about thirty-eight such retail shops established in this manner in 1972. Fierce competition reigned between the wholesalers. Once Gel-Tat entered the halal meat business it was even more successful. None the less, it was dissolved in 1973, and the same people founded Elfi, a larger wholesale enterprise with more shareholders. This time they included coffee houses and casinos in their trade chain. Four years later in 1976 another major event occurred when one of the principal partners of Gel-Tat founded a competing wholesale firm, Unita. Unita soon controlled seventy-eight grocery stores, thirty-one coffee shops, and several casinos in Berlin. It opened offices in Istanbul and Rize and a small textile factory in Gaziantep in the south-east of Turkey. This line of development was significant for the establishment of Turkish business in Berlin because it laid the foundation for other large-scale chains, and it was the first to exploit the traditional Islamic elements on a larger scale. Halal meat and halal foods became compelling advertising slogans and were used effectively to gain ground. As a consequence, between 1976 and 1984, larger Islamic business complexes could be established by the firms of Helal Gida, Elif Gida and Hicret.

Most of the Turkish wholesale companies have investments in a number of other areas. It is not, however, a stable business. There appear to be a number of 'ups and downs'. Only a few have managed to survive over a ten-year period. None the less, produce remains an area which is still considered attractive and profitable, and many workers continue to dream of setting up their own business. This has also led to the mushrooming of small grocers in Turkish quarters throughout the city, followed by expansion and bankruptcy. Between 1981 and 1985, there were 3206 new business registrations and 2052 liquidations among Turks in Berlin, so that almost two-thirds of the new openings yearly are matched by dissolutions.[12]

Religion and business expansion
The roots of Turkish business and its expansion are clearly related to the need for halal meat in the Islamic community. The development of the produce market among Turks is not only associated with religious needs, it also lends support to the conservation of a traditional way of life among certain sections of the population. Turkish entrepreneurs were immediately aware of the potential for a high demand by a conservative section of the community for halal meat and other foods prepared by Muslims, and they did not hesitate to take advantage of this opportunity. Following Gel-Tat's success with halal meat on a wholesale level, others began to look at serving the needs of the orthodox Islamic community.

Three important and widely known religious business chains emerged between the early 1970s and the mid-1980s: Helal Gida, Elif Gida and Hicret. They have all established a variety of lines of activity in addition to foods. They provide a number of community services, travel agencies, sports activities such as karate lessons for the young, and Qur'an courses, the last aimed at the political socialization of children. Between 1975 and 1980 they were so successful in this area that, if one so desired, it would have been possible to fulfil most of one's needs for commercial or social relations within the Islamic community, avoiding all contact with non-Muslims.

Each of these chains also represents dominant religious orientations and factions within the Turkish Islamic community. They have all had an interest in the politicization of the community. They have supported and provided resources to the political parties and grass-root organizations in Turkey. The division between various groups was so evident between 1975 and 1980 that each group had one or more of their own mosques, Qur'an schools, sports clubs and community centres, etc. They competed among themselves, and this was reflected in the attendance patterns of participants. Instead of attending a nearby mosque or sending children to the Qur'an school of that mosque, people would travel further, into another district, to be able to reach 'their' mosque. Business chains became the arena for the religious and political power struggles of various Islamic and conservative factions.

Helal Gida was the first chain business to address itself directly to the Islamic community. It was established in late 1971, with five supermarkets, restaurants, and travel agencies. Although it did not own more than four or five shops, Helal Gida established a financially potent monopoly among Turks in Berlin. It also had rigid control over the religious community through its financial support of the Islamic cultural centre, which provided all the educational and religious services mentioned above.

Later, Elif Gida and, later still, Hicret emerged as additional chains to safeguard the Islamic community, and compete for the market and factional power. Elif was established in 1978 with the initiative of three members of the Helal group. Two supermarkets and one restaurant was the result. This group projected the image of an even more conservative organization, but it was in actual fact another political-religious faction. Its purpose was to expand the religious/political view of the 'nationalistic outlook' (Milli Gönüs), a grass-root organization of the nationalist (MSP) party in Turkey. They could not expand as planned, since Helal Gida also began to support the same party, and Elif could no longer justify its own identity.

The Hicret group appeared in late 1980. It emerged under the leadership of a well-known imam. He was able to organize a joint stock company with 5000 to 20,000 DM contributions from some 200 Islamic brothers. People say that about four million DM was collected in this way in a few days. They began by taking over Elif's retail trade and soon expanded into the restaurant and travel agency business. With its more fundamentalist orientation, the Hicret group approached the Islamic Bank (Saudi Arabia) and secured credit of a substantial sum—it is said about five million DM. At the time they were to have bought a plot of land to build the largest mosque in Berlin. This possibility caused enormous excitement among the leaders of Hicret and the Islamic community about the possibility of creating a prestigious focus of identity for the Turkish Muslims in the city. But Hicret's expectations were short-lived, the Islamic Bank, dissatisfied with the business style of Hicret, forced the group to dissolve late in 1983. Thus, Hicret became bankrupt, unable to even repay the original capital to its shareholders.

A new business chain entered the market in 1983. Misir Carsisi, named after the covered bazaar in Istanbul, is owned by one man and has the same four lines of activity as the others (supermarket, restaurant/snackbar, travel agency and a mosque with a Qur'an school). It is located in the heart of Kreuzberg next to the largest mosque in Berlin, which is now in the hands of the Nationalist Outlook (MSP) group. Misir Carsisi appears to take the official line of the Turkish state about Islam, as a non-political religion which respects the secular state. The members of the community of the neighbouring mosque associated with the former Hicret chain strongly oppose this new competition. They warn that Misir Carsisi may be the Trojan horse sent to the centre of the Berlin community by the Turkish consulate general.

As a matter of fact, the Turkish government was, through its general director of religious affairs, in consultation with persons in the Berlin Turkish business community in late 1985 about launching a relatively modern joint venture with some religious and some commercial components. If established it is to be called the Hittite group. Hittite, of course, symbolizes another, and less Islamic source of Turkish identity! It would adopt the official view of the Turkish state about religious affairs.

Today, it appears that these chain businesses have lost some ground. There could be several reasons for this, such as the weakening of the ideological hold of Islam on the owners or intensive competition for a limited market and the lack of sophisticated management skills which multi-faceted chains require. Whatever the reason, the expansion of business ventures by Turks in Berlin continues nevertheless. A breakdown of the large holding companies does not seem to stop the founding of new mosques. Only time will tell if the religions-business as a chain trade has reached its limits.

There is no doubt, however, that business circles in Turkey are also interested in obtaining a larger share of the market in Germany. This is especially feasible and attractive for the large Turkish monopolies, who may present a major challenge to the local worker-turned-entrepreneur. It may also be an additional reason for the efforts to rally Turkish businessmen together in Berlin. Some thirty Turkish businessmen gathered together in early 1983 to form an association of Turkish entrepreneurs. Their twofold objective was: (a) to help one another to take advantage of benefits available to them from the German government; and (b) to develop and increase trade connections with Turkey. Following teachers and other professionals, businessmen have become another occupational group seeking the advantages of forming their own associations to be able to negotiate with the government and their counterparts in German and Turkish societies.

Formal associations among Turks

The formal associations organized by Turks in Germany reflect the entire political and religious spectrum to be found in Turkey. In fact, there is a greater range than could be found officially active in Turkey, since numerous organizations were first publicly brought to life in Germany, which would have had difficulty existing back home. Some 100 different associations and forty or more mosques have been founded by Turks in Berlin. A few Turkish worker associations were begun with the advent of the first migrants in the 1960s; they were followed by the growth of religious and politically conservative associations in the 1970s. Between the late 1970s and mid-eighties there has been an even more rapid multiplication of formal organizations. It is also during this period that the nature of associations has begun to change. Until around 1981 it was possible to categorize the majority of Turkish associations within one of the two extreme poles of Turkish society. They were either affiliated with one of the Turkish worker associations attached to one of the left-of-centre Turkish parties, or they were more religiously oriented, some aligned with the extreme right parties.

The orientations of Turkish formal associations reached a turning point in Berlin in November 1981. This change of orientation was stimulated by a governmental decree to curtail the rights of non-European Community foreign parents to bring their children over fifteen years of age into the country. Since this was a short time before the 1982 national elections, politicians were also focusing on issues of assimilation or return of foreign workers in their campaigns.[13] Foreigners, especially Turks, became scapegoats for the rapidly rising unemployment which was being felt everywhere. For the first time Turks of all political shades joined together to organize the largest demonstration they had ever held in Berlin to protest against a policy of the German government and not about Turkey or internal Turkish issues.

Until 1981 the majority of Turkish associations in Berlin were primarily oriented towards Turkish society. Even the Turkish worker associations which provided some services to help workers in Berlin were marked by the political divisions of Turkey. With the exception of sports clubs and mosques, most of these groups had a small membership and were usually run by a core group of less than twenty young persons. The leaders of these associations were usually students, teachers or other young professionals.

The Turkish worker associations are closely affiliated with the Turkish political parties. Of these, three groups organized on both a local and national level are the most important: FIDEF (Federation of Turkish Associations in Germany), HDF (the Progressive People's Association), and KOMKAR (The Association of Kurdish Workers). (A description of these associations and their sub-groups can be found on p.118.)

The Islamic associations were founded abroad at a period of extreme political tension in Turkey. Since they are often affiliated with certain international Islamic movements and because of their opposition to secularism, they were considered a threat to the principles of the secular Turkish republic. Their emergence in Germany profited from the freedom of expression permitted in the democratic system they found abroad.

Several different types of Muslimism have been identified as relevant for Turks in Berlin and other parts of Germany (Elsas 1983): fundamentalists, traditionalists, mystics, secularized Islamic groups with an orthodox basis, which range from conservative to progressive, and the Alevi.

The majority of Turks in Germany are probably Sunni, the officially recognized religious faith. Of these, it is the traditionalist Süleymanli movement with its Islamic cultural centres which claims to represent over 60 per cent of the 160 branches throughout Germany. This is also the group associated with the MHP Party (Nationalist Party), the latter led by Turks and considered to be the main support for the 'Grey Wolves'.

The radical fundamentalists, heavily supported from Libya, are estimated to appeal to about 6–10 per cent of the Turks in Turkey. These are associated with the MSP (National Salvation Party) of Erbakan. They claim about 8000 Qur'an school pupils in Berlin. Finally, the secularists claim to have about 500 members in Berlin, and about 600 Qur'an school pupils.

In 1980 nineteen Islamic associations and mosques overcame their divisive orientations to establish the Islamic Federation. One of the main goals of this unification was to establish a counterpart in Germany which could claim to represent all Turkish Muslims, and thus be officially recognized, as the Christian and Jewish faiths are, to formally teach the Islamic religion to Turkish children during the normal school day in Berlin schools. This goal has not yet been achieved since it is the Turkish state which alone claims the right to represent the teaching of Islam to Turkish pupils. Despite rumours about the changing weight of religion and secularism in internal Turkish affairs, it is unlikely that this issue can easily be resolved juridically. In the meantime the need for recognition by German authorities and the

German public has at least forced a good share of the Sunni splinter associations to try to find common ground.

Exact figures on the attendance of mosques and participation in Islamic associations do not exist. Most of the information available is based on out-dated surveys, and estimations of the organizations themselves.[14] However, the rapid growth of the number of mosques in Berlin can probably be taken as an indicator of growing participation as well.

Less is known about the religious organization of Alevis, whose members are both ethnic Turks and ethnic Kurds. There are some estimates that they contribute to about a quarter of the Muslim population in Turkey today. It is not clear what their share is among Turks in Germany. To our knowledge there exists only one formal organization of Alevi in Berlin. This says nothing, however, about their number, since they have the most active informal networks. There appear to be a number of Alevi among the Kurds in Berlin. Their religious organization is not based on mosques and Qur'an course instruction. It may be especially difficult for the Alevi to evoke new kinds of formal institutions abroad, since their religious leadership is based on a family hereditary system and tied to old tribal structures. On the other hand, their religious-ethnic identity lends strength to their informal social networks which appear to be extremely efficient despite the extensive mobility and fragmentation caused by migration. In Berlin there have been some attempts to recreate traditional ceremonies, attracting Alevi of very different regional and ethnic composition. The confusion of ethnic and religious belongingness appears to become more critical abroad. The first generation who were responsible for organizing these events, is particularly concerned about losing the second and third generations to political and ethnic movements.

An important and controversial association founded in Germany is the nationalist and separatist movement of the Kurds (KOMKAR). They co-operate with other non-Turk Kurdish groups in Germany and claim that about 250,000 Kurdish Turks live in Germany. Recently they have also begun to address the social and cultural problems of Kurds by opening up a neighbourhood centre in Berlin to serve the needs of the nearby Kurdish families.

This centre has also suffered from the religious conflicts between Sunni and Alevi. Nevertheless, the formerly quiet presence of Kurds among Turkish migrants has become more and more apparent. Although only a small share may be militant and organized in Kurdish associations, this trend is reflected in other ways. For example, community centres which previously were simply entitled as services for 'Turkish' women, girls, or youth have changed their names to centres for women, girls, youth, etc. 'from Turkey'. A few of these provide special literacy courses in Kurdish, an activity not possible in Turkey.

Among the most important and energetic associations emerging to meet the needs of the workers abroad are those developing among specific ethnic and/or religious groups. These associations appear to function as 'interest' groups, attracting members from specific minorities (Islamic sects, Islamic splinter groups, Kurds, etc.) channelling their need for belonging (a meaningful collective identity) into their special ethno-religious identity. More and more these seek to press for certain rights for their members. They are interested in the survival of a specific identity, for example Kurdish or Turkish Muslim identity, and not that of Turkishness in general. These groups have a social as well as some personal stake in associative affiliation. Nevertheless, the actual influence they have on the younger generation is not yet clear.

These specific ethnic religious groups strive to gain political ground and search for financial support and connections. These objectives were especially important in the second part of the 1970s. During that time certain associations were used as material and social links to Turkey. Some groups were involved in smuggling and supplying arms in support of street-fighting at home. They later provided channels for the escape of political refugees, activists and criminals abroad. Since the military gain of control in Turkey in 1980 and the crackdown of the German government on extremists these activities have also diminished.

Associations organized by Turks in Germany are entering a new phase. In addition to ideologically oriented associations there are others, which may have begun with an ideological basis, but which have evolved to take on a broader scope.

There are about thirty sports associations with some 3000 members in Berlin (Romann and Schwarz 1985). Many of these were offshoots of political or cultural associations. These are mainly football clubs which serve an important function vis-à-vis the Turkish minority abroad. They attract a large public, overwhelmingly larger than any equivalent German teams. Their successes and defeats are the object of intensive attention in the weekly sports section of the German edition of Turkish newspapers printed abroad. These associations were organized, however, to serve the needs of an adult population. The majority of Turkish young persons under fifteen years of age are members of German sports associations. This fact, however, is difficult to interpret, since almost half of the under-fifteen-year-old members of German sports associations in certain city districts are foreigners, and most of these are Turks (Romann and Schwarz 1985:

51). Little is known about the situation in the other districts.

A number of cultural activities exist within as well as independent of the formal associations. Since their existence is not as lucrative as business ventures, they suffer as much or more from ups and downs; the numbers involved are tenuous. In 1983 there were nine amateur and one professional theatre groups, several bookshops and libraries specializing in Turkish literature, as well as three publishers. In addition to several folk-dancing groups, there were also two associations each for Turkish classical and folk music (Basegmez 1983). Students, professionals, exiled Turkish artists and other intellectuals have been responsible for many of these initiatives. Since the end of the 1970s Berlin is considered to be the centre of Turkish cultural life outside the home country.

In addition to associations, institutions of Turkish mass media are active in Germany. Five of the largest Turkish newspapers print European editions in Frankfurt. Three of them have special editions for Germany. They reach about 40 per cent of the Turkish population in Germany (Oepen 1984). Since late 1985 cable television makes three hours daily of the Turkish national television programme available to some 6000 Turkish households in Berlin. The Berlin government estimates that these programmes reach about half of the Turkish population in the city.[15] There is no doubt that this development which brings current Turkish conditions closer to Turks abroad is also in the interest of the Berlin and Turkish governments. Both are concerned about the radicalization of the population which may occur in the diaspora, where extremist positions have found a more liberal context and economic base than would have been possible inside Turkey.

Participation in associations

The kinds of formal organization among Turks in Berlin further indicate the heterogeneity of the networks and orientations among the first generation. Not only does there exist one association for about every hundred Turks in Berlin, but these numerous associations have quite distinct orientations, which imply a different focus with respect to the symbols of collective identity. As far as the significance of membership and participation in these diverse organizations is concerned it is very difficult to reach clear-cut conclusions. Preliminary observations in Berlin would lead us to conclude that none of the associations has a large membership, and that most of them are run by a core group of about five to twenty-five young persons. Associations, however, may play a much larger role than their formal membership would indicate. Through their programmes, public interventions, and activities they may involve more persons than their immediate members. A representative study in the Frankfurt area sought to differentiate between knowledge of the existence and activities of a number of ethnic organizations, and contact with them, and active membership (Schoeneberg 1985). It found that about 40 per cent of the nationalities studied had contact with at least one association. In this regard, Turks were not much different from the Greeks and Italians; however, Turkish nationals who had contact were much more likely to be active than the other nationalities. Almost half of the Turks who had contact (20 per cent of those interviewed) claimed to attend activities at least once a week (Schoeneberg 1985). This does not indicate anything, however, about the orientations of these activities and the identity options which may be offered by the associations they attend.

If one attempts to ascertain which orientations are predominant, it becomes clear that these remain very polarized. In Frankfurt, it was the Turkish People's House[16] which was the most well-known among all Turks (68 per cent), but only visited by less than 20 per cent of the sample. Among the religious associations, it was the Islamic Cultural Centre of the Turkish Federation (MHP) and the Faith Moshee which were the most well known (45 per cent and 42 per cent respectively). However, less than 10 per cent indicated that they had ever attended either place (Breitenbach 1984). One finding of the Frankfurt study which would also agree with the observations in Berlin is the difference between members of Islamic and the more secular political associations. Members of Islamic associations tend to be older and blue-collar workers, while the members of the more secular associations are usually younger and better educated.[17]

Thus, although the radius of influence of the activities of Turkish associations may extend rather widely, the population they reach may differ qualitatively. Among the second generation still attending school in Berlin, membership in formal associations is generally limited to sports clubs (football teams, karate or judo courses). Participation in Qur'an courses has also been widespread. While less than one-fifth of Turkish youngsters in Berlin schools had attended Qur'an courses in 1975 (Wilpert 1980), a recent study (Wilpert 1986) indicates that participation may have increased to about thirty per cent of the school youth in the past decade. Those who attend do so usually under pressure from parents who may be sensitive to the social control of their environment. On the other hand, it has evidently become more common for Turkish women and young girls in Berlin to wear scarves in public. The children who have experienced the anti-authoritarian atmosphere of German schools not only frequently reject the strict discipline and rote learning of these courses, they have evidently at times been armed with replies, which frequently arise in the family interviews: 'How can we be expected to learn three additional languages (Arabic, German and English) and continue to keep up our school work?'[18]

As mentioned at the outset, none of the associations described has, until very recently, attempted to address itself to issues of civil rights within German society. There have been no organizations of parents, such as are found among the Spanish and the Greek, to lobby for better education or mother-tongue instruction for their children. The two organizations most recently constituted for the purpose of demanding certain rights have not yet had the opportunity to prove that they will be able to mobilize the grass roots.

The leaders of these new types of association are first-generation academics and professionals, who cannot help but reflect the gulf in Turkish society between the peasant hinterland and the urban élites (Kiray 1982). Thoroughly secularized as they are, this also entails a certain distance, at times genuine denial, of the legitimacy of the Islamic aspirations of some of their compatriots, and especially of the active splinter groups organized around mosques and associated with conservative tendencies in Turkey. There are, however, more and more efforts to overcome this distance and increased willingness to recognize the real religious needs of many families.[19]

Conclusions

In this transitional period, there still remains a great deal of scepticism about the possibilities of influencing Turkish or German society. As has been seen in the decade between 1970 and 1980, all factions of Turks were influenced by the hope that through their activities in Germany they could alter the political balance and social structure of Turkish society. With the advent of the military regime in Ankara and the widespread control of all political movements, these aspirations have diminished. Since 1981, there has been a turn toward issues in German society, although little of this has been at the initiative of the first-generation workers and their children. Even now, many of the first-generation activists express an attitude of powerlessness to mobilize to achieve changes in Germany or Turkey, and both orientations, 'here' and 'there', do continue to exist.

The level of political organization among the workers themselves is rather low. Aside from the militant but small Kurdish minority, grass-roots organization in the form of collective pressure groups is not very common in the Turkish countryside. The migrant workers live in a political limbo, due to their extended temporary migration, prolonged 'myth of return' and lack of electoral rights in receiving or sending country. Long hours and demanding working conditions leave little energy for formal activities. Cafés, casinos and video programmes are more attractive, and since there is a great deal of informal social interaction between families, little time and need is left for the formal.

None the less, despite the existence of a modern welfare state which provides the most basic social services in terms of health, education and social security, Turks have found it necessary and opportune to set up their own services to mediate between individuals and German institutions. These, however, may become less important as German facilities become staffed with Turkish mediators. Like the translators in factories and courtrooms, there are more and more Turkish-speaking social workers, educators, legal and nurses' aids, in the latter case it is often the second generation who begin to assume these roles.

The investments of Turks in business activities in Berlin have created a *de facto* territorial base, which makes it possible for those persons who choose to do so to socialize in a predominantly Turkish milieu. These economic roots certainly integrate Turkish institutions into German society. It also, however, guarantees a prolonged interest in the existence of a Turkish clientele oriented towards specific Turkish cultural products. This has drawn another line of dependency between Turkish and German societies.

The formal associations which have most rapidly emerged in the migration context represent groups which are either suppressed or do not have the legitimacy to function as freely as they would like to do at home. Germany and other European countries provide an open space for the expression of suppressed ethnic and religious identities countervailing the secularist movement and aspirations for national, cultural homogeneity of the Turkish nation state.[20]

Religious groups have been able to appeal to a number of families to strengthen original values. They exercise social pressure in the densely populated areas to educate children in Qur'an courses. The Islamic Federation has been formed to regroup the splinter Islamic associations and to lobby for religious rights and the opportunity to be officially recognized to teach Islamic religion in German schools. This movement has occurred as a reaction to the position of the German public and educators to the 'undemocratic' methods of Qur'an schooling. Thus, we find the conditions of German society fostering some transformations in the social organization of the religious groupings to meet new needs in the foreign context. This is counterbalanced again by the role of the Turkish government and its interest in maintaining an economic link and ideological control over its citizens abroad.

As long as both the Turkish and the German states continue to provide the legal basis for the existence of a stratum of politically marginal foreign workers in German society, the Turkish minorities and splinter groups will continue to have a vested interest in the mobilization of particular sub-group identities. The construction of a homogeneous collective will prove difficult. What will be the symbols of Turkishness? Language and religion will not easily unite the whole. Perhaps a basis for ethnicity will instead be created through the common experience of the second generation. Although their socialization continues primarily within their sub-groups, secondary socialization occurs outside with other Turks in German schools. Peer relations among Turkish males result from school, work, leisure and street-corner life. And both daughters and sons begin to press for marriage outside the sub-group.

In spite of the ideological and cultural diversity among the Turkish population in Germany, insecure futures at home and in Germany encourage families to develop double strategies: to keep one foot in Germany while investing at home as well.[21] New forms of social organization are in process. Among the youth, values may change, but feelings of ethnic belongingness may increase. The settlement and stratification of the Turkish collective suggest a basis for leadership in the formation of new formal associations in the future. Will the coming of age of the second generation be able to break through this standstill?

Appendix: Turkish Associations in Berlin

General associations

Turkish Association for Culture and Social Work (TUBIKS) TUBIKS was established by liberal and social democrat academics and professionals in the mid-1970s to tackle community problems. Their policy aims at the integration of Turks, especially the second generation. They are trying to form a 'Turkish lobby' in Berlin with the hope of achieving democratic and social rights for the Turkish minority. The aims of TUBIKS appear to be identical with those of the 'Turkish Community of Berlin'. Considering the members active in both, it is reasonable to think that these two associations are the same; TUBIKS is the older association.

Turkish Community of Berlin/Berlin Türk Cemaati (TCB) Claims to represent thirteen Turkish associations in Berlin, from centre right to centre left, and to serve the community as a whole. This appears to have the recognition of the city government.

Its stated aim is to help the community to develop a pressure group. Although it is not commonly known to an average worker, since it is organized from the top down, it is trying to establish itself as the representative of the community. The recently established 'Turkish Chamber of Commerce in Berlin' (Verein Türkischer Kaufleute) was, for instance, an initiation of the active members of this association. In 1983 it had some sixty members, of whom about twelve were active.

Turkish Science and Technology Association/Berlin Türk Bilim-Teknoloji Merkezi (BTBTM) A students' association in the Berlin Technical University. As is the case with most university-based associations, its main aim is academic and social. But it has, from 1975 onward, been engaged in political debates, depending on the political views of the active members. It has, since 1975, maintained its liberal to social democratic identity, keeping left and right extremes out. Currently it has some seventy-five members, but only twenty active members. This is not many if one considers the size of the student body, which is about 750 in the Berlin Technical University.

Turkish Union/Berlin Türk Toplulugu (BTT) BTT is an association for progressive and left-democratic Turkish organizations in Berlin. Its goal is the equal treatment of Turks living in Berlin in all spheres. The BTT and the TGB are the two major secular associations which compete for public recognition of their voice as representatives of Turks in Berlin. Both organizations are run by first-generation Turkish intellectuals.

Leftist associations

Progressive People's Association/Halkci-Devrimci Birliği (HDB) A social-democratic organization. Founded in 1973, it has since developed into a federation. It has an effective network within Germany and international connections in Europe, especially with Scandinavian countries, as a member of a social democratic family in Europe. It was once more closely tied to the social democratic party in Turkey, but has recently begun to act independently. It claims to have 400 members in Berlin and fifty active volunteers, mainly academics, teachers and qualified workers, but it represents more than that number. In addition to various forms of legal and social counselling, it runs a theatre and folklore group, a sports club and a women's chapter.

Turkish Centre/Türk Merkezi Established in 1979, this is a Marxist-oriented association with international ties. The centre defines its objectives in the spheres of culture, education, leisure and understanding for Turks, Germans and other nationalities. It offers a number of courses for young people and adults, theatre, folklore, Saz-music and sports activities. At first it functioned almost like an umbrella for various orthodox associations (for example, Association for Turkish Socialists, Association for Artists, Women's Association, Association for Radical Workers, etc.), which are all represented in the centre. It has intellectual support of many academics and the educated and a wide membership among immigrant workers. It offers language courses for workers and their families, provides certain recreation facilities such as drama, music (singing and playing instruments), folklore, crafts, and assists workers in their daily legal and social problems. Although the membership is in the region of 50, more people attend and enjoy its social and recreational activities.

Kurdish Cultural and Counselling Centre   This centre was founded in 1984 to serve the needs of Kurdish-speaking Turks in Berlin.

Workers' Youth Association/Isci/Genclik Birliği   A revolutionary grass-root organization, associated with other groups in Europe and in Turkey. It is the extension of the Turkish Dev-Yol (revolutionary path), having a large membership in Germany and publishing a monthly news-bulletin, of which over 10,000 copies are distributed in the whole of Germany. The active members are, however, mainly those who have completed their education in Turkey or those who escaped from the military coup of 1980. Active membership of the association is sixty to seventy, but they seem to have many more sympathizers.

Other political associations
These present more or less the same picture as the above-mentioned Workers' Youth Association. They are all extensions of similar associations or groups in Turkey, with the same ideological factions and divisions. They were, however, brought to function under more powerful federations, which would cover all the similar (i.e. leftist) associations of Europe.

— *Federation of Turkish Socialists in Europe*/Avrupa Türkiye Toplumcular Federasyoriu (ATTF) is a large pro-Moscow federation, with strong links with the outlawed Turkish Communist Party (TKP).

— *Federation of Turkish Workers in Europe*/Avrupa Türk Isci Federasyoiu (ATIF) is a small pro-Albanian, Maoist proletarian revolutionary federation.

— *Federation of Democratic Workers' Associations*/Demokratik Isci/Devrimci Federasyoiu (DIDF) covers varying political groups from social democrats to orthodox Marxists, but is dominated by radical Alevis and Kurds, who would disassociate themselves from the 'Shematic' leftists.

—In 1977, various federations formed an umbrella federation called FIDEF *(Federation of Turkish Associations in Germany)*. This was mainly a workers' federation and excluded students. Then, the leftist students were brought together under a federation: *Federation of Turkish Students in Germany* (ATOF).

—*Populist-Progressive Federation* (HDF) is an outgrowth of HDB, a social democratic association. It is one of the most active organizations in Berlin, with wide intellectual membership.

—*The Association of Kurdish Workers* (KOMKAR) acts like a federation for the whole of Germany. This separatist organization is a reasonably well-organized 'federation' with a few thousand members. They do not disassociate themselves from the leftist associations, but also have members who are considered rightists. The organization is involved in activities concerning the welfare of the Kurdish immigrants, a repressed group, and the development of a collective consciousness to open ways to establish a separate state in the Kurdish section of Turkey.

—Another Kurdish separatist and militant association is *Bir-Kom*, the association of Kurdish apocu (those escaping the military repression of 1980) leftists. This group has nothing to do with immigrants; it works for the separation of the Kurdish region. They cannot be active in Turkey and organize themselves for future rebellion.

Rightist associations

These may be studied in two categories, religious and non-religious (ideological) but, in general, religion is the starting point. In this sense, they are all religious associations, but some use religion as a tool for political expansion, whereas others are organized for religious solidarity and expansion. They both use the mosque as the centre of their activities, but the former have further political and ideological ambitions.

Rightist political and religious-oriented associations

—*Independent-Turk*/Hür-Türk is a right-to-centre association, with strong ties to the ruling justice party (AP) in Turkey. They consider themselves as 'nationalist' and not religious, but they represent a large religious faction, the Süleymanli movement, as well as the liberal section of the National Salvation Party (NSP). The association is known to have provided considerable financial support to the rightist political movement in Berlin and in Turkey, but has not been involved in open political disputes.

—*Greater Ideal Association*/Büyük Ülkü Dernegi is an extension organization of the Turkish Grey Wolf movement which works in collaboration with the rightist party MHP, Party of the National Movement. It is the main rightist youth organization which has been involved in organizing political struggles to gain ground and to be able to support the organization in Turkey. There is another smaller association for adults and people in power. This is called *Turkish Union*/Türk Cemaati and has more of a religious tendency.

—*Turkish Association in Berlin*/Berlin Türk Ocagi is the extension organization of Greater Ideal Association. It functions as a training and social club of the core association.

—*Turkish Students' and Youth's Association*/Turk-Genc is another association functioning as an extension of Greater Ideal Association. It is run by university students and other youth of the extreme right.

All the above associations have been brought together under a large umbrella organization: *Federation for the Turkish Idealists' Associations in Europe* (ATÜDF). The centre of the federation is in Frankfurt. In Berlin, it is not very strong, but it is well organized in Europe. It is estimated to have about 110 associations with 26,000 members in Germany. The rightists in this federation have recently been organized in the Turkish Congress Centre in Berlin. This centre provides facilities for all rightists. It has meeting halls, game-rooms and regular personnel. The centre offers its halls for large meetings like weddings, circumcisions and other occasions, and tries to expand through such social contacts. In this sense, the centre acts as a social institution established to handle community problems and to organize community activities.

Religious and religious-political associations   Religious associations are organized around mosques and act, in essence, as Islamic missionary organizations to be able to serve the faithful and to expand. As they do not have formal counterparts in Turkey, they have developed their own expansionist culture abroad and, as such, become conservative cultural centres for their followers. They have, on the other hand, established close links with the religious and conservative parties in Turkey, becoming one of the financial sources of these parties, but mainly of the National Salvation Party (MSP) during the 1970s. They are among the best organized associations in Berlin.

One of the most important Islamic umbrella organizations in Berlin is the *Islamic Federation* which was founded in 1981 and regroups about twenty mosques and religious associations in the city. The Islamic Federation was set up as a public institution (öffentlich-rechtlicher Verein) to assume leadership as representatives of all Muslims in the Federal Republic of Germany and West Berlin. Their objective is to obtain recognition to teach Islamic religion in the public schools as the more homogeneous Catholics, Protestants and Jews do for their members. The German legal and political institutions would definitely be interested in offering legitimate religious courses for Turkish Muslims in Berlin schools, to prevent the supposed success of the clandestine Qur'an school movements in the store-fronts throughout the Turkish neighbourhoods of the city.

The federation has a foundation to manage its financial matters. It is said that the foundation has an annual budget of about DM 500,000, which is used for religious development, political expansion and Qur'an schools, and for the economic development of the community.

Apart from the mosque-based associations, there are a few non-mosque religious associations. Such associations are extension organizations of the mother organizations in Turkey. They are generally affiliated to one of the mosque groups as well as to the religious party (MSP).

—*Association of Conquerors*/Akincilar Dernegi is a grass-root organization, representing young Muslims and aiming at preparing Muslim youth for the future and preserving the Islamic tradition. It is more of a political association and has close links with the religious party (whichever it is) at home. It has a relatively large membership of a couple of hundred and is much concerned with community affairs and with the maintenance of the Islamic way of life.

—*Nationalist View Association*/Milli Görüs Teskilati, *Islam Students' Association*/Müslüman Talebeler Camiasi, and *Turkish Culture and Solidarity Association*/Türk Kültür ve Vardimlasma Dernegi are also grass-root organizations with direct links to the dominant religious party in Turkey.

—*Islamic Culture Centre*/Islam Kultur Merkezi (ICC) is the religious organization of the Suleymanili group and sympathizes with the centre-to-right party (now outlawed) AP, the ruling party before 1980. It is well organized in the Federal Republic of Germany, but not in Berlin. It owes its development to its organization around a mosque. This has direct links with the conservative party. There is some division between ICC and the rest of the religious parties.

—*VEPIFM* was founded to further control of religion by the state. It is organized around a mosque, sponsored by the Islamic Union, without political involvement. The mosque has a large attendance. Most of those mosques not belonging to the federation are members of the Islamic Union, which is the official representative of the Islamic religion sponsored by the Turkish state. This group has about six mosques in Berlin, but none in Kreuzberg.

Notes

1   The observations in this paper are based on several years of research with Turkish migrants in Berlin and returnees in Turkey (Gitmez 1979, 1983; Kudat *et al.* 1974, 1976; Wilpert 1983, 1986). Within the context of a research project about the future prospects of migrant families at the Berlin Technical University financed by the Volkswagen Foundation, Ali Gitmez has collected a series of migration histories of first- and second-generation Turks in Berlin. In addition to this, we have conducted numerous expert interviews, several group discussions among second-generation youth and villagers, and participant observation in the Turkish community. In the same study, foreign youth and families were interviewed about their future aspirations and social networks. Preliminary results are reported in Wilpert (1983b). Efforts were made in 1986 to bring preliminary observations up to date.
2   The federal German government sponsored a repatriation scheme between October 1983 and September 1984. It is reported that 189,000 Turks left the country during this time. This policy for non-European Community migrants waived the two-year waiting period for the refund of payments into the German social security system. Those who withdrew their pension gave up further rights to retirement benefits and the possibility of returning to the Federal Republic of Germany.
3   According to a 1974 survey in Berlin (Kudat), 27 per cent of the Turks were employed at that time in skilled positions, 5 per cent as foremen. The majority (98 per cent) were manual workers (65 per cent in manufacturing) of whom 43 per cent were in the metal industry. According to the Bundesanstalt für Arbeit, over 45 per cent of the Turks officially recruited in 1971 were skilled workers before departure (Bundesanstalt für Arbeit 1972).
4   Between 1976 and 1980, the number of applications of foreigners for refugee status multiplied by ten, from 11,000 to over 100,000. And in 1980, the year of the military coup in Turkey, over 50 per cent of the applicants were Turkish nationals (Korte and Schmidt 1983: 23).
5   Another factor which added to the attractiveness of Berlin was the cost of living addition to the paycheck (Berlin-Zulage) and the fact that there were housing possibilities for families and couples in the deserted buildings of the urban renewal areas. At that period, the urban housing shortage was serious in many German industrial areas.
6   Since 1981 the regulation is that, when the child of a foreign worker marries, their spouse may only enter the country if they themselves have been residents of Germany for the previous eight years, they are at least eighteen years of age, and they have been married for at least a year.
7   According to Lescot (1938) the Yezidi religion is a mixture of Zoroastrianism, Muslim ritual, Sufi mysticism, and Brahmanism. About six million Kurds are estimated to live in Turkish Kurdistan, about 30,000 of these are thought to be Yezidis. Wrongly stigmatized at times as devil worshippers, Yezidis have suffered religious persecution, and may seek refugee status in Germany (Schneider 1984).
8   According to a Berlin study (Schuleri 1982), before 1980 more than half of the applications from foreigners to establish a business were denied. This is supposedly no longer the case. Many of the first businesses were started without the necessary residence permit. Someone who is eligible, usually a German citizen, would be paid to be the nominal 'straw boss'.
9   Quoted from Harnisch and Ayanoglu (1983).
10   In 1981 less than 5 per cent of the Turks in Berlin had obtained this status. In 1984, almost four times that number (or 18 per cent) had a 'right to stay' (*Aufenthalts-*

berechtigung). At least eight consecutive years in Germany is required to achieve this (Der Senator für Gesundheit, Soziales und Familie 1985: 84).

11 According to Berlin Government Administration for Commerce and quoted in *Der Tagesspiegel* (22 November 1985).

12 This turnover is equally high—if not higher—among the other nationalities. It is especially pronounced in the restaurant trade among Italians and Yugoslavs where there has been an 80-to-90 per cent turnover in this four-year period (see Table 5.1, p.100).

13 cf. discussion in Wilpert (1980).

14 The discussion on religious activity among Turks may be found in Elsas (1983). These findings are taken from surveys conducted in the Federal Republic of Germany in 1979.

15 As quoted in *Der Tagesspiegel* (22 November 1985).

16 The Turkish People's House is a secular establishment which has been in existence since 1966 and which identifies with the Turkish Kemalist movements for popular education. Breitenbach (1984) points out that contrary to the Kemalist movement it recognizes language groups among Turkish nationals, indirectly recognizing the Turkish minorities.

17 Only persons over eighteen years of age were interviewed, and of these only 13 per cent claimed membership in an ethnic association (Breitenbach 1984). If second generation is defined as born or raised from entrance into elementary school in Germany very few would have been in this category. The majority of these youngsters are only now beginning to reach adulthood (compare the presentation of associations on pp. 115-121).

18 The significance of observations made about the wearing of scarves is also not easily interpreted. There is no easy measurement. We rely on impressions. If this is true, it may mean that it is preferable to identify oneself as a Turk. And Turks more than Germans remain the reference group. Although pressure to wear scarves is exerted by the religious groups, scarf-wearing itself is a more common custom than that of attending Qur'an schools.

19 This has been recently demonstrated in the initiatives of Turks of all political orientations to mobilize support for a Turkish cultural centre with a mosque in an urban renewal district (so 36) in Kreuzberg (Harnisch and Ayanoglu 1983).

20 The boom in Islamic organizations is a reaction to the official state secularism in Turkey. For the first time during the Turkish republican era Turkish religious groups have found a tolerant and supportive setting.

21 According to the most recent data from the Deutsche Bundesbank (1985) the amount of remittances transferred from Germany to the sending countries has not noticeably wavered between 1981 and 1984. Turks have transferred an average of DM 3,350,000 yearly in this period, with slight decrease in 1983, the year that the German government offered the limited repatriation scheme. Remittances began to drop between 1975 and 1978, but increased sharply thereafter.

References

Abadan-Unat, N. *et al.* (1975) *Migration and development*, Ajans-Türk Press, Ankara.

Basegmez, O. (1983) 'Bauchtanz und Basar—Türkische Kultur in Berlin', *Zitty*, 17/1983: 28–33.

Benedict, P. (1976) 'Aspects of the domestic cycle in a provincial Turkish town', in J.G. Peristiany (ed.), *Mediterranean family structures*, Cambridge University Press, pp. 219–41.

Breitenbach, Barbara von (1984) *Die Funktion von Vereinen im Integrationsprozess von Arbeitsmigranten*, Bericht uber ein von der Stiftung Volkswagenwerk gefordertes Forschungsprojekt, Mimeo, Frankfurt.

Breton, R. (1964) 'Institutional completeness of ethnic communities and the personal relations of immigrants', *American Journal of Sociology*, 70, pp. 193–205.

Bundesanstalt für Arbeit (1972) *Ausländische Arbeitnehmer*, Nürnberg.

Bundesanstalt für Arbeit (1973) *Repräsentativ-Untersuchung 1972*, Nürnberg.

Darkow, M. and Eckhardt, J. (1982) 'Massenmedien und Ausländer in der Bundesrepublik'. Erste Ergebnisse eines ARD/ZDF-Projekts, *Media Perspektiven*, 7.

Decker, Frauke (1982) *Ausländer im politischen Abseits. Möglichkeiten ihrer politischen Beteiligung*, Campus Verlag, Frankfurt.

Der Beauftragte Der Bundersregierung für Ausländerfragen (1985) *Bericht zur Ausländerpolitik*, Bonn.

Der Regierende Bürgermeister von Berlin (1972) *Eingliederung der Ausländischen Arbeitnehmer und ihrer Familien*, Berlin.

Der Senator für Gesundheit, Soziales und Familie (1985) *Miteinander Leben. Bilanz und Perspektiven*, Berlin.

Deutsche Bundesbank (1985) 'Überweisungen ausländischer Arbeitnehmer in ihre Heimatländer', *Ausländer in Deutschland*, no 4, p. 3.

Duben, Alan (1982) 'The significance of family and kinship in urban Turkey', in C. Kagitcibasi (ed.), *Sex roles, family and community in Turkey*, pp. 73–99, Indiana University, Bloomington.

Dubetsky, Alan (1976) 'Kinship, primordial ties, and factory organization in Turkey: an anthropological view', *Int. J. Middle East Stud.*, 7, pp. 433–51.

Elsas, C. (1983)Religiöse Faktoren für Identität, 'Politische Implikationen christlich kultureller Eigenarten im Zusammenleben von Türken und Deutschen*, pp. 39–142, Rissen, Hamburg.

Engelbrektsson, U. -B. (1982) *The force of tradition. Turkish migrants at home and abroad*, Acta Universitätis Gothenburgensis, Gothenburg.

Freiburghaus, D. (1974) *Die Bedeutung der rechtlichen Struktur des Wohnungsmarkts für die Wohnungsversorgung der ausländischen Arbeitskräfte*, Wissenschaftszentrum Berlin.

Freie Planungsgruppe Berlin (FPB) and Prognos AG (1980) *Wohnraumversorgung von Ausländern und Entballung überlasteter Gebiete durch städtebauliche Massnahmen*, Studie im Auftrag des Regierenden Bürgermeisters von Berlin, Berlin.

Gericke, R., Bischoff, D. *et al.* (1985) *Leitfaden zur Ausländerarbeit in Berlin*, Sozialpadägogisches Institut Berlin.

Gitmez, A.S. (1979) *Disgöc Öyküsü* (The myth of external migration), Mava Publication, Ankara.

Gitmez, A.S. (1983) *Disgöc ve Dönenler: Beklenenler, Gerceklesenler* (External migration and return: expectations, fulfilments), Alan Publishing, Istanbul.

Gokalp, A. (1980) *Têtes Rouges et Bouches Noires*, Société d'éthnographie, Paris.

Harnisch, U. and Ayanoglu, Ö (1983) *'Mit-Bürger-Beteiligung' am Görlitzer Bahnhof*, Im Auftrag der Internationalen Bauausstellung Berlin.

Iskender, S. (1983) *Medien und Organisationen. Interkulturelle Medien und Organisationen und ihr Beitrag zur Integration der türkischen Minderheit*, Express Edition GmbH, Berlin.

Karpat, K. (1976) *The Gecekondu: Rural migration and urbanization*, Cambridge University Press.

Kendel (1982) 'Kurdistan in Turkey', in Gerard Chaliant (ed.), *People without a country*, pp. 47–106, Zed Press, London.

Kiray, M. (1982) 'Changing patterns of patronage: A study in structural change', in C. Kagitcibasi (ed.) *Sex roles, family, and community in Turkey*, pp. 269–94, Indiana University, Bloomington.

Klitzke, D. (1982) *Das 4. Programm. Studie zum türkischen Videomarkt*, Express Edition GmbH, Berlin.

Korte, H. and Schmidt, A. (1983) *Migration und ihre sozialen Folgen*, Vandenhoeck & Ruprecht, Göttingen.

Kudat, A. (1975) 'Patron-client relation: the state of the art and research in Eastern Turkey', in E.D. Akarli and G. Ben-Dor (eds), *Political participation in Turkey: Historical backgrounds and present problems*, pp. 61–87, Bogazizi, Istanbul.

Kudat, A. (1975) *Stability and change in the Turkish family at home and abroad* Wissenschaftszentrum Berlin.

Kudat, A., Wilpert, C. *et al.* (1974) *International labour migration: a description of th* *preliminary findings of the West Berlin migrant worker survey*, Wissensch aftszentrum Berlin.

Kudat, A., Özkan, Y. *et al.* (1976) *Internal and external migration effects on the experi* *ence of foreign workers in Europe*, Wissenschaftszentrum Berlin.

Lescot, R. (1938) *Enquête sur les Yezidis de Syrie et du Djebel-Sindjar*, Beirut.

Magnarella, P.J. (1979) *The peasant venture – tradition, migration and change amon§* *Georgian peasants in Turkey*, Schenckmann Publishing Co, Cambridge/Mass.

Mehrländer, U. (1972) *Beschäftigung ausländischer Arbeitnehmer in der Bundes* *republik Deutschland unter spezieller Berücksichtigung von Nordrhein-Westfalen* Westdeutscher Verlag, Opladen.

Mehrländer, U., Hofmann, R. *et al.* (1981) *Situation der ausländischen Arbeitnehme* *und ihrer Familienangehörigen in der Bundesrepublik Deutschland. Repräsentativ* *Untersuchung 1980*, Bundesminister für Arbeit und Sozialordnung, Bonn.

Oepen, M. (1984) 'National report of the Federal Republic of Germany', in T Hujanen (ed.), *The role of information in the realization of the human rights o§* *migrant workers*, pp. 125–54, Tulkaisuja, Tampere.

Rebentisch, M. (1986) 'Am besten wäre ein Verhältnis von 50 zu 50', Zwei türkisch« Jugendvereine suchen Kontakt zu Deutschen — Türkischkurse angeboten, *De* *Tagesspiegel*, 23 February, 1986.

Romann-Schüssler, D. and Schwarz, T. (1985) *Türkische Sportler in Berlin zwische* *Integration und Segregation*, Berlin, der Senator für Gesundheit, Soziales un« Familie.

Sassen-Koob, S. (1979) 'Formal and informal associations: Dominicans and Col ombians in New York', *International Migration Review*, vol. 13, no. 2, 314–31.

Schneider, R. (ed.) (1984) *Die kurdischen Yezidi. Ein Volk auf dem Weg in den Un* *tergang*, Pogram, Göttingen.

Schoeneberg, U (1985) 'Participation in ethnic associations: The case of immigrants i» West Germany', *International Migration Review*, vol. 19, no. 3, pp. 416–37.

Schuleri, U.K. (1982) *Ausübung eines Gewerbes oder Handwerks durch Ausländer* Verwaltungsakademie Berlin (Mimeo).

Sozialdata (1980) *Befragung deutscher und ausländischer Haushalte zur Ausländer* *integration in Berlin*, Der Regierende Bürgermeister von Berlin.

Spies, U. (1982) *Ausländerpolitik und Integration*, Peter Lang Verlag, Frankfurt.

Statistisches Bundesamt (1983) *Strukturdaten über Ausländer in der Bundesrepubli* *Deutschland*, W. Kohlhammer, Mainz.

Statistisches Landesamt Berlin (1975) *Die Ausländer in Berlin (West) 1960 bis 1973* Kulturbuch-Verlag GmbH, Berlin, Sonderheft 234, 5/1975.

Statistisches Landesamt Berlin (1983) *Ausländer in Berlin (West) 1960 bis 1983* Kulturbuch-Verlag GmbH, Berlin, Sonderheft 342, 12/1983.

Statistisches Landesamt Berlin (1984) *Berliner Statistik*, Berlin 7/1984.

Thomä-Venske, H. (1981) *Islam und Integration*, Verlag Rissen, Hamburg.

Trommer, L. and Köhler, H. (1981) *Ausländer in der Bundersrepublik Deutschland* Deutsches Jugendinstitut, Munich.

Unel, M. (1983) 'Muhammed, Marx und Atatürk — Türkische Politik in Berlin', *Zitty* 18, pp. 12–16.

Wilpert, C. (1980) *Die Zukunft der Zweiten Generation — Erwartungen und Ver* *haltensmöglichkeiten ausländischer Kinder*, Hain, Königstein/Ts.

Wilpert, C. (1982) 'Structural marginality and the role of cultural identity for migran« youth', in European Science Foundation (ed.), *Cultural identity and structural mar* *ginalization of migrant workers*, pp. 117–29, Strasbourg.

Wilpert, C. (1983) 'From guestworkers to immigrants' (Migrant workers and thei» families in the FRG), *New Community*, vol. XI, nos 1/2, Autumn/Winter pp 137–42.

Wilpert, C. (1983) 'Wanderung und Zukunftsorientierung von Migranten-familien', in C. Wilpert and M. Morkokvasic (eds), *Bedingungen und Folgen internationaler Migration*, pp. 3–274, Technische Universitat Berlin.

Wilpert, C. (1987) 'Acculturation in urban areas: Labour migration and the settlement of Turks in Berlin', in D. Frick *et al.* (eds), *Urban settings*, Walter de Gruyter, Berlin.

Wilpert, C. (1987) 'Zukunftsorientierungen von Migrantenfamilien: türkische Familien in Berlin', in H. Reiman and H. Reiman (eds), *Gastarbeiter*, Westdeutscher Verlag GmbH, Wiesbanden.

Yalman, N. (1969) 'Islamic reform and the mystic tradition in eastern Turkey', *Archiv. europ. sociol.*, X, pp. 41–60.

Newspaper Articles

Die Nachrichtensendung aus der Türkei ist umstritten, *Der Tagesspiegel*, 22 November 1985.

Videofilm warnt Türken vor den Gefahren einer Kreditaufnahme, *Der Tagesspiegel*, 22 November 1985.

Konflikt um kurdisches Zentrum, *Der Tagesspiegel*, 29 November 1985.

IG Metall verlangt kommunales Wahlrecht fur Ausländer, *Der Tagesspiegel*, 8 January 1986.

125

6 Portuguese Associations in France

Marie-Antoinette Hily and Michel Poinard

Density and goals of the Portuguese associative movement in France
Almost 900,000 Portuguese nationals, or one-tenth of the population
of Portugal, reside in France. They are the most important community of foreigners in France and represent almost 17 per cent of all
migrant workers. They are characterized by the paradox that despite
their numbers they abstain from involvement in protest movements
against the rising tide of xenophobia and racism. The most committed Portuguese leaders criticize the reserve of their community:

> We constitute the main flow of immigration into France but we are the
> only group which either does not know how to or does not wish to partici-
> pate, collectively, in crucial debates on basic immigration issues.

None the less, the Portuguese are the community which has established the most dense and active network of official associations,
who did not wait to begin to organize themselves until the left came to
power and provided the institutional framework for the organization
of foreigners in 1981.

The object of this chapter is to investigate these two facets of the
Portuguese community in France, its quietness and apparent 'integration', as well as its active ties to the mother country. This will be
accomplished by way of an analysis of the functioning of associations,
their leadership and strategies. Is this passivity and the image of
the Portuguese as 'foreigners without problems', as opposed to the
'unassimilable arabs', proof of their integration? Or, on the contrary,
should not the very close ties which they continue to retain with their
country of origin lead us to conclude that this community is above all
concerned with preserving its identity? Is it not precisely the strength
of their feelings of belonging to Portugal which motivates the agility
they demonstrate in their use of the institutions of French society?

Substructure and resources of association life
At the end of 1982 the Secretary of State for Immigration compiled a
register of 769 associations (see Table 6.1). If one relates the number

126

of associations to the size of the immigrant population in France, there are nearly 1230 potential members per association.

Table 6.1   Evolution of Portuguese associations in France

1971	23	1973	82	1980	473	1982	769
1972	58	1975	101	1981	620	1985	850*

* This is an estimate based on the most recent calculations of the SPACA

In 1982 alone, 192 new associations were discussed by the Servicio de Programaçao e Apoio as Comunidades (SPAC)—planning and support service for the communities. This number represents an increase rate of 32 per cent, offset, in actual fact, either by the dissolution or by the non-response of forty-nine associations which no longer reply to the enquiries of the Portuguese co-ordinating service.

It may be true to say that this associative network does not maintain a permanent mobilization of the entire Portuguese community, that the burden of management often falls on to the same shoulders, and that apart from the presence of the unremitting 'old faithfuls', that of other members is episodic. However, the fact remains that this movement currently channels the essential expression of Portuguese autonomy in France; the expansion allows a certain number of activities to take place; the movement is capable of mobilizing the core of the community at certain critical periods; and even those who are critical or who take issue with this movement are compelled to go through their local association in order to keep in touch with life back home.

An additional aspect of their uniqueness springs less from the discovery of a 'network', since all other immigrant communities have set up their own networks, but more from the extent and degree of cohesion manifested by this network. To the indigenous French population, the discrete nature[2] of this community seems to be reflected in reality by its sense of 'identity', by its concern to reconcile the 'Portuguese character' with a strong capacity to achieve a 'functional integration' in the day-to-day life of the local French community. This is done in order to work, to find accommodation and to gain the support necessary for the success of their own goals.

On the whole, a Portuguese immigrant has no reason to doubt his own national identity and his arrival in France does not entail entering into relation with a society which maintains conflictual and impassioned links with his own society at home. Unlike North African immigrants, the Portuguese immigrant does not have to face the after-effects of decolonization.

One may consider that this balance achieved by the Portuguese community has been established as a result of two conditions: the first of which concerns the social organization of the community and the other which has to do with the symbolic resources mustered within its organized network.

Role and durability of informal networks
Since the advent of capitalism, the history of economic migrations has been marked by the *individualism* of a person planning to improve personal conditions as well as those of his family by seeking work in the most dynamic regions of his own country or of foreign countries. However, this relative freedom, which certainly does not remain untouched by the pressures generated by poverty and which contrasts with the large-scale population movements of previous ages and with the collective transfers imposed by wars, is after all realized neither by chance nor without the support and complicity of communities in the countries of origin. Whether it is a question of internal migration[3] or of emigration across national frontiers an active solidarity with those at home compensates for the disappointment of leaving one's home and eases the transfer of the newcomers by smoothing out administrative problems and by providing initial accommodation or employment. The importance accorded to such clusterings in certain areas, whether based upon family, village or religious ties, explains the professional specialization of certain national or regional minorities. For example, those coming from the Aveyron region work in the Paris 'lemonade' industries, while others from the Balearic islands can be found in the greengrocery trade in Lyons. It also explains the partial transfer of a village community to certain towns or suburbs in France and the continuation of intense communication with the home country after the initial tide of migration ebbs away.

The establishment of entry networks   The Portuguese colony has not escaped this informal and spontaneous form of collective organization focusing upon the *elementary protection* of newcomers; it seems, in fact, that the particularity of the emigration patterns of its own citizens has reinforced such practices.

Firstly, until 1970 at least, most migrants came from a highly-structured rural milieu where, beyond the generalization of very small holdings, community-based agricultural practices persisted (cf. the exploitation of the Baldios in forest pastures). Above all, cultural attitudes, a sense of belonging and a hierarchy of values resulted from the village community's concern for its own sense of identity.[4] In so far as one usually marries into one's *aldeia* or, furthest from home, into one's *freguesia*, family and local solidarities overlap and are thus reinforced, so that upon emigration to another country forms of mutual aid extend beyond the limits of the family circle.

Secondly, this emigration towards Europe and especially into France, is rooted in a migratory tradition. Prior to agricultural mechanization in the south, it was usual for peasants from the *Beiras* to go harvesting or olive-picking in the vast regions of Alernejo. Since the end of the nineteenth century, Portugal has been forced to balance its economy by exporting its workforce to the United States, Latin America and Canada. Faced with emigration and uprooting, folk ways have developed to organize departures, control the behaviour of wives left behind and regulate money sent from abroad. Furthermore, after the First World War, when a Portuguese contingent won renown through fighting with the Allies, approximately 30,000 persons, often ex-soldiers, settled in France, constituting the first wave of Portuguese immigration into the country.

While the economic crisis of 1929 halted this first wave of immigrants and necessitated the repatriation of the majority of Portuguese whose marital status, upon arrival in France, had been single, others remained settled without ever entirely breaking relations with their home country. After 1960, with the resumption of immigration into France, it was usually the 'veteran immigrants' who began to re-initiate the process by taking upon themselves the task of recruiting workers from their native villages on behalf of their employers. This was the case, for example, in St Ètienne where a community from São Bras de Alportel in the Algarve emerged as a consequence of a recruitment drive launched by a foreman working for a large BTP (Bâtiments et travaux publics) company. Chain migration provided the basis of Portuguese concentration in Villefranche de Rouergue in the region of Aveyron. Others established themselves as leaders of a nascent community, as in the case of a naturalized Portuguese iron-monger in Tarascon/Ariege.

Finally, the majority of immigration to France has taken place outside of the legal, institutional framework of the Portuguese state. This immigration, which by definition remained illegal from the Portuguese government's point of view, entailed the establishment of entry points in order to cross national frontiers, the transportation of potential workers in France and the provision of material support for the settlement of these workers. It is in this way that frontier towns, which, since 1955, were the first to encourage emigration from Portugal, put to good use their experience gained as smugglers in ensuring border crossings by others.[5] Thus it is also that during the early 1960s the Portuguese population conglomerated in the departments of France which favoured and facilitated the legalization of clandestine immigrants. The department of Puy de Dome is the primary department, outside the Paris region, whose population includes a Portuguese colony.

On the whole, all studies[6] undertaken on Portuguese emigration during this period stress the importance of solidarity networks, based as much upon family as upon village ties, in guaranteeing first the arrival and then the survival of newcomers. Thus after initially settling in the Pau region, where a small community has rooted itself, the people of Queriga (a district of Viseu) moved on to settle in Orsay. As Maria Beatriz Rocha Trindade stresses:

> Individual behaviour tends to be subordinated to the maintenance of the whole, the small nucleus of which the latter are members . . . the limited groups of men without their families, who live in dormitories or barracks, organise their daily activities upon a quasi-family model. The fact that they are often already related to each other, entertain old ties of friendship or that they share similar regional backgrounds, means that the restrictive environment in which they live only serves to reinforce existing ties. Their lives are, in general, communally organised, certain daily tasks are performed by each person in turn.

When it comes to weekend relaxation, the people of Queriga pay a blind accordion player, also a native of their village, to provide music for an open-air 'ball' which takes place near the Town Hall, on the pavements of Orsay's main street.

There exist, parallel to these popular networks, other instances within which one attempts to regularize one's situation and thus alleviate the problems connected with a clandestine life: the Portuguese church is, firstly, one such instance upon which Salazarism has conferred the task of moral supervision of the rural population and which cannot remain indifferent to the scale of emigration and the ensuing dramas.

Since 1966 the church has organized meetings on issues pertaining to Portuguese emigration, has set up commissions in France in order to gather the faithful for a Portuguese mass and has requested local priests to open the pages of their parish newsletters to article writers reflecting the lives of their immigrant parishioners. Thus it is that the priest from Queriga regularly visits his flock in Pau and even records personal messages from them during his pastoral tours, which are then delivered to the villagers back home by means of a loudspeaker attached to the church tower. It is difficult, all the same, to assess the influence the church has wielded during this period and more so because the conservatism and paternalism of Portuguese Catholicism often lies in contradiction with the conciliar modernism of the French priests or with the militancy of members of Catholic workers' action groups.

Relatively unknown and more discrete still was the role played by

130

militant anti-Salazarists opposed to the colonial war. While their resistance networks may not be as important as the popular networks, they were often the initiators of associative practices and they trained a number of political leaders who returned to Portugal after the *coup d'état* on 25 April 1974.

The social role of informal networks   Progressively, towards 1970, after the rigours of clandestine life lessened, after freedom of movement had in fact been instituted within France and after emigration had become widespread in Portugal, it was still the energy of the informal networks, coupled with the industrious individualism of these workers, which placed the Portuguese community ahead of all the colonies of foreigners established in France and which hastened its unnoticed integration into the norms of local society. Even if the study of the course of migrations shows that certain individuals experience their departure as an effective and uncompromising break, the majority of family ties remain intact: this is the moment when, with averages of approximately 65,000 newcomers per year, emigration of families reaches its highest level and the most complex forms of solidarity are put to the test on either side of the frontier. Sometimes an immigrant is joined by his children of working age while his wife remains in Portugal with the younger children, whereas at other times it is the grandmother who joins a family and contributes to the upbringing of her grandchildren while their mother joins the labour market. Conversely and more frequently still, because of the high rate of female employment within Portuguese society, the wife alone may join her husband while the children are left in the care of relatives or of brothers and sisters who have not emigrated. However, in exchange, such a couple would arrange for the arrival and facilitate the initial establishment of their nieces or nephews.

In fact, family ties have constituted the mainstay of migratory strategies which have been elaborated during this period. Leaving behind children in the mother country is also a way in which parents choose, for their children, social advancement through the Portuguese education system. This, in turn, diminishes within these children the desire to emigrate later on. It is equally a way in which couples indicate that their stay in France will not be definitive and that they will retire in their country of birth. In addition to all this, the social standing of those immigrants who have returned to Portugal equally underlines the importance of solidarity networks.[7] Economic success, the capacity to continue to accumulate this success by setting up shop or a small transportation business, depends most often upon the social circumstances of immigrants prior to their departure and those members of the family who have stayed behind in the mother country are able to detect the best profit-making opportunities and hence contribute to the making of viable investments. Thus, acting upon the advice of their brother, who was an employee of the Municipal Chamber in Braganza, three immigrants acquired, upon their return, a bar-cum-restaurant, a butchery and a jewellery boutique all in the same street.

Interwoven with family ties, village ties retain their influence upon the conduct of immigrants: having organized journeys and entry networks, the villagers continue, once their kith and kin arrive in France, to contribute to the determination of conditions measuring success and the volume of savings to be accumulated before one can retire properly. Consequently, individual fortunes, reflecting the success of emigration, are in essence collective ones. Certain *aldeias* have been more successful. This is exemplified by the density of construction of new buildings, the renovation of commercial structures and the epidemic proportions of 'property speculation fever'. On the other hand, in certain regions of Portugal (for example the industrial belt of Lisbon or the vast plains of Alentejo) which do not have a tradition of migration, the effects of emigration appear slight and less profitable. This is explained by the fact that those who emigrated from the industrial zones of Lisbon already possessed a working-class mentality before their departure and rapidly modelled their lifestyles upon those of the native proletariats into which they were integrated, while those agricultural workers, from the Alentejo plains, generally preferred emigrating for shorter periods at a time, according to the availability of seasonal employment. All in all, workers' savings capacities were insufficient in both cases.

The durability of informal networks   The closure of the frontiers and the curbs on immigration since 1974 have not led to the dissolution of the ever-changing links formed between France and Portugal. Although, as time passes, the influence of the communities of origin upon the daily lives of immigrants in France diminishes, there is a certain envy or resentment of the latter. In the meantime, intense ties still prevail. The speed of communication links has dissolved distances and has initiated a sort of continuous coming and going. The Portuguese, 'here' and 'there', never cease to meet, visit or telephone each other. The traditional means of travel by train or by air are now complemented by countless coach services operating directly, or very nearly so, between the majority of French regional towns and major areas of Portuguese emigration.

Summer holidays have become a time for reunions with the community of origin and it would seem that some sort of ritual is being established to 'return to one's roots'. It begins with the race for Portugal, with each person making it a point of honour to get there as quickly as possible. In her gripping text, Rosa de Guimaraes,[8] a second-generation immigrant herself, denounces this 'tunnel race', of which the starting point is a French town and the finishing line the village of origin. There is total unawareness of any intermediate French or Spanish territory. While this 'who dares wins comedy' may arouse increasing irritation on the part of receiving friends and relatives, the village fête remains a high point for the demonstration of brotherhood. The fête, which is usually held in August so that those who have emigrated abroad or elsewhere within the country can be present, continues to celebrate traditional customs and events (for example, processions, ceremonial masses, fireworks and the village banquet) and the local ball which, in the past, was strictly forbidden by the church. In certain villages of *Beiras* the fête even becomes a rite of village membership where no adolescent is accepted as a member of the *aldeia* unless he participates in a dangerous rustic bullfight which takes place in the village square converted into an arena for the occasion.

Complementary to these changing traditional networks of exchange and communication, which are in transformation, are others of which commercial relations are gaining the most importance. One observes the development of a powerful banking network which channels the flow of billions of francs sent to Portugal each year by Portuguese immigrants in France. While the Franco-Portuguese bank has reserved for itself the traditional functions of mercantile banking in particular, all other major Portuguese banking groups have, progressively, set up establishments in France: the Banco Pinto and Sotto Mayor (with not less than two and a half billion bank accounts) has operated since 1972, the Borges and Irmao bank (with two billion deposits) since 1974 and more recently the Caixa Geral de Depositos and the Espirito Santo group. The banks only have a few branches (the largest has twenty-three) but their main efforts are geared towards a door-to-door canvassing of Portuguese residents so much so that one local branch in a large south-western French town, with more than 2000 depositors on its records, claims to have registered almost all the Portuguese residents in the area and regards its own statistical data as the most reliable means of localizing the Lusitanian population. The influence of this banking network far extends the mere drainage of savings, as these establishments follow closely or even support the development of the associative movement. The conglomeration of Portuguese immigrants within one area facilitates a bank's task of door-to-door canvassing. In exchange for publicity given to the bank by a local association, the bank may 'sponsor' a number of activities (for example it may purchase football vests or provide a refreshments counter at the occasional local ball etc.).

Although this phenomenon remains unremarked, it is also certain that networks for the commercialization of Portuguese products (beer, wine, handicrafts) are currently being established, and that the Portuguese associations constitute privileged places from which such products are sold. In addition to this, with emigration channels doubling up as channels for smuggling, it would not be presumptuous to point out that a network of more or less lawful 'trafficking' has been formed between the two countries. This sort of trade is made possible by the fact that the growth of Portugal's invisible economy contributes to the total amount of currency in circulation, which exceeds by 30 per cent the official figure for gross industrial earnings.

Thus it is, on the whole, understandable that the considerable size of the Portuguese community in France, the extraordinary entanglement of links between the two countries as well as the endless comings and goings of immigrants have rendered contacts a common phenomenon. Whereas one might imagine that illegal immigration in France mainly concerns poverty-stricken Turks, Pakistanis or Mauritians who, in their ignorance of the law, get duped by dishonest smugglers, it would seem (based upon the results of the 1981 amnesty offered to all illegal immigrants) that 15 per cent of those offered regularization of illegal status were Portuguese, in third place after Moroccans and Tunisians respectively.

The belief that the way into France is always open, the assurance that one will be among one's compatriots is so widespread in Portugal that Rosa, the young barmaid in Alain Tanner's film *Dans la Ville Blanche*, can disappear in order to end the futility of her existence, by announcing her departure for Paris. The story does not make it clear whether Rosa's plan was realized or not—everybody else, however, accepted it as entirely plausible.

The establishment of an institutionalized network

The proliferation and general use of migratory know-how   The figures in the introduction indicate the spectacular progression of the life of associations within ten years. The Revolution of the Carnations constitute a decisive turning-point in this process, since the greatest progress was made after 1974. This demonstrates the political dimension assumed by the associative network which is formally recognized in the country of origin as well as in the host country. In light of their immediate past and recent settlement, the Portuguese are assured that the assertion of their identity will be tolerated and that possession of a community centre, recognized by all others, would not fuel xenophobic reactions. It is important to note, for example, that despite the current intensification of racism, not a

134

single Portuguese association has fallen victim to attacks of vandalism or to the ransacking of its premises. This is not the case for immigrants from the Maghreb.[9] However, while the law which pertains to associations has been liberalized since 1981, and was immediately taken advantage of by the Portuguese, the growth of their associative network took place prior to that date, in keeping with the changes which occurred in Lisbon. On the one hand, since the fall of Salazar, successive governments, albeit with some contradictions, have taken a positive line on migration. Even the title of the liaison service, planning and support service for the communities, reveals the objective of maintaining links with the diaspora, to promote the work of associations. On the other hand, and more importantly, the renewal of democracy on the shores of the river Tagus and the explicit acceptance of pluralism thereby implied has enabled the Portuguese in France to participate openly in the affairs of their community without the risk of facing reprisals on their return home, in the event that their political opinions contradict those of the incumbent government.

The distrust which existed in the Portuguese community prior to 25 April 1974 is comparable to the case of the Moroccon community leaders who face harassment (or even imprisonment) as a result of their opposition to the Rabat-controlled Association of Moroccan Workers. This suggests that among immigrants the emergence of an autonomous associative network, which openly asserts its national identity, may be dependent upon the existence of a pluralist democracy in the country of origin.

Distribution of associations: regional disparities   The most salient fact to emerge from a look at their addresses is the extreme unobtrusiveness of the Portuguese associative network, not only in large towns and suburbs but in the country at large. There are 115 associations registered in towns with under 20,000 inhabitants, thirty-two in smaller towns of under 5000 inhabitants and four in the villages. This dispersion points out that, despite the concentrations of the Portuguese in certain areas of residence the Portuguese colony, the most important foreign worker group in France, is largely scattered throughout the French territory. It also emphasizes the extent to which the associative phenomenon has become one of the favoured means for the Portuguese to cope with their stay in France and to preserve their autonomy while at the same time participating in local structures.

However, the distribution of this network is not uniform throughout France and does not directly correspond to the map of the Portuguese presence. The 1981 data show a sharp division, on both sides of a line running diametrically from Le Havre to Nice, between the industrialized north, which has a dense associative network, and the rural south with fewer associations. Taking into consideration their clandestine past and the fact that the Portuguese settled down initially in areas which had a more liberal attitude towards regularization of illegal status, it appears that three regions played a particular role in all this: the northern region extending to the Oise and Champagne Ardennes; an indeterminate landmass centring upon that part of the Loire Valley between Tours and Orleans; and the triangular block of land which has as its three focal points Clermont-Ferrand, Lyon and Grenoble, and which then extends beyond the eastern side of the Massif Central, the Saône Valley and the Alps, and which in itself unites more than half of the associations established in France around 1970. From 1981 onwards, it has been those zones that already have the most highly structured associative networks which have experienced the generation of new associations. For example, one finds long-established settlements and twice the national average of associations in the regions of Nord-Pas-de-Calais or Champagne Ardennes. New associations have also been established in regions where Portuguese settlement is recent or especially where there are a small number of communities; as, for example, in the case of the Languedoc-Roussillon region, home to only 7000 Portuguese inhabitants, where in addition to the associations of Nimes and Montpellier, new ones were set up in Mende, Carcassonne, Perpignan and particularly Brittany, where the small 4500-strong community is provided for by eight local associations.

Despite its relatively large Portuguese population, the south-west region of France has been slow in the development of associations. This delay, however, is indicative of the reasons governing the formation of the associative network. First of all, the Portuguese communities, sizeable though they may be at a departmental level, are often scattered throughout rural areas (one-third of the Portuguese in Aveyron or Gers inhabit such areas). Very small communities have no need of institutional representation, as a local café may serve as the favoured venue for informal meetings.

Secondly, during the history of illegal immigration, this particular region had of necessity become the initial point of entry for the Portuguese before they could settle down in other parts of the country. A number of immigrants from various parts of Portugal stayed on by chance and then firmly rooted themselves in this region of France despite the fact that no apparent links could be found between their villages back home and the French towns they had settled down in. Thus, although small numbers of people from Minhotes, the Algarve and the Transmontane region and people from the *Beiras* found themselves in close proximity to each other, the situation was not conducive to the development of associative life, which was normally founded upon informal village solidarity.

Finally, it is possible that these patterns of regional disparity closely followed those of French associative life and that the influence of some traditional local dignitary, particularly in the southwest, with an established network of clientele, inhibited the formation of organized groups. In this case, the Portuguese (separated in both geographical and cultural terms) would only have recognized later on the advantages of being organized and of being considered as autonomous groups receiving a minimum of support from French militants organized in nearly 1500 associations,[10] such as trade unions, support committees, literacy centres, all positively contributing towards the welfare of immigrant workers. Conversely, six associations have been officially registered in a town where a real political willingness to integrate the Portuguese in local affairs is displayed (see below).

The splintering of associative life   Despite the current geographical extension of the associative process (as illustrated by the example above), growth is achieved essentially in areas where a network is already established, so that the setting up of one association creates a precedent for the creation of a second or third association. At the end of 1982, 485 associations registered outside the Paris region were scattered among 328 towns or agglomerations, but, while 243 of these were concentrated in one, the remaining 245 (*sic*) were found situated in just eighty-five boroughs. An acceleration of this process has taken place if one considers that during the previous year 173 clubs were dispersed among sixty-five towns with more than one association per town. This sort of distribution would seem to be justified in towns of more than 100,000 inhabitants where the Portuguese are scattered out in peripheral areas, but how does one explain the existence of three or four associations in places such as Melun sur Yèvre (population of 7000), Gray (population of 8000) or Cerisay (population of 4800)?

At the same time, there is not a single authority which has the means to unite or to federate this specific associative phenomenon. The SPAC is certainly a favoured representative of the Lisbon authorities, whose task it is to organize the Portuguese community, but its role, undermined by lack of funds, is restricted to the enlisting of new associations, to prompt aiding of associations (through occasional but sparing grants, the loan of films, the setting up of libraries, dispatching of newspapers) and to the registration of complaints made by local leaders. While the French representatives of the Conseil des Communautés (the communities' council, working in an advisory capacity, for the government, on problems facing immigrants) are responsible for associations in a very general sense, they are not appointed by their fellow members (of the Conseil des Communautés) to formally represent associations. In addition, attempts made and realized by certain political parties (for example the Portuguese Communist Party—PCP) and other left-wing organizations to establish affiliated associations have been modest and are even declining. The Associations des Originaires du Portugal (AOP, associations for persons of Portuguese origin), set up by the PCP, currently has seventeen branches in France but, of these, twelve are concentrated in the Paris region while others (for example, that located in Roubaix) remain inactive. There also exist forty associations bearing the epithet 'France–Portugal', but it is doubtful, considering the neutrality of the appellation, whether all these associations are affiliated to the one in Paris.

The example of Roubaix and the life of Portuguese associations, analysed at great length by Antonio Marrucho,[11] throws light upon the reasons for this dispersal of associations. The Portuguese community (numbering 4621 persons in 1975) in the town of Roubaix (where immigrants account for ten per cent of its population) constitutes the second largest group of immigrant workers, and with fifteen associations (of which eleven are officially registered) it holds the record for 'association boom'.

Apart from the powerful Amicale des Parents Luso-Français de Roubaix (the Roubaix Luso-French parents' association), the largest parents' association in France with nearly 1000 members, whose initial concern for the teaching of Portuguese has expanded to include a host of cultural activities (theatre, cinema, library service, etc.), there are four football clubs, four folk-song and -dance clubs, three clubs which enliven local life on a modest scale and three unregistered associations with strictly religious purposes (mainly devotees of Our Lady of Fatima). In consequence it is not so much the type of activities undertaken which define Portuguese associationism as the fact that such activities are in themselves undertaken at all. The strength of the feeling of sharing a common identity allows for a flexibility of forms or places in which the community can feel at home. The associative movement has passed beyond the stage of 'instinctive defensiveness', displayed when confronted by an unfamiliar or unknown society, to a stage where it has acquired privileged means to gain recognition and assert itself on its own terms. Thus it is that the present period affords the possibility for the existence of Portuguese pétanque (a type of bowls) clubs (as in Pau) together with Portuguese modern and classical dance associations (in St Etienne) and the 'Linda de Suza' fan club (in Paris).

In order to justify the lack of cohesion within Portuguese associationism one must also take into account the political dimension. On the one hand, although the movement is steeped in community or village customs, one may suppose that it has inherited (from Salazarism) an absence of democratic traditions. Ordinary members contribute little towards the running of their local association and often it only takes the departure of an association's founder for that association to go into decline. Conversely, the individualistic attitude of members leads to scant appreciation of the commitment displayed by those in charge of running the association: their indifference is viewed suspiciously, and suggestions of dubious schemes or misappropriation of funds ('they only do such and such because it is personally beneficial') frequently poison the life of the richer clubs and cause splits to occur. Lastly, it is often those very groups, continuously holding power and retaining control over elective procedures and modes of conflict resolution, as set out in official regulations, which turn out to be incapable of resolving internal tensions. On the other hand, the political wheeling and dealing of associative life, concealed as it may be from the outside observer or even the rank and file militant, often determines the commitment of leaders who initially came over in order to fight against Salazarism and the colonial war, and who now maintain that the most effective means by which Portuguese politics may be influenced is through control of the associative network.

'Portuguese character' and integration in local life   Despite the quarrels and rivalries which abound within associations, their assertion of their Portuguese character remains their cardinal value. Eighty-nine per cent of associations make this explicit in the adoption of Portuguese names and in their internal affairs. When native French persons are members their presence is minimal or occasional (invitations to festive occasions or to dances). In contrast, the question of naturalization does not seem to pose a problem: members are not obliged to state on their membership forms whether or not they have renounced Portuguese nationality, nor are community leaders expected to step down from their positions upon naturalization. Also, while the fact of being Portuguese increases one's standing, very few associations (less than 7 per cent) emphasize their worker or immigrant status, which serves to define the Portuguese in the eyes of the French population. It is in fact quite evident that the associative movement expresses a refusal of proletarianization and a desire to underplay the economic reasons for the arrival of the Portuguese in France, such as the better material conditions of life in France. This is one of the reasons why the Portuguese associative movement has been remarkably tactful in its protests against the rise of xenophobia and furthermore has been very reluctant to take part in solidarity campaigns with

other immigrant nationalities. This also explains why the politically active have been obliged to conceal, though without much success, their political strategies, since these ex-peasants refuse to adopt a class consciousness or working-class instincts. Thus committed to associative life they write:

> . . . we should question our own political strategies and aspirations if we seriously wish to end our marginality or quit, in certain cases, nationalist ghettos and move towards comradeship, collaboration, collective action and coexistence with the French population and other immigrants. (CEDEP 1982)

More surprisingly still, from the point of view of the emigration history and of the importance of informal village networks, there appears to be an absence of reference, in the names of associations, to regions or localities: hardly 5 per cent of associations consider that they bring together natives of Alentejo (for example the Celebre Coral dos Progressistas do Alentejo de Roubaix) or of another province or even of a Portuguese town or village whereas surveys reveal the importance of local affinities in the emergence of associations. In fact, tensions founded upon regional differences may persist— 'People from the Beiras are uncivilized—they come to watch us dance but are happy to drink only with each other,' affirms the leader of a small-town Pyrennean folk group which is exclusively composed of people from Viara do Costelo and its surrounding areas.

The absence of references to regions in the names of associations may be explained by the absence of the regional dimension in Portuguese culture. Beyond recall of old names and some very typical provinces (Tras-os-Montes, Algarve, Alentejo), specialists and especially geographers have always found it exceedingly difficult to divide Portugal into homogeneous regions. In popular culture it is one's attachment to one's village which is predominant. For example, when an emigrant says 'a minha terra' (my land) he or she confounds the whole of Portugal with his or her native area. Thus, the group of progressive singers of Alentejo was formed, symbolically, after 25 April 1974 at the height of the agrarian reform programme. For the members of the group, the singing of songs (typical of the Alentejo region) within the community signified support for the agrarian reform programme and in turn transcendence of the regionalist setting. Logically, therefore, as the reform programme has now lost significance so also the group's interest has waned and its members recognize that they are carrying on without an aim in mind and that the number of their performances is diminishing.

Another explanation, according to the Portuguese, for this absence of regional references is the ignorance of the French with respect to Portugal. If an association were to carry a local or regional Portuguese name then passers-by noticing the association's name-plate or people in the locality would not immediately recognize its Portuguese connections. As for the members themselves, it is sufficient that they meet friends and neighbours from their native region at the local association headquarters!

However, this argument, which is aimed at doing away with the regionally orientated recruitment of certain associations in the name of efficiency, in fact emphasizes the extent to which the official associative movement remains the favoured choice of the Portuguese as a means by which to assert themselves as such in the host community. Since informal networks are always dependent upon family and village connections, it is quite understandable that the official associative networks make references to the national origins of immigrants. As Portugal is the oldest nation-state of Europe, its nationals are not for one second in any doubt as to their national identity.[12] On this level, the Portuguese are aware of belonging to a country whose existence is indisputable, whose history is glorious and whose language is one of 'empire'. These powerful sources of identity, reinforced by the explicit and unyielding support given to associations by successive governments of the Revolution of the Carnations feed this collective consciousness which has always contributed to the success of Portuguese emigration. Not only has such support laid the foundations for the burgeoning of associative life after 1974, but it is also indicative of the rebirth of democracy in Lisbon and of the promise given to all Portuguese citizens, at home and abroad, of the freedom to belong to the organization of their choice. Curiously, whereas Portugal has never before held as much dialogue with its emigrants and attempted to define their place in national life,[13] it is only at the present time that such misunderstandings have occurred and that frustrations have developed within the community.

Beyond the economic reasons which have led Portugal to give special consideration to its diaspora, this latter phenomenon has acquired a new dimension in relation to the definition of national identity. M.B. Rocha-Trindade (1983) affirms that Portugal has discovered:

> . . . in the self-actualisation of Portuguese citizens, living abroad and dispersed over all the continents, the psychological substitute for an ex-empire which was of global dimensions . . . The concept of Portugal, identified with that of its population, is superimposed upon the usual definitions of sovereignty or of territorial unity.

Consequently

> . . . the notion of emigration, as dynamic flow, loses importance and is

replaced by the value attached to the interactions between Portugal and her communities which result from this flow: policies geared at supporting communities are replacing emigration policies.

Additionally, while the Ministry of Emigration Affairs is undergoing a restructuring and expansion process, a series of legislative and statutory measures are aimed at furthering links between the emigrant communities and national political life (through the election of four MPs to parliament, the establishment of a communities' congress and council) and at the resolution of problems encountered by Portuguese citizens in maintaining contacts with their native country (for example, problems regarding dual nationality, validity of Portuguese qualifications, transfers of funds, admission of goods acquired abroad, etc.). All these policies are particularly based upon the explicit recognition of the associative movement:

Given the fact that Portuguese emigration is composed of large numbers of widely dispersed persons, the only agency which allows for bi-lateral communication, at the present time, is that constituted by local structures organized along associative lines. . . Whatever their objectives may be, the associations exist as the favoured channel of dialogue between the Portuguese state and its emigrant communities. (Rocha-Trinidade 1983)

Thus by way of clear and singular official discourse, founded upon a broad consensus of 'the ruling class' (political, church and local civic dignitaries, intellectuals, media representatives), emigrant communities are assigned the task of representing the greatness of their native country and of replacing a lost empire; the symbols of national identity inhibit Portugal from conceiving of itself as merely a small and obscure quadrilateral piece of land surrounded by neighbouring Spain. Some signs of the emergence of such symbolism within the official order are demonstrated by:

—the title given to the ministerial department dealing with emigration matters: 'the Office of the Secretary of State for Emigration and Portuguese Communities';
—the use of the term 'diaspora', borrowed from Jewish use, in reference to Portuguese communities;
—the issue of postage stamps and the erection of monuments as tributes to emigrants;
—the recognition of 9 June as an official public holiday —'Remembrance day for Portugal and the communities'—when the president of the republic, together with other intellectual authorities, leads the country in paying tribute to the richness of emigrant culture and to the virtues of loyalty and courage as represented by this culture. This ceremony takes place in a town usually chosen because of its location in a zone of emigration.[14]

142

This new official ideology, widely propagated through the media, deserves some interpretation. Emigrant causes are provided with seemingly consistent support and associative life is encouraged because it is regarded as the most effective means by which cohesion is maintained between emigrants and their native land. In addition, and although it poses some difficulty, financial aid is made available to its diaspora. At the same time, a kind of mythology emerges and surrounds the diaspora. This is because Portugal 'invents' for itself such communities on a scale befitting its dreams of grandeur, striving constantly to retrace an imaginary continuum from the glorious Age of Discovery to the contemporary era of rural exodus. The life of associations, such as that which has emerged in Brazil, Venezuela and the USA, wherein rich community leaders of Portuguese origin encourage cultural, sporting and charity events commensurate with their personal prestige and success, is thus implicitly approved of as the associative norm. Through its management of national identity, the Portuguese state in fact assumes that it has the right to define the standards by which 'Portuguese character' is measured, standards which are all the more élitist in nature since the support given to the communities reflects the state's concern about its own fate. This attitude, which may appear as honourable, inevitably becomes a source of irritation and increasing conflict for the more rural and humble communities of Europe.

While the increased prestige offered to emigrants carries with it a firm sense of identity, it is the conditions under which it is expressed that cause frustrations and misunderstandings, for example:

—communities which have never found access to an intellectualized culture are discouraged by the prescription of high cultural standards;
—cultural discourse coupled with the enoblement of a mythicized 'Portuguese character' undermines the political scale of things as well as the right of opposition accorded to emigrants, thus rendering them incapable of exercising such a right in reality;
—the Portuguese state's claim that it manages the affairs of communities only emphasizes its incapacity, firstly, to help communities whose demands are defined in relation to the means offered by French society to its own associations and, secondly, to prevent emigrants over a period of time from feeling like foreigners in their own country.

As a consequence, since 25 April 1974, successive governments have brought in new dispensatory legislation which works increasingly in favour of emigrants. Such action has been undertaken for the following reasons: to compensate for the contemptuous attitude of the Salazar regime towards emigrants and to recognize in law the significance, at national level, of the diaspora, by virtue of the fact that the money sent back home by emigrants contributes towards the maintenance of a healthy balance of payments.[15] Thus, under the new legislation, savers are offered interest rates of 30 per cent on investments, while borrowers pay interest at 12.5 per cent. In addition, emigrants benefit from paying lower fiscal charges on money transfers, lower customs duties on goods brought into Portugal, and from reduced air fares, etc.

Such dispensatory measures have, on the one hand, led to public hue and cry in a period of economic crisis, provoking charges that 'emigrants are a privileged group'. On the other hand, emigrants never cease to increase their demands (for example, the right to be exempted from national service, the right to receive unemployment benefit if a person returns to the country without having found work) in the apparent belief that each demand and acquired right draws them close to their country, reflecting their belongingness in material terms. It is for this reason that one of the most frequent demands made by associations concerns the free repatriation of corpses. The expression of the desire to be buried in one's village cemetery indicates the belief that death matters extend beyond the concern of the family or community of origin.

> The nation-state is faced with a demand, put forward by emigrants, which has to be dealt with within the realm of civic culture; furthermore, it is required to submit itself to the principle of bilaterality and to recognise the double existence of emigrants by setting forth a principle which embraces that of burial rights.[16]

The question of permanent bilateral affiliations must be studied through examination of the constant dialogue held between the associative movement, which is anxious to play a role in the future of Portugal, and the Portuguese nation state. The firm integration of Portuguese associations in the local life of France contradicts neither the continuance of dialogue nor the demand to remain part of Portugal.

Cultural resources of associations: the expression of 'Portuguese character'[17]

It is not possible to reduce all that is preached and practised within associations to an eclectic combination of notions derived from a variety of sources. Cultural practices occur on several different scales. The factoral analysis of responses to questions addressed to some twenty associations (chosen according to a limited survey of 500 associations in 1980) indicated a hierarchical relationship between activities and associations. Firstly, associations may be differentiated by their diversified use of resources. Associations range from those whose activities are extremely limited to those providing a great many and varied activities. Secondly, associations differ according to the types of activity and the priority certain activities are given. Thus activities linked with library services, cinema and dissemination of information are located at the bottom end of the scale while the teaching of French, social and political meetings and activities linked with drama, arts and crafts are all situated at the top end of the scale. Publications (excluding those of newspapers), the teaching of Portuguese and the celebration of traditional holidays constitute an intermediary category of activities.

Finally, activities such as football, indoor games, balls, folk-song and -dance, publication of Portuguese newspapers, observance of religious occasions, organization of variety shows and communal outings are not included within the same framework. The hierarchy applies only to these activities which may be termed as 'complex', that is, to those activities whose organization requires technical and intellectual know-how as opposed to those which do not require such support and which may therefore be termed 'popular' activities.

The results of the survey tend to suggest that the life of associations fulfils two functions. Firstly, it has the function of preserving traditional forms of socializing and secondly that of maintaining a cohesiveness between immigrants in the urban setting. The more recently established associations in the large northern towns or within the Paris area have attempted to initiate and develop the more 'modern', intellectually orientated activities such as photography, drama and craftwork. The reason behind the launching of such activities is to attract and to retain young members, as well as to prove that the Portuguese association shares the same standard as French cultural organizations.

In the large associations it is significant that when young people are delegated responsibilities by those in charge, these responsibilities generally entail the setting up of a dramatics club, the management of a magazine or of the association's newsletter, or the running of craftwork activities. Not only does this give the association a 'modernist' aspect along the lines of the French maisons de la culture (municipal arts centres), but it also expresses a willingness on the part of the association to call upon young people to contribute their expertise.

However, all these activities assume a new sense within the associative framework. Thus drama consists mainly of Portuguese drama whose clear aim it is 'to bring about an awareness of Portuguese culture and also of immigration problems'. Examples are drawn from classical Portuguese literature as well as themes such as generation conflicts or the development of feminism. Drama is, however, a 'complex' activity and organizers complain that it is often costly and requires skills and resources which are unavailable to them. It is often only the large associations which are able to provide premises for rehearsals and which have the resources to attract a sizeable audience. In addition, the risk that such an activity represents is indicative of the divergent conceptions of organizers about drama. While for some it constitutes a vehicle of prestige and an object of attraction, others criticize it as too 'political' or lacking in interest in both senses of the term. Moreover, it provokes the hostility of those who wish to retain the private character of associations, who mistrust the initiatives of youth and especially intellectuals who aim to create a politically orientated theatre group, as a privileged means for the politicization of immigrant workers. Nevertheless, drama is considered to be a 'serious' 'intellectual' activity which allows for the internalization of the insights of high culture on an emotional plane. This explains the importance of drama to associations which are prospering. Not only does it enhance their prestige, but it provides an activity for their members directed at the Portuguese and performed by Portuguese.

Another example of such an activity is the teaching of the Portuguese language. The importance that teaching and preserving the mother tongue has for group solidarity in the immigration context is well known:

> Of all the aspects of national belongingness it is language which combines closely existential choice, the schema of institutional totalisation and the symbolic resources that both the former mobilise.[18]

It is also a precious but threatened source of identification. To be maintained it requires the full attention of the family, and its promotion in schools and associations.

In the above factoral analysis, the teaching of Portuguese ranks lower than complex activities. One might have expected it to be more widely taught given its symbolic importance, but it is also an activity which is costly and requires teaching staff which are often difficult to obtain. One of the main conflicts between the associations and the Portuguese state concerns mother-tongue teaching. Out of the twenty associations of the survey sample, eight provide Portuguese language classes mainly geared towards primary and secondary school age children. The teaching of Portuguese language is one of the highest priorities of the associative movement. Not only do associations call for an increase in the number of teachers but they also expect teachers to take part in associations for 'the overall mobilization of community life'.[19] Portuguese parents who are active in the associations value the teaching of Portuguese as 'decisive' for the future of their children. Catani stresses that even an approximate knowledge of one's mother tongue 'has nothing to do with the level of language needed in order to be accepted as a native in the country of one's parents'.[20] In fact, it is this very problem which mobilizes the Portuguese: how to avoid a situation in which ignorance of the language does not accentuate the gap between generations and especially that the new generation is not estranged from Portugal and an eventual return home? The association can do no more than represent the interest of parents, by at times providing Portuguese language classes itself and by applying pressure upon the respective French and Portuguese authorities to develop such classes in schools. In so doing, the association counts on its own reputation within the community, its legitimacy and also its long-standing position. One may wonder, however, what difficulties the associative movement faces in relation to these demands. Has it the means to take on or to control the teaching of Portuguese?

On the one hand, a discrepancy exists between the demands for the teaching of Portuguese and the number of people who actually follow courses in schools. On the other hand, the Portuguese state is unable to respond satisfactorily to such demands. As a result, associations are obliged to take a position in an institutional debate. They can either continue to ask for a greater number of Portuguese teachers in French schools, in which case the teaching of Portuguese becomes the concern of the Education Nationale (French Ministry of Education) or they can attempt to take upon themselves the teaching of Portuguese. In opting for the latter course, the associations run the risk of forfeiting their autonomy as they would then depend upon decisions taken in Lisbon and would place themselves purely in a position of making demands upon the Portuguese state. In the meantime this situation has been altered by the circular of 13 April 1983 on mother-tongue teaching to immigrant children, according to which mother-tongue teaching would receive the same status as other subjects. The associations saw themselves as being gradually divested of their power and control unless they used their own resources to support mother-tongue teaching on their own premises. These two examples are sufficient, although more could be cited to illustrate that the logic behind these activities corresponds to that of any sphere in which the responsibility must be assumed by trained or professional group leaders.

If it is true that the associations gain prestige from their capacity to promote activities described as 'modernist' which appeal to the youth, they also pride themselves on not having ignored in the least the more popular activities which can be provided within the associative framework. These activities constitute that which is conveniently termed the 'substratum' of the life of Portuguese associations. It is not an exaggeration to claim that the bar is the pivotal point of any association worthy of its name, for this is the place where one drinks, debates and plays traditional games (cards, billiards) as well as modern ones (table-tennis, computer billiards). Men without families certainly favour the café as a meeting place but it is also true that the existence of a bar, materially represented by a real bar counter, ensures the institution's continuance. On the one hand the bar's drinking hours determine the association's ability to attract, while on the other hand, bar receipts provide the association with two-thirds of its budget and support of other activities.

In symbolic terms, the bar in fact assumes the role of the *tasca* (local village taverns back home). Whenever possible, when costs are not high, association organizers offer for sale Portuguese drinks (Sagres beer and *vinho verde*—local wines) together with appetizer snacks (salted lupin seeds, *tremosos*, fish croquettes, cocktail sandwiches) which make up the charm of Portuguese snack bars.

The bar is also exclusively a meeting place for men. In the villages back home, amidst a rural environment characterized by subsistence farming, leisure time, that is individual or familial inactivity, was non-existent. There were no books, no television, in a world enclosed by illiteracy, and there was no vacation time either (the Portuguese word *feira* refers first and foremost to 'festival' or 'fair' and it is the emigrants who have coined the word *vacancas* to take into account a concept which has become a new reality for them). On return home from the fields, the peasant always found something else to do: tending to the livestock, repairing tools, tinkering about here and there. Apart from time spent at religious festivals or at the market, the only moments when one did not work, when the body relaxed, were those spent at the *tasca*, drinking with other men and discussing minor local events. In general, the women did not frequent taverns. It was either at the grocer's (*la loja*), at the wash-house or after mass that bonds of feminine sociability were forged.

Now one witnesses the establishment and progression of the same relationships and functions respectively around the association bar. The Portuguese man, whether he works in a factory or in construction, discovers certainly the rupture between work and leisure but his plans for amassing wealth often lead him to regard leisure as a waste of time. Apart from watching television, the Portuguese family is slow to give in to strictly private and individual activities; all the surveys show that where associations are non-existent, Sunday afternoons are taken up with visiting one's compatriots.

Therefore the association bar is at once the place where traditions are protected and where the process of transplantation into French society is eased. As a place where men may rightfully relax, the bar allows frequentation at little cost. Since it belongs to the association, it does not appear to contradict the concern about savings—especially since it doubles as a job market for informal work. Here one receives news from home, and gathers positive experiences of one's compatriots.

Finally, the bar also provides a meeting place for adolescents. In Portugal, youths frequent the *tasca* or, in larger towns, the bar, where they meet after school and before going to support their football team. The association bar preserves this role of providing a physical and symbolic meeting place as well as the role of transmitting the sociability of father to sons. This is why the bar's wall-display consists of tourist posters of Portugal and images of most significance in group history (photographs of the football team, the Portuguese flag, winners' trophies, pendants). Even when the bar is often a converted premise, certain people find fault with its bistro-like style as well as the behaviour of its clientele. They regret that they are unable to bring along French friends because it would give them an unfavourable impression of Portugal. They would wish to give the bar a more chic, more exotic appeal, to transform it into a place which would continue to reinforce the image of Portugal as a land of sunshine holidays. This rests on the belief that it is only through sterilization of their identities that poor countries can attain a certain reputation.

The celebration of festivals, communal dinners and the ball are the highlights of the life of associations where, in contrast to the bar, the entire community experiences traditional forms of social mixing. The communal dinner which the Portuguese refer to as the *refeicao da connaternisacao* (brotherly meal) is without doubt the most intense part of the festivities, where emotions are at their highest and when community leaders evoke the collective historical experiences of the community in their speeches. The non-acceptance of an invitation to the dinner signifies, in fact, that one no longer considers oneself as part of the association, for in Portugal this celebration constitutes a traditional practice for maintaining group solidarity. In the banquet hall, community bonds are strengthened around the table as Portuguese dishes prepared mostly by the women are consumed. In addition to bringing together the community the feast also has the function of table companionship and the products consumed have emotional connotations. These products are imported directly from Portugal or are bought from Portuguese companies in France. The food is carefully selected and it is full of symbolic significance. Preserving ties with their native soil means for the Portuguese obtaining its fruits. Portuguese cuisine cements the link with Portuguese soil which has never been severed.

The ball represents another privileged moment of encounter between the Portuguese. As in the case of any village dance today, modern music alternates with Portuguese rhythms and the young are afforded the opportunity, under the watchful eyes of mothers and in an approved environment, to look for a partner. The combination of French customs (the speaking of French between youngsters, dancing to rock music, etc.) and Portuguese customs is possible through the mediation of the association. Catani (1983) sees in this mediation one of the main criteria for the existence of associations.

> This mediation, the hierarchy of different levels which would otherwise meet with direct opposition, is not unique to the ball. It touches upon all aspects of the life of associations, as much in the latter's internal functioning as well as in its links with the host community.[21]

The ball therefore forms part of a cultural strategy. In this respect it is possible to talk about a privileged place for the management of the symbolic process and a way of controlling of priorities: to dance to French or American music for most of the time, but remaining Portuguese in one's choice of future marriage partner.

Football and folk-dancing must be viewed in the same perspective of bilaterality. Both activities stem from the same line of logic—that of legitimizing self-affirmation through recognition from the host society. Moreover, these activities constitute a continuation of practices which were firmly encouraged and developed at the time of *l'Estado Novo*. Under the Salazar regime sports clubs, folk-dance and musical groups were in fact the main forms of collective activity tolerated. Their vitality within associations is astonishing. On the football pitch it is the community's honour which is at stake, whereas when Portuguese dance groups are invited to take part in French festivals or receptions, it is once more the pride in demonstrating these Portuguese dances that reinforces community belongingness.

The associative network reveals itself as a particularly efficacious means of preserving the community's intimacy and in ensuring that it is surrounded by discretion. Membership of associations allows the Portuguese to drink, eat, interact with each other through activities engaged in at home or at local festive events in spite of the fact that Portuguese cafés, restaurants and even small shops are practically non-existent, although the number of open-air stalls is increasing. The village-based community, however, while constantly incorporating the lessons learned from emigration into their shared migratory know-how, has always made way for collective initiation into modern ways of life. The associative network has assumed this latter function by providing the framework for the exchange of experiences and for the realization of all material and symbolic links forged between informal networks and Portugal. It is for this reason that the life of associations is not the nationalist ghetto referred to in the denunciations of certain leaders, but rather the interplay of various definitions the Portuguese themselves give to their own identity. Here one discovers another function of the associative movement: that of promoting national identity (as opposed to local identities). In attempting to integrate paying members of various origins, associations are unable to avoid conflicts which at times take a violent turn. Contrary to expectations these conflicts, which are mostly politically determined, often constitute a supplementary factor for unity. This does not prevent associations from very often having to tread a fine line in order to maintain stability in the face of opposition and confrontations. The definition of cultural and national identity, poised between symbolic and political poles, raises the question of the role of community leaders in the associative movement.

Actors and forces at play within the associative movement

The role of community leaders[22]

The period following 25 April 1974 (which was marked by the victory of democracy, the process of decolonization and also the reunification of families) witnessed the appearance of new factors linked with different political strategies within the associative movement. Consequently there emerged two types of leader. Within the smaller associations which were more likely to provide single activities (football, folklore) grass-roots leaders tended to emerge. They are in a way *de facto* leaders who perpetuate or resume activities formerly practised in Portugal:

> When the association was formed, there were a number of us young men who wished to do something. We wanted to continue playing football in France because it was something we knew how to do.[23]

Recognition of these organizers is founded mainly upon their distinctive qualities: devotion to and time spent at the club. The chairman becomes a sort of Jack-of-all trades, often supported by his wife or other family members. Thus 'M' considers that without him 'the association would fold up', but in fact he is criticized by others of 'running just about everything' and of acting simultaneously as chairman, treasurer, organizer of functions, football team manager, etc. The dangers and advantages to association members, as a result of a personalized leadership, are well assessed. On the one hand dedication (by the leadership) makes up for the individualistic attitude of members: 'They only come to eat, drink and attend the ball, when it comes to helping out, everyone disappears'.[24] On the other hand, while appreciating the dynamism provided by this type of leadership the members are aware of the limitations of this style of operation in which there exists a permanent risk of conflict. Acknowledged and opposed, at the same time the leader is criticized for endangering the association: 'If "A" leaves, the association will cease to function'. As 'A' does not take kindly to such criticism he regularly threatens to resign. Thus one understands better the character of this type of association which is based essentially upon good fellowship in an atmosphere of delicate equilibrium, and which combines individual responsibility with collective sharing of symbolic resources.

In the case of larger associations which offer diverse activities, where responsibilities are heavier and tasks are more important, the administrative organization is necessarily different. Leaders are expected to be able to respond efficiently to all manner of requests made by a heterogeneous membership representing various interests. The diverse political currents manifested within these associations are more conspicuous than in the smaller associations because the stakes are higher. As a result it is necessary to take into consideration the influence of ideologies upon the practices of leaders.

Of all the major Portuguese political parties, the Portuguese Communist Party (PCP) has traditionally accorded the most attention to problems caused by emigration which is viewed by them as an irreversible process. The PCP regards the necessity of exile from one's country to be a result of the incapacity of the ruling classes and parties to construct an economy which satisfies common needs. This criticism, recurrent in the party press (*Avante, Diario*), is expressed in their calls for the full political, economic and social rights of emigrants.

At the same time, Portuguese Communist emigrants who, in contrast with their Spanish counterparts, entertain close relations with the French Communist Party, do not directly translate party policies into the activities of their associations. Needless to say, when they take over the leadership of an association their first move is to subscribe to the party press—*Diario*, or at least a newspaper with left-wing sympathies (for example *Diario di Lisboa* or *Journal di Fundao*). The members of the association consider them to be efficient organizers concerned with sustaining traditional customs.[25] Thus, in an association in the south of France, showings of Eisenstein's films are accompanied by gatherings around the bar, card games, etc. In the words of one member: 'Their goal is to get people to read the newspaper while they are selling codfish.'[26]

Electoral strategies favouring the exercise of political rights by emigrants in Portugal are symptomatic of the ideology being developed by Communist party members. Paradoxically, they may only call for greater political rights because, in general, emigrants tend to vote for right-wing parties. This is a difficult contradiction which can only be overcome by an increase in the political awareness of emigrants. In practice, penetration of the political sphere has to take place in an inconspicuous manner in order to sway people from the Salazarist legacy of reactionary traditionalism to the modernism of the left. The main problem using the same imagery as above consists in being able 'to sell the newspaper as something more than just wrapping for codfish'. An activist's remarks serve to illustrate this point:

> The majority of people come here to dance, to enjoy themselves. . . . I would like them to come to cultivate their minds. One has to try, learn a little, realise what Portugal is all about . . . but they don't like that. . . . People aren't interested in anything. I would like them to take an interest, find out what life's about. They never look around them. I don't mean everyone's like that . . . take me for instance, I'm an exception. . . . I like to enjoy myself but then I also like to think.

The second political current to assert its presence within the associative movement is the CEDEP (Collectif d'Etudes et Organisation de l'Emigration Portugaise, collective for the study and organization of Portuguese emigrants) which unites militants of various ideological backgrounds. This group was formed in the early 1980s 'in order to organize action study projects and to create a dynamism within the Portuguese immigrant community in France'.[27] The group's manifesto puts forward a new vision of relations between immigrants and between Portugal and France. Its analyses are at once within a perspective of pragmatism and of cultural pluralism. The resultant assertion of such analyses is that 'we are Portuguese from France' rather than 'Portuguese in France'. The CEDEP came into existence after an attempt to unite Portuguese associations while striving to avoid organizational inflexibility in the light of numerous failures to create a national federation of associations. The group therefore endeavours to develop an understanding of associative life and of the problems facing immigrants.

> The CEDEP embodies a new dynamism aimed at removing immigrant workers from their marginal position in order to allow them to feel more at ease within urban life. Convinced of the soundness of this approach, the CEDEP seeks to be instrumental in such a way as to render this section of the population an acceptable component of French society as much on economic and financial levels as on the social, political and cultural levels. They want to accomplish this without bringing about the depersonalisation of immigrants, the expected outcome of assimilation. This must be carried out within the framework of a decentralised society, open to inter-ethnic and intercultural exchanges, where dissimilarity is recognised and viewed as a gainful contribution to social and cultural life.[28]

CEDEP recognizes the multinational nature of the working class in the organization of its activities.[29] How does one participate in trade union and political struggles, develop pluri-cultural activities, preserve one's identity and culture while living in France? Its fight against nationalist ghettos calls for solidarity with various immigrant communities in France. The media, in particular independent radio stations in the Paris region, shared with organizations of Maghreb immigrants, constitutes the favoured vehicle for such political messages. The group's concern with grasping the new realities of immigration as well as second-generation discourse, leads it to defend a 'modern' associative dynamic.

> It is a case of determining, as firmly as possible, new forms of intervention which would progressively allow Portuguese immigrants (young and old) to really live together with French and other ethnic groups. New forms of intervention would also lead to improved social, cultural, political, economic integration in a new society based upon complete respect for the values of all minority communities.[30]

Hence the group's proposals are necessarily preceded by a strengthening of institutional ties between various Portuguese associations in France. This is carried out so that the associations assume greater efficiency, are able to make their weight felt in French society and thus avoid a weakening of the associative movement.

> The associations are unable to widen the scope of their activities as they have at their disposal neither trained group leaders nor the material means, and they receive no financial support or special services because they are insufficiently developed and representative. (CEDEP 1982)

The CEDEP reiterates this report by describing the associative movement as 'encapsulated' and 'atomized'. The youth represent the future and continuity of the Portuguese character in France; they must become 'modern Portuguese men and women'. Hence the concern regarding the capacity of associations to survive through their participation and initiative.

Upon examination of CEDEP's position and declarations, one might ask where the concept of Portuguese identity fits into this sort of strategy. One finds a very clear-cut distinction between identity and ideology. The CEDEP clearly defends the advancement of the Portuguese language. In fact, in common with active student associations of the Paris region, it tends to interpret folk culture within an intellectual perspective 'in order to bring together those who cling on to their roots, those who rediscover their roots and those who create new roots'. Inevitably they cannot avoid the secular puritanism that is characteristic of syndicalists. One organizer of an association close to the CEDEP was indignant about the fact that an association's acivities could be centred around the bar and that it could be just part of a catering network. He very grudgingly recognized that it was only through folkloric activities that his association came back to life after going through a crisis.

Consequently, the CEDEP, whose survival is due to the political commitment of a small number of militants, primarily Parisians, sets out in unequivocal terms the problem of getting across its propositions to the majority of Portuguese immigrants. For whom should new associations be developed? How does one prevent conflicts from weakening associations which have been abandoned by the militants either because 'they are fed up with selling codfish'[31] or because they are bored?

The 'correct' ideology does not necessarily help one to find an adequate reply to such questions. The life of Portuguese associations may be considered, in the words of B. Hervieu,[32] as 'the dramatization of identity'. The interchange or confrontation between cultural as well as political expressions constitutes the web of a drama within a movement that has too often been presented as a homogeneous whole. Portuguese associations, as they have been observed, often operate in a patchwork fashion. That which may be considered as an imbalance, thus compromising the future of the movement is paradoxically, in fact, its richness and dynamism. The Portuguese associative movement is not a closed or ossified system, but rather the expression of oppositions which counterbalance each other through apportionment of the symbolic wealth of common belongingness. The Portuguese can, within this context, define themselves somewhere in between the symbolic pole and the political pole. The future of the associative movements of immigrants is linked with the political evolution of French society.[33] In fact the immigrant communities form the only set of actors, physically present amongst the French, who compel French society to situate it outside the national political arena which is less and less capable of assuming the international solidarity for the ties with which it is interdependently linked.

The burgeoning of the associative movement, the marked polarization of the community towards sources of national identity and the role of the movement's leadership are all in keeping with a particular historically determined phase of immigration which fits in with the needs of first-generation immigrants. At present it is men around forty years of age who control community life and who structure it to suit their own interests. These are the people who tolerate a functional integration into French society while planning a hypothetical return to their country of origin. It is on these two levels, that of the evolution of the community and that of the evolution of Portugal,

that the assertion of the Portuguese character is becoming problem
atic.

The youth
In order for the community to survive it would be essential fo:
children to retain the values of their parents. Up until recently thi
was not an apparent problem. But now an increasing number o
children who were either born in France or who arrived at a ver
young age, are reaching the age where they have to make a decisiv
choice as to where they belong. Admittedly the vigour of Portugues
identity still imposes itself upon the youth; this is partly explained b
the strength of the family structure and by the fact that the Port
uguese continue, for the most part, to marry within their own com
munity. Additionally, even if Portugal is regarded merely as th
country of their parents' birth, young people keep going back durin
the holidays combining family reunions with seaside holidays. Fin
ally, at least until 1981, applications for naturalization remained in
significant.[34]

Certainly young people are in a position to serve as transmitters fo
the current association leaders. On the one hand, they have to b
regarded as capable of assuming, in their own time, responsibilities o
administration and organization; on the other hand, the fact that the
identify themselves as Portuguese remains the only guarantee of th
survival of Portuguese communities in France. Hence, the life o
associations aims, firstly, to ensure, as an extension of family life, a
socialization process which is not viewed as a strict reproduction o
Portuguese customs and values, but as an initiation into the relation
ship between the systems of values of the two societies. Thus th
diffuse efficacity of the associations is more bound up with the multi
dimensional function of mediation, between the countries of origi
and of residence, between generations and between ideologies, tha
with the role of conservation or refuge. In other words, identity man
agement, which the associations tend to assume, is exercised in a var
iety of ways, which returns us to the typology discussed above.[35]

The smaller associations, with their limited list of activities, do no
apply particular strategies to gain the participation of young people
Significant exceptions to this are those associations which have a
number of folk activities. In general, in smaller associations activitie
revolve mainly around the bar, table football, pin-ball machines
football practice and dances. Moreover, with the exception of team
sports, the youth participate irregularly in activities. Youth initiative
hardly find room for expression within smaller associations, since th
resources which would enable youngsters to meet and organize ar
insufficient. By contrast, the larger associations offer a diverse range

156

of activities which have a 'modern' orientation: photography, drama, arts and crafts etc. The reasoning behind such initiatives is not just to recruit and retain the young, but to offer activities available elsewhere within French cultural organizations. The Portuguese association also wants to better its image in the public eye and improve its standing *vis-à-vis* the local council. However, large associations do experience problems in training and supervision. The responsibilities delegated to young people by organizers usually consist of setting up drama groups, editing association newsletters and running craft workshops. This is a practical way in which a 'modernist' image of the association can be linked with an appeal to the abilities of youngsters. Such activities do not, however, hold great attraction for the majority of young people. It is only a minority of students and young professionals in tertiary sectors of the economy who appreciate the cultural and at times militant potential of such activities. Thus, drama consists mainly of plays done in Portuguese, which combine ideas inspired by classical tragedies and efforts to present productions about immigrants often in a humorous light. But associations of this kind, which allow young people to express themselves in such complex forms, are rare.

Conversely, one finds that communal festivities, dances and dinners are the activities in which young people participate most, even if it is only to meet with one another in a quiet corner or on the dance floor. These simple activities, uniting one and all, allow young people to express spontaneously the practices and choices which attach them to their country of origin, to speak their own language or to choose a partner who has a better chance than elsewhere of becoming a future spouse.

In most places one observes a growing involvement of young people in folk-dancing, the intricacies of which they attempt to master. In one association in south-eastern France folk group rehearsals take place every fortnight. The research involved in putting together a musical repertoire and the choreography of scenes demands more than the simple attendance at a ball or the dated projection of rural culture. It is a matter of acquiring real skills with symbolic significance and hence of rejecting the status of a passive consumer in associations.[36]

Moreover, such folk groups increasingly perform at festivals and local fairs. Thus it no longer becomes a question of performing only for their own people, but one of promoting their cultural belongingness. Activities such as these fit more than might be expected into a modern framework, for they go along with the regionalist aspirations now in vogue within the host society. These activities allow for conciliation between symbolic and commercial interactions, and through

a meaningful return (to cultural roots), they also reinforce the legitimacy of the associative movement *vis-à-vis* the country of origin.

Less obvious than this perhaps, but an essential element in the
association's contribution to shaping the sense of belongingness of
the young, is the teaching of the Portuguese language.[37] Students
sometimes take charge of classes for children and as a result increase
their own desire to improve their language of origin. Finally associations often provide a place where young people can interact with one
another, where they can come and 'lend themselves to symbols which
prove that their common identity is not an imagined phenomenon'
(Oriol 1984). It remains a fact, however, that not all associative practices appear attractive to young people: this is mainly the case of the
'association bistro'. The latter provides no attraction for the youth
because it is the haunt of adult males and excludes young women. But
young people also condemn the obsession with profit-making which
prevents the association from closing at weekends in order to participate in organized trips. They want associations which are more open
and more modern but which would not prevent the staging of what
they consider as 'traditional' cultural activities: folk-dancing community balls, countryside picnics and football with the participation
of exclusively Portuguese teams. Sport is by far the most popular of
activities within associations. (There are more than a thousand clubs
listed.) Games with French clubs stimulate and invigorate cultural
and national belonging and bind the honour of the community.
Nevertheless, many organizers regret the lack of enthusiasm amongst
young people who forget to attend training sessions or who prefer to
join the better equipped French clubs. Thus one returns to one of the
major problems facing associations: the fact that their capacity to
promote new activities rests upon the accumulation of financial resources without which they could not hope to compete with the
better-off French organizations. The demands put forward by associations to their government tend therefore to increase the operational
means of association structures and thereby to offset the apathy of
the youngsters. This is why the teaching of Portuguese is a very apt
example.

In addition to the outstanding importance of language as a consti-
tutive element of cultural belongingness, the demand for the provision of schooling appears to be the true test of the country's commitment to support its people and the assurance of continuity. To
have command of one's mother tongue is regarded not only as pos-
sessing the potential to return and to reintegrate oneself in one's
native country but also as giving proof of one's Portuguese character
and unfailing attachment to Portugal. The demand for schooling is
strong and continual but often of no avail. At primary level only 40

per cent of children learn Portuguese with the help of teachers from Portugal. At secondary level this percentage is reduced to 20 per cent. This is because there are fewer Portuguese students at this level, and also because the demand for Portuguese language teaching represents more an expression of the wishes of individual leaders than that of the majority of the members of associations. The largest associations ensure the provision of classes by paying their own teachers, recruited mainly from second-generation immigrants who have either successfully completed higher studies or who are currently following courses in further education.

Moreover, it is the latter who play an active role within associations and who involve themselves more in cultural activities often initiated by them, for example drama, newsletter publishing, private radio stations, etc. Their involvement in associations has a double objective: to offer their services to the associations, but also to use these positions as spring-boards for the eventual furtherance of their professional capacities either in France or in Portugal. In fact, one observes the development of an entire movement which has its roots in the Portuguese associations as well as in certain French institutions, and which is geared towards providing the latter associations with organizers who are professionally trained in the handling of administrative duties and the organization of socio-cultural activities. This nascent logic would direct the evolution of the associative movement along the same lines as that of the municipal youth clubs and cultural centres. This orientation could not take place, however, without raising the issue of the relationship between intellectual and popular culture. There is in fact the danger that a process of over-institutionalization could reduce and transform the type of 'Portuguese sociability' which currently exists within associations and which we have already described.[38] The fact remains that this is only one consequence of over-institutionalization. Another foreseeable outcome, analogous to that of the evolution of Portuguese communities in the USA, is that leadership positions within associations are monopolized by persons who have succeeded in attaining social status as small-scale employers or as businessmen or tradesmen. In this event the role of associations would be confined to promoting the prestige of local dignitaries.

Portuguese youngsters are protected by two 'safety barriers', as it were: family customs and associative practices which favour and strengthen the common migratory know-how which has been kept alive throughout the history of migrations. This cultural heritage defines an entire body of practices and strategies which lead one to conclude that Portuguese youngsters remain in no doubt as to their identity. This has never been more evident than at the present time.

These practices affect the behaviour of young people in two ways. On the one hand, there is a tendency among young people to conform to a group model, in other words, to express collectively their cultural belongingness, and on the other hand, there is silence or discretion about the norm which does not necessarily permit individual cultural expression indicating the differences within French society.

In this, the Portuguese differ from young intellectuals of the Maghreb countries if only in terms of cultural production expressed by the media. At best, Portuguese youngsters don't appear as more than good managers on the level of socio-cultural discourse.

Conclusion

The principal trait of the life of Portuguese associations is currently its all embracing character, its capacity to totally engulf the aspirations of its members and to transcend these aspirations through common reference and deference to Portuguese identity. Portuguese identity welds together the status of immigrant with that of worker within one's representation of oneself in the country of residence, and leaves as secondary the potential antagonisms which could arise through allegiances to different regional backgrounds. This strong national sentiment or conviction that one is a member and a representative of an old and very 'respected' country cements social and expressive ties within the group. This is best illustrated, for example, within the warm atmosphere of festive events, of the community dinners and of the ball. It is this sense of national identity which furthermore facilitates external relations with others such as local councils, schools, sports federations and even labour markets.

The association assures the group a dependable space, as an identity resource, while acting as a mediator *vis-à-vis* French society. In this way the association appears as a reflection and image of the village (back home) and offers a response to the cultural dominance of the French surroundings. Although it is controlled and run by young adult immigrants of the first generation whose plans and scale of values remain centred upon their country of origin, the Portuguese associative movement does not constitute a nationalist ghetto.

The expansion of the movement and the diversity of activities in which its organizers and members are involved, even its instability, are in a way collective interpretations, and they have the function of making their way, of appropriating the host society.

Today one observes dynamism and flexibility but the focus bears upon Portugal, not a bilaterality of references.[39] In addition there still remains a potential hope of returning home, although it may prove to be hypothetical or illusory and Portuguese immigrants *in*

France do not regard themselves as Portuguese *from* France.

Conversely, a relevant and often fruitful attempt has been made to establish an organized space with the objective of resisting the often hostile pressures from 'the institutions'[40] of the two state apparatuses (French and Portuguese) which define migration policies and which set the norms for membership which their subjects are obligated to interiorize. 'The organization' is a means of acquiring some autonomy. Opposing institutional rigidity, it rolls back or, rather, abolishes the barriers which tend to assign each person his place in society and thus constrain choice. It is also synonymous with extra-territoriality, or rather with the tendency toward extra-territoriality, since the emigrant community, in order to reach its own objectives, with respect to marriage, linguistic and economic strategies or to ensure its reproduction, tends to break with the governing norms of the two states. One gains a better understanding of why the intense negotiations which associations often conduct with their French counterparts on a local level, meaning the representatives of town-halls, schools and churches, may be accompanied by a relative passivity with respect to basic immigration issues which are being discussed in the midst of French society.

On the other hand, one also gains greater insight into the way in which the extreme value attached to national belongingness can go hand-in-hand with progressively harsher criticism of the manner in which the Portuguese state governs and with increasing demands for exemption from the obligations which are normally expected of Portuguese citizens.

However, if 'the organization' allows for mutual compatibility of membership which would otherwise remain exclusive, it also runs the risk of being trapped by its own indecision. Consequently, the Portuguese associative movement can be regarded as a somewhat desperate attempt to prolong a temporary state of affairs as well as an attempt to institutionalize in the long run the benefits from a privileged period in history of the convergence between a migratory movement on a hitherto unrivalled scale and the prosperity of a system believed to be crisis-free.

In order to define the critical sources of identity for the younger generations, the Portuguese community must question its own evolution and its capacity to preserve autonomy. This is necessary, since the economic crisis and the growing uncertainty of the job market renders capital accumulation strategies, such as remittances to the country of origin and all other strategies which have been perceived as constituting an implicit refusal of proletarianization, untenable. Moreover, the longer the period of residence in France is prolonged and the more community dynamics intensify, the more the 'organized' will be influenced by the institutional pressures of the host society.

Consequently, two axes, which are not mutually exclusive, become apparent within the framework of this associative movement, since it will lose its capacity to express the 'global character' of the community to reconcile between 'warmth and experience' and to accord stature to future leaders. Similarly to the leadership structure of Portuguese associations across the Atlantic, key posts will be monopolized by persons who have reaped success within the community (small businessmen and tradesmen). This conforms to the mobility norms and corresponds to the values, such as inter-class mobility and the ideology of free enterprise, of a liberal, capitalist host society. Existing tensions with the Portuguese state will be ironed out with the affirmation of a proper Portuguese character. Also, Portugal's entry into the Common Market will help to make the associations a good ground for the promotion and prestige of local leaders who at the same time are able to reconcile the search for respectable 'roots' with a concern for profitable business ventures which will guarantee the continuation of ties across national boundaries.

On the other hand, other associations will be invested with the capacities of young intellectuals, who are currently emerging at the interface of French and Portuguese cultures. This young intelligentsia has already proved to be the energy within associations, because it is capable of operating in both social and cultural systems. Moreover, it considers itself capable of crossing cultural boundaries and of risking a synthesis.

There is no doubt that original cultural expressions can emerge (within the framework of drama and cinema for example), but the standards of leadership adhered to by these leaders will be based upon that existent within the host society. This standard, neither neutral nor indifferent, and which expresses the pre-eminence of 'institutions', albeit discreetly, is, in this case, capable of recognizing and of encouraging incidental 'differences' when these do not undermine the rule of the state and the primacy of intellectual culture. It is possible for a 'pluralist culture' to become the ultimate phase of integration into a society imbued with a sense of its own mission to civilize—where reference to 'Portugueseness' becomes obligatory but emptied of its meaning.

Notes

1 This text reports and expands upon some of the conclusions arrived at by the ATP CNRS 054 in their work entitled: 'Les variations de l'identité': etude de l'évolution de l'identité culturelle des enfants d'émigrés Portugais en France et au Portugal' (edited by Michel Oriol), *Rapport* vol. 1, no. 14, 1984.

2   Hily, M.A. and Poinard, M. (1984) 'Un million de silencieux, les Portugais', *Politique Aujourd'hui*, no. 4, February–March.

3   This is such a generalized phenomenon that it is referred to in all works treating the subject of emigration. For works treating the subject of internal migrations see Beteille (1974). For works synthesizing ideas on international migrations see Georges (1974) and Tapinos (1974). The two latter works provide important bibliographies.

4   V.Cutileiro, J. (1977) *Ricos e Pobres no Alentejo*, Sá da Costa, Lisbon.

5   Poinard, M. (1983) 'Emigration et Developpement Rural: Le Cas de FOIOS', paper presented at conference on Emigraçao na Regiao Centro, January.

6   Rocha-Trinidade, H.B. (1973) *Immigrés Portugais*, ISCSPU, Lisbon.

7   Poinard, M. (1981) *Le retour des travailleurs Portugais*, La Documentation Française, Paris.

8   De Guimaraes, R. (1981) 'La deuxième génération: Aspects scolaires et culturels', in *Aspects culturels de l'émigration Portugaise en France*, paper presented at the conference of Sèvres, 18–19 December, ICEI Paris.

9   Woodrow, A. (1983) 'Musulmans en France', *Le Monde*, 12, 13, 14 July.

10 Associaçao Cultura Popular Portugal Novo de Colombes (1981) *O Movimento Associativo Portuguese en Franca*, Colombes.

11 Marrucho, A. (1982) *L'Immigration Portugaise dans la ville de Roubaix*, MA dissertation in geography, Lille.

12 Oriol, M. (cd.) (1984) *Les variations de l'identité. Etude de l'évolution de l'identité culturelle des enfants d'émigrés Portugals en France et au Portugal*, IDERIC, European Science Foundation, Nice.

13 Rocha-Trinidade, M.B. (1983) 'Le Dialogue Institué', paper presented at conference on the life of associations in immigrant communities, held by the European Science Foundation, Florence, October.

14 Hily, M.A. and Poinard, M. (1985) 'Les Jeunes et la Dynamique associative', paper presented at a round table meeting on the topic *Générations Issues de l'Immigration*, held at Lille, 12–14 June. The communities' commission which meets every year must discuss government policy on emigration and it is important to note that according to a decree (and discussion in Lisbon) associations have to be recognized by Portuguese consulates before being allowed to nominate their representatives.

15 Moulier, Y. (1981) 'Les remises des Portugais dans l'argent des émigrés', *Travaux et Documents de l'INED* (J.P. Garson, ed.), no. 94, PUF.

16 Catani, M. (1983) *Une hypothèse de lecture des relations entre parents et enfants: émigration, individualisation et reversibilité orientée des choix*, ERMI, Paris.

17 This section is based on Hily, M.A. and Poinard, M. (1984) 'A propos des associations Portugaises en France ou l'identité condensée', *Revue Suisse de Sociologie*, no. 2.

18 Oriol, M. (ed.) (1984), see note 12.

19 Marrucho, A. (1982), see note 11.

20 Catani, M. (1983), see note 16.

21 Catani, M. (1983) *Identité et culture. Hypothèses théoriques et perspectives interdisciplinaries dans l'étude des communautés Italiennes en France*, European Science Foundation, Strasbourg.

22 This section is based on Hily, M.A. and Poinard, M. (1985) 'Fonctions et enjeux du mouvement associatif Portugais en France', *Revue Européenne des Migrations Internationales*, vol. 1, no. 1, September.

23 Extract from interview, Hervieu, B. quoted in Agulhon and Bodiguel (1981).

24 Extract from interview.

25 It is the case that one of the sample associations, which is led by Communist party militants, does not make the impression of a typically political organization either as a result of responses to items on the questionnaire or according to the graph drawn from the factor analysis. Similar to a strategy found in other emigrations,

'sound' politicization occurs indirectly: by the politicization of certain cultural activities and through the confidence invoked by militants.

26 The codfish is the national dish of the Portuguese. As for newspapers, the most regularly and widely read of all newspapers is *A Bola* (a newspaper devoted to football).

27 Extract from a duplicated document produced by the CEDEP Paris, 1982.

28 CEDEP, see note 27.

29 Consequently he condemns the reticence of the Portuguese in involving themselves in immigrant struggles. This is the only Portuguese organization which took part in the demonstration of the 'Beurs' in December 1983. ('Beur' is the self identification of activists among the descendants of North African immigrants in France.)

30 CEDEP, see note 27.

31 Expression used by a youth leader.

32 Hervieu, B. quoted in Agulhon, M. and Bodiguel, M. (1981) *Les associations au village*, Ed Actes Sud, Paradou.

33 It is regrettable that the political debate on the role of the associative movement was postponed in France after its initiation at the end of 1981.

34 The new law on Portuguese nationality entitles Portuguese nationals to hold dual nationality. One may therefore adopt the nationality of one's country of residence while retaining the nationality of one's country of birth. Consequently many have taken up French nationality as a means of overcoming administrative problems without feeling that they have betrayed their native country.

35 Hily, M. and Poinard, M. (1984) 'Le réseau associatif Portugais et les expressions de l'identité', in Oriol M., see note 12.

36 Oriol, M. (1984), see note 12.

37 Remember, that the teaching of Portuguese language ranks in the middle of the scale which rates activities according to their complexity. It ranks therefore much lower than that of French language teaching. It should also be mentioned that the oral practice of Portuguese, constantly reinforced by the commands of adults, is widespread.

38 Hily, M.A. and Poinard, M. (1984), see note 35.

39 For the sense in which this term is understood by researchers studying the Italian associations in France and the strategies deployed by transalpine peoples, cf. Catani, M. (1983), 'L'Identité et les choix relatifs aux systèmes de valeur', *Peuples Méditerranéens*, no. 24, pp. 117–26.

40 'The institutions' are characterized by the monopoly of various sanctioning criteria used to demarcate group limits. This logic of domination is reinforced by the fact that individuals find themselves trapped in modern institutions within a system, which is broken up by its own logic and does not allow them to find a place of their own which they can relate to as a whole. As a reaction to this alienation, the organized space facilitates the circulation of accepted symbols and exchanges. It establishes a social space in which (the experience of) the whole (totality) can be taken over by the subject without continuing to centre upon an official national discourse (Oriol, M. (1984) p. 179, see note 12).

References

Agulhon, M. and Bodiguel, M. (1981) *Les associations au village*, Ed. Actes Sud, Hubert Nyssen, Paradou.

Associaçao Cultural Popular Portugal Novo de Colombes (ed.) (1981) *O movimento associativo portugues em Franca*, Colombes.

Beteille, R. (1974) *Les Aveyronnais*, Poitiers.

Catani, M. (1983) *Identité et culture. Hypothèses théoriques et perspectives interdisciplinaires dans l'étude des communautés italiennes en France*, ESF, Strasbourg.

Catani, M. (1983), 'L'identité et les choix relatifs aux systèmes de valeur', *Peuples Méditerranéens*, no. 24, pp. 117–26.

Catani, M. (1983) *Une hypothèse de lecture des relations entre parents et enfants: Emigration, individualisation et réversibilité orientée des choix*, ERMI, Paris.

CEDEP (1982) (extract from a duplicated document), Paris.

Georges, P. (1974) *Géographie des migrations internationales*, PUF, Paris.

Guimaraes, R. (1981) 'La deuxième génération: Aspects scolaires et culturels', in *Aspects culturels de l'émigration portugaise en France*, paper presented at the Conférence of Sèvres, 18–19 December, ICEI, Paris.

Hily, M.A. and Poinard, M. (1984) *Le réseau associatif portugais et les expressions de l'identité. Les variations de l'identité: étude de l'évolution de l'identité culturelle des enfants d'émigrés portugais en France et au Portugal*, IDERIC, FES, Nice–Strasbourg.

Hily, M.A. and Poinard, M. (1984) 'Un million de silencieux. Les Portugais', *Politique Aujourd'hui*, no. 4.

Hily, M.A. and Poinard, M. (1985) 'A propos des associations portugaises en France ou l'identité condensée', *Revue Suisse de Sociologie*, no. 2.

Hily, M.A. and Poinard, M. (1985) 'Fonctions et enjeux du mouvement associatif portugais en France', *Revue Européenne des Migrations Internationales*, vol. 1, no. 1.

Hily, M.A. and Poinard, M. (1985) *Les jeunes et la dynamique associative*, paper presented at a round table meeting on the topic 'Générations issues de l'immigration', held at Lille, 12–14 June.

Marrucho A. (1982) *L'immigration portugaise dans la ville de Roubaix*, MA dissertation in geography, Lille.

Moulier, Y. (1981) 'Les Portugais', in J.P. Garson and G. Tapinos (eds), *L'argent des immigrés: Revenus, épargne et transfert de huit nationalités immigrées en France*, *Travaux et Documents de L'Ined*, no. 94, PUF, Paris.

Oriol, Michel (ed.) (1984) *Les variations de l'identité. Etude de l'évolution de l'identité culturelle des enfants d'émigrés Portugais en France et au Portugal*, vol. 1, vol. 2, IDERIC, FES, Nice.

Poinard, M. (1981) *Le retour des travailleurs portugais*, La Documentation Française, Paris.

Poinard, M. (1983) *Emigration et développement rural: le cas de FOIOS*, paper presented at the conference on Emigraçao na Regiao Centro, January, Coimbra.

Riegelhaupt, J.F. (1983) 'O significade religioso do anticlericalismo popular', *Analise Social*, no. 72-73-74.

Rocha-Trindade, M.B. (1973) *Immigrés Portugais*, ISCSPU, Lisbon.

Rocha-Trindade, M.B. (1983) *Le dialogue institué*, paper presented at the conference on the Life of Associations in Immigrant Communities, European Science Foundation, Florence, October.

Tapinos, G. (1974) *Economie des migrations internationales*, A. Colin, Paris.

V.Cutileiro, J. (1977) *Ricos e Pobres no Alentejo*, Sá da Costa, Lisbon.

Woodrow, A. (1983) 'Musulmans en France', *Le Monde*, 12, 13, 14 July.

7 Italian Immigrant Associations in France

Giovanna Campani, Maurizio Catani and Salvatore Palidda

Introduction*

For a long time the rare studies of Italian immigration in France emphasized the progressive slackening off of the migration stream, and the integration or even assimilation of the Italians. Italians were considered to be devoid of any interest, since no 'Italian problem' was thought to be left in France.[1]

None the less, although the majority of Italians have been assimilated and statistics reveal few new arrivals, there are certain signs which indicate the vitality of the Italian community in France and the maintenance of an Italian ethnic identity:

—The migration network of kin and fellow villagers continues to thrive. The fact that the migration chain still exists proves that the old migrants have experienced socio-economic success and are in a position to respond to the requests of fellow villagers. This fact also throws light on the maintenance of networks with the place of origin.

—There are about one hundred Italian 'regional' associations in France today, and forty-eight free radio stations which broadcast in Italian or Italian dialects. A regional association means that its members come from the same region of Italy, very often from the same village. Generally, they consider that nationality is less relevant than common origins. Hence, these associations include members from both French and Italian nationalities, and they sometimes welcome other immigrants but mostly they establish a socio-cultural and socio-economic relationship with the French population in the municipality of residence.

—A substantial number of city councillors and even mayors are of Italian descent, and even if they have French nationality, they have not forgotten their origins. In fact for the local French authorities, shopkeepers, entrepreneurs and artisans of Italian origin

* by Giovanna Campani

or of Italian nationality are not only voters or at least taxpayers, but are members, often leaders, of Italian communities who inform a sector of public opinion and the cultural life of the commune. In other words it is possible to speak of pressure groups of Italian origin at the local level.

The Italian immigration in France provides a variety of cases. Since it is a rather complex phenomenon sweeping generalizations must be avoided; however, it would be wrong to limit ourselves to a simple sociology of everyday life.

Obviously, in the light of this complexity, the study of the phenomenon of associations is not in itself sufficient to reach a comprehensive and sensitive understanding of the entirety of Italian migration to France, but it certainly makes it possible to evaluate some of its most significant aspects.

With which theoretical instruments should the phenomenon of associations be studied? We have chosen an interdisciplinary framework. Italian migration in France cannot be properly understood without knowledge of its historical context. We will therefore analyse its evolution with respect to its century-long history and give special attention to the current period which has witnessed the upsurge of regional associations since 1970.

This historical analysis will be complemented by a socio-political and a socio-anthropological approach. The former studies the different political strategies of the two nations *vis-à-vis* migration and the political strategies of the migrants themselves. The latter discusses relations within the associations, of associations to the larger host society, and the maintenance of networks with the villages of origin in their various dimensions as well as their significance for families and individual migrants.

The generations of Italian immigration in France (1830–1985)*

Integration, assimilation, family networks and communities
In our research we have criticized the simplistic view of Italian immigration in France which uses the notion of integration too loosely. In common speech 'integrated' is taken to mean all the groups of foreign origin which do not create problems for the indigenous population.[2] As a result of this ambiguous use of the term 'integration' it has acquired a second connotation: 'a desirable and desired norm, i.e. an adequate justification of an institutionalized practice'.[3] In this way it is possible to speak of the 'Italian model' of 'successful immigration' compared to other more recent immigrations, such as the immigration from north Africa.

* by Giovanna Campani

167

The current opinion among lay persons and even sociologists which says that there is no 'Italian problem' left in France is not merely the result of a kind of a 'socio-centric' approach which sets as a point of reference 'an adequate justification of an institutionalized practice'. The interpretation is based on the notion of invisibility as developed by Duncan and Lieberson (1959). The invisibility of the Italians is a real phenomenon. But this invisibility is more directed by French public opinion, than by their fellow villagers and compatriots.

Thus, invisibility does not necessarily imply that the cultural traits of the nation of residence have been internalized, but only that they have been understood. This would clarify and modify the classical definition of assimilation (Herskovits 1950), whereby assimilation implies the internalization of cultural traits and norms.

Our research indicates that whilst Italians are almost all integrated in the sense that they have found their social and economic place in France, they are certainly not all 'assimilated' according to the full meaning of the term. The assimilation of the Italians is an historical process: the Italian migration in France has a century of history marked by such events as the unification of Italy, two world wars and Fascism. Without ignoring the role played by a certain cultural proximity,[4] it would seem that the historical context has been one of the major determining factors in the process of assimilation. We shall investigate how the process of assimilation has touched the majority of Italians in France. If assimilation did succeed for a long time among a large share of the Italians in France, another section of the Italian population escaped this process. Those who escaped were primarily immigrants who came after the Second World War, most of whom originated from southern Italy and the islands of Sardinia and Sicily. And, also, others who chain migrated as family networks and communities of immigrants.

Here the expression 'family networks' is used to refer to a set of families who have the same local origin, who are related to each other by kinship in both the biological and social sense of the term. Through endogamy, they aspire to the reproduction of these social relations. The family network is at the centre of the community; 'community' refers to life within a common geographical space as well as interaction between different primary groups (that is, between different family networks) and the general acceptance of common norms and values. From an anthropological point of view the community is a symbolic system where the relation to one's ancestors is a fundamental element of the auto-perception of the local society.

To understand the phenomenon of family networks and community it is necessary to take into account some historical and sociological factors specific to Italy; in particular its belated national unification, its regional divisions with their structural, social and cultural implications, which remain important today. The regional differences have had a significant influence on the migration process. From a geographical point of view, instead of speaking of Italian emigration it would be more correct to speak of 'migratory entities' (Beteille 1981) when referring to migration from Sicily, Sardinia, Pouilles, the Comino Valley, etc. The fact of coming from a particular area determined the type of trajectory in the migratory process. Over the years, persons from these regional 'migratory entities' continued to belong to family networks and communities. In such cases the experience of migration did not have a destructive effect on the culture of origin. Some cultural traits, such as the organization of the family, were the condition for success of the migration project. The migration project is shared by the whole family, and is pursued as well by the children, and in this way is transferred from one generation to the next.

The different epochs of Italian immigration in France

The Italian economic migration[5] to France dates back to 1830 but flows continued from well-defined regions of origin until the mid-1960s. Although Italian migration ranks only fourth in size today, it was the most important migration stream between 1901 and 1962. There were already 330,000 Italian residents in France in 1901, and the peak of 808,000 was reached as early as 1931.

Except for critical times (the 1888 trade war, Italy's alliance with Prussia and Austria, the Aigues-Mortes massacre in 1893[6]) France was the European country which during the whole pre-First World War period absorbed the greatest amount of Italian labour. The average yearly intake was very high: around 30,000 a year between 1860 and 1880, around 35,000 between 1881 and 1890, around 24,000 between 1891 and 1900 and around 57,000 between 1901 and 1910.[7] Throughout this time, Italians were the largest colony in France. They were often concentrated in certain regions (the Paris area, the south-east, Lot-et-Garonne, Morelle, Alsace), and they generally came from northern Italy, which almost always preferred emigration within Europe, whereas overseas emigration was more frequent in the south.

Between the two world wars France absorbed 80 per cent of the Italian labour emigrating to Europe, as well as a large section of political emigration: altogether 1,192,118 Italians emigrated to France between 1922 and 1942. Returns to Italy were numerous in that period (822,558), indicating the great mobility of this labour force. Only a minority stayed and settled in France. Political emigration characterized this period, although it is insignificant when compared to the total number of Italians residing in France.

Emigration was slowed down by Fascism in the 1930s and then by the war. After the Second World War, the migration flow to France became very important again, until 1962. Most of the immigrants came from northern and central Italy. From then on it decreased. Peaks of immigration were reached in 1947: 51,339 Italian workers, in 1956, 1957 and 1958 respectively 52,782, 80,315 and 51,246. The migration flow after 1958 came from more southern areas. Sicily, Calabria, Sardinia and the Pouilles provided the majority of the immigrant labour force. Meanwhile, most of those who had arrived before the war became naturalized.[8]

Since the end of the 1960s, Italian immigration has stabilized: few arrivals, few returns, relatively few naturalizations. It essentially consists of families—the number of children increasing until 1975. However, according to the last census (1984) the share of the young has diminished and the 'ageing' of the Italian population appears to be definitive.

Italians have attained a higher socio-economic status than other groups of immigrants; there are many skilled workers, professionals, artisans and entrepreneurs among them.[9] This socio-economic mobility of Italians must, however, be differentiated according to the regions of France.

Living standards and housing conditions vary substantially from one region of France to another. For example, in the north and the east of France, where Italians have worked in sectors with low job mobility (textiles, mines, steel industry) and where the economic crisis is severe today, their small margin of 'superiority' in the hierarchy of immigration is not comparable to what is to be found in other regions and especially in the large urban agglomerations such as Paris, Lyon or Marseille.

Throughout these periods Italians have been confronted with changes in immigration policies implemented in France and the varied reactions of the French population. Schematically, one could say that Italians have been affected by a policy of assimilation alternating with one of ostracization. On the other hand, Italy virtually never had an emigration policy towards the Italian population in France. Here, there was not so much at stake as in the colonies of the Americas.[10] Italians were therefore often abandoned by Italian authorities in their confrontation with French society and institutions. Yet the relationships between the Italians and the French community reveal that they followed parallel rather than divergent patterns of development, but these relationships are very difficult to schematize and to generalize about.

Whilst the history of Italian migration has been affected by xeno-phobia and racism—for example, the casualties in Aigues-Mortes (the massacre of Italian workers) and elsewhere—between the end of the nineteenth and the beginning of the twentieth century, immigrant Italian mountain people (from the Alps and the northern Apennines) who went up to Paris in search of employment got on well with French people from other regions, the internal migrants from Auvergne and Savoie.[11]

Some authors claim that the assimilation of Italians can be essenti-ally explained through their cultural and religious similarities and through the spontaneous friendships and affinities which are sup-posed to bring them close to the French.[12] We would argue somewhat differently: assimilation was the result of a combination of variables. Cultural proximity did not necessarily mean assimilation; for in-stance, these very mountain people from the Alps and the northern Apennines who made friends with their counterparts from Auvergne and Savoie have generated very solid family networks and communi-ties still in existence today, a hundred years after the first immigrants arrived, and at the same time they have refused assimilation. Their grandchildren are still very attached to the village of origin. For them migration was part of a tradition, it was perceived as a seasonal ex-odus, as one of the possible modes of working to support family and community. In this case, migration did not destroy the traditional life of the villages. On the contrary, it made possible the continuation of family and village networks.

On the other hand, for other immigrants coming from regions much more 'distant' from France, in every sense of the term, than the Alps or the Apennines, assimilation and 'gallicization' were *sine qua non* conditions of a successful integration in French society, es-pecially if they sought upward social mobility. This means that cul-tural proximity is only one of the factors which explain assimilation.

In our opinion the following conditions contribute as well to influ-ence the extent of assimilation:

—*French policies* defined as assimilationist or as forced accultura-tion. The assimilative force of French society is declining today, due to the general crisis of values, of the educational system and of absolute identification between the political and the cultural unity of the nation-state.

—*The historical conjuncture* which confronted immigrants with in-ternational crises in which they had to make a choice (war, Fas-cism). It is particularly interesting to examine how 'economic' immigrants lived through the rupture of two world wars and the intervening years of Fascism.

171

—*The migrants' origin* and the history of their migration: the migration stream drifting towards France was essentially a rural labour force shed by the dislocation of the old rural society and the introduction of capitalist forms of production in the north of Italy. When the migrants came from areas where the traditional societal relations endure, assimilation became much more difficult.

The history of Italian immigration led us to formulate the hypothesis that the majority of immigrants from northern Italy underwent the same general process of proletarianization as the peasants in that region. Those immigrants who were to become the industrial proletariat, and at times the agricultural proletariat, in France had already experienced the introduction of capitalism and the dismantling of their previous social conditions in their own country. The 'classical' process of proletarianization experienced by the majority of immigrants from the north is not a negligible factor in their assimilation in France. Particularly, the context in the period of the two world wars, reinforced the 'subjective' aspects of proletarianization. Class conflict was intense. Nationalism, but also parochialism, was loaded with negative connotations, so that immigrants identified with their class straight away.

Another variable related to the subjective aspect of proletarianization and class consciousness is the affiliation of Italian immigrants to the French working-class movement, particularly trade unions and political parties.[13] There is no doubt today that the left-wing affiliations of Italian immigrants facilitated their assimilation, given the strong national connotations of the French working-class movement, especially since the foundation of the Second International.

Although belonging to networks and communities was not always a barrier to integration into the French working class, it is true that the best instances of Italian participation in the French trade union movement or in the resistance were those Italians who had thus become assimilated and whose children became assimilated, whilst at the same time remembering their origins.[14] For the members of networks and communities, the village constituted a refuge at all times of crisis, particularly during wars. Their participation in political events in both nations was passive most of the time. That is explained by the importance of primary structures in their system of values. The family and the village were much more important than the nation.

The socio-political dimension of Italian immigration in France*

General remarks
This section discusses the forms of organization among Italian immigrants in France at different historical periods. There are no specific studies on the history of Italian associations in France. There are, however, studies by historians mentioning associative life in the past, which, together with the results of our research, provide useful elements for an outline analysis.

It is difficult to recover the historical 'memory' of old forms of organization or of collective actions in the past. Few associations have a long history and only 4 per cent of associations existing today were created before 1945. In the past, organizations were rarely created by 'economic' immigrants, or those who did not choose assimilation, or who were members of family networks or communities. In general, one can say that the creation of associations results from what is at stake in the migration phenomenon for the country of origin, for the host country, or for the political and trade union forces of the two countries. Until 1910 the immigrants themselves rarely made use of the various interests they represented.

Organizations among Italian immigrants in France may be differentiated according to their ties to principal institutions within either society; those identified with are:

—the public authorities in their country of origin
—public authorities in the host country
—parties, trade unions and the church in the country of origin
—parties and trade unions in the host country
—organizations created by immigrants themselves.

In reality, this distinction is a rather formal one, because each organization is more or less subjected to the interaction between different processes and different protagonists depending on which interests are at stake.

It is only the organizations created by immigrants themselves, however, which follow a logic which gives reference to local roots in the two nations and puts the interests of the immigrant group before national interests. Traditional national organizations, on the contrary, give preference either to the interests of the country of origin or to those of the host country.

For the Italian public authorities, emigration has always been a precious source of foreign currency. Since Italian immigration in France tended to stabilize, little money was sent to Italy, which is one reason why Italy neglected this immigration. Today, thanks to the

* by Salvatore Palidda

173

socio-economic success of a sizeable proportion of Italian immigrants in France, a certain share of Italy's foreign markets is secured. Migrants promote the consumption of Italian national products and have a positive influence on French tourism in Italy. Italian authorities have recognized this change and speak of the emigrants as the 'best ambassadors of Italy'.

For the political parties, the trade unions and the church, emigrants constitute a clientele which they try to organize in order to appropriate resources apportioned to emigration by the state. Their electoral support is a minor interest. For the church, in particular, emigration is also the vector of its universal presence, of its ecumenical vocation.

As far as the French public authorities are concerned, they have often encouraged immigration for well-known demographic and economic reasons, even if it meant reducing it in times of crisis. Their objective was to assimilate the immigrants and especially their children. The attitude of French political parties and trade unions towards immigration has varied a great deal over the years. At times it has been considered as an advantage for the country, at times as the cause of all evils. In general, left-wing parties and trade unions have tried to recruit immigrants and this has been an important channel of assimilation.

Torn between the policies of countries of origin and those of the host country, immigrants have often been limited to a passive role. Only very recently new forms of associations began to claim the autonomy of the immigrants, and to assume a role which cuts across societal and national boundaries.

Associations in the history of Italian immigration: 1900–60
Until the end of the last century, Italian associations in France were rather few and, as is noticed by Bonnet (1976) about Lyon, they involved a limited fairly middle-class clientele.[15] This is the case of the Société Italienne de Secours Mutuel (Italian mutual aid society), authorized since 1965, and also of cultural organizations with government banking and under the chairmanship of the consul, like the Union Muscale Italienne, created in 1885 as well as the Armonia Italienne.

Between the end of the nineteenth and the beginning of the twentieth century, the presence of political immigrants (anarchists, socialists, trade unionists, who had escaped from police repression in Italy) stimulated political life and the life of associations among Italians, who had often been up until then passive victims of xenophobia and racist outbursts. Associations began to thrive: in 1900 in Marseilles alone there were twenty-two Italian associations. Sometimes the

Italian authorities took a suspicious view of these associations. The historian Serra relates Ambassador Tornielli's concern over a group of sixty sacked Italian workers, led by an anarchist, who had levelled threats at Italy, France and the company that had sacked them.[16]

The internationalist trade union movement constitutes a very interesting page of history, but it will not be repeated. It is the first and last time that immigrant workers made their voice heard at an international level, although an international workers' movement would be more suited to their very situation as migrants. The activists of the time expressed their plight as 'victims of the migration policies of both countries, international capital, and "the bosses"'. Italians, especially in the Marseilles region, were the largest constituent group of the international trade union and actively participated in strike activities.[17]

Left-wing leaders like Guesde, who had made racist comments about Italians fifteen years before, referred later to the outstanding mobilization of the Italians.[18] The internationalist trade union movement laid stress on workers' unity before their national origin, but this did not last. With the third international, working-class organizations began to emphasize national objectives. Moreover, the strong national character of the French labour movement positively influenced the 'gallicization' of its activist foreign members.

In the 1930s there was an important Italian participation in French left-wing organizations: between 1935 and 1936 Italian CET members numbered 130,000, that is over 15 per cent of the totality of Italian immigrants in France. This is a fairly high number, which was not equalled in the following periods, with the exception of specific areas or sectors such as the mines or steel works in the north or in Lorraine during the 1950s.[19] At the same time, the influence of the Italian Communist Party is estimated at 50,000 which results from a significant input of political, or both political and economic immigrants.

During the Fascist period, Italian forms of organization in France were divided along political lines; on the one hand, the anti-Fascists to be found in the parties of the left or in a few organizations (the Fratellanza Romagnola, the Fratellanza Reggiana),[20] on the other hand, official organizations set up or supported by the Italian government. Fascism attempted to link immigrants to a nationalist project, opening the *Case del Fascio*. During the Fascist period Catholic missions took root in France, whereas few had existed before the First World War. The missions took advantage of the treaty between the church and Fascism (the famous *Concordato* signed in 1928) to establish their presence in the immigrant milieu, and this grew in importance as a reflection of Christian Democratic governments after the Second World War.

If this is the general picture of Italian associative life, it must not be forgotten that the majority of immigrants neither joined nor participated in the different associations, whether Italian or French. This absence of participation continued after the Second World War. The new post-war immigration reinforced the trend towards depoliticization, since most immigrants were workers with families originating from the south and the islands. They ignored all forms of political life, importance was attached to primary structures, such as family and personal relations.

Until 1950, moreover, the majority of Italian immigrants lived in very modest economic conditions. They had to work very hard with the hope of settling in France in the best of possible conditions. Because of the wars, hostility on the part of the French was strong during the immediate post-war years. Immigrants did not want to incite further hostility by calling public attention to themselves.

After the Second World War, France encouraged assimilation, while Italy did not take much interest in its emigrants. In fact, to the contrary, the policy of Italian public officials was in favour of emigration abroad. The church was left with a monopoly on activities among the immigrants. It was only at the end of the 1950s that significant changes occurred in Italy's social policy which had repercussions for immigrants abroad.

1960–85: The regional associations
During the 1960s Italian immigrants experienced considerable socio-economic success. This was due to two factors: their know-how in the host society which allowed them to take advantage of the economic boom; and the particular nature of the Italian immigration whereby the entire family has an economic role and works towards upward social mobility.[21] It is access to this new social position which allows links to be re-established with the place of origin. Before that, a return visit had not been possible. It is not only a question of spending holidays there, but of investing savings. To own a house in the village and another one in France constitutes a status symbol.

Italy had also experienced an economic boom during this period and the standard of living in Italian society began to catch up with other European societies. At the same time Italian emigration, which continued throughout the 1960s, no longer centred on France, but emigrants went to Switzerland and Germany, where wages were higher. The Italian government began to develop a social policy towards its emigrants modelled on its internal policy. The budget devoted to migration grew. The money appropriated is partly used to support the diplomatic corps, which is responsible for immigrants, and partly to help organizations and affiliates of political parties and trade unions.[22]

Between 1960 and 1970 Italian parties created numerous organizations abroad: associations supposed to be national such as the ACLI (Italian Workers' Christian Associations) linked to Christian Democracy,[23] the F. Santi Institute linked to the PSI (Italian Socialist Party), the FILEF (Italian Federation of Emigrant Workers and their Families) linked to the PCI (Italian Communist Party). (As a result of the agreement between PCF and PCI, in France the FILEF became AFI-FILEF, a Franco-Italian association.) All these organizations have a weak influence on Italian immigrants in France, but they help to make immigrants receptive to political practices.

In addition to national associations, the *patronati* also have a foothold among immigrants. These are para-trade union organizations which have a monopoly on the bureaucratic procedures needed to obtain retirement pensions and other benefits to which immigrants are entitled. In many cases, the *patronati* fall within a system which could be almost called *clientelare*.[24] This system consists of distributing a proportion of the state budget through retirement pensions, allocations and other credits by way of organizations more or less manipulated by the parties in power.

In the 1970s the immigrants began to seek their own autonomous representation through the regional associations. These sprang up and grew quickly, while national associations linked to parties, trade unions and the church underwent a crisis of affiliation and credibility. The political logic of the regional association is completely different from that of the national associations. The most active regional associations are the ones founded by a native of this or that village: the regional dimension is often that of a small village. The creation of an association institutionalizes the success of a family network or a community. In other words, after a few years, socio-economic emancipation needs to be paralleled by socio-political affirmation in the place of origin as in the place of residence. It is this economic emancipation that stimulated the passage from the informal family network and communities to the formal during the 1970s.

The role of associations in the French areas of residence is to obtain recognition as groups of immigrants accepted and supported by the local administration. Recognition is also desired from the political and administrative authorities in the region of origin. In both cases, recognition is sought for a formal 'entity', with its economic, electoral and symbolic weight. The development of regional associations also coincided with two institutional phenomena:

— A new interest in Italians, in those places where they are numerous, expressed by French local administrators. This new interest coincides with the new status of EEC countries' nationals which gives an advantage to Italians compared to other immigrants.

— Regional decentralization in Italy and the creation of regional councils for emigration and immigration (consultative organizations). This entailed financial decentralization for tourism, schools, social and cultural activities, and allowed leaders of associations to qualify as representatives of an interest group to be heard in planning.

The political dimension of regional associations is sometimes expressed through the pressure applied by local groups. Some of these associations have a real importance on the local administrative level through pressure mechanisms *al italienne*, that is, limited to civil society which appears to have become 'infiltrated' by a network of non-codified relationships similar to the pattern of primary family relationships.[25] The result is that local migration policy comes into existence which results from the *de facto* interaction between local administrators and leaders of associations, and these are often people with a socio-economic role in the community.

Family networks and communities have, over the generations, constantly readapted their particular configuration of local and family values. And it is exactly these values, on the other hand, which have guaranteed the immigrants the achievement of a certain socio-economic success, while maintaining their ethnic identity.

The same has happened with regional associations. Because of the policy of decentralization in Italy, the value placed on local and village common origins has assumed a regional dimension also. Strict localism includes ideological features, which correspond to another period in the national socio-political system. Although the combination of cultural traits and values obtained in such processes of readaptation may very often be inadequate because they are syncretic and may provoke anomie, there exist numerous cases of adequate combinations.

It is obvious that immigrants are more or less influenced, although indirectly, by the development of the political game, in particular the credibility crisis of the electoral system, the workings of the relationship between civil and political society, the centrifugal tendencies of modern western societies and finally by the ethnic movement and the phenomenon of association.

Immigrants are also affected by the crisis of the nation state, as well as the internationalization of capital, culture, politics and economics.

Although all this turmoil has not yet been clearly articulated in speeches or organizations, increasingly one can observe a combination of localism and 'cosmopolitism', which represents a specifically 'immigrant' socio-political dimension.

Organizations and the institutional affiliation of Italians in France: an attempt at a typology

Having rapidly traced the historical course of organizational forms and the evolution of the socio-political dimensions among Italian immigrants, from syndicalist internationalism at the end of the nineteenth century, through anti-Fascism between the world wars, to the 'localism' of regional associations, it is now necessary to discuss the types of organization and their currently existing structures. According to the register established by the Italian ministry of foreign affairs, there were 322 Italian associations in France in 1980. This census is, however, not reliable enough, since associations are included which no longer exist, and recent developments are not taken into account. In our estimation the associations which Italian immigrants have joined in France are today more numerous. But, as will be seen later, it is necessary to differentiate between different types of association. According to the ministry register, there would be a total of 45,000 members in all the associations together. In our estimation there are fewer. While regional associations alone may count from 20,000 to 25,000 official members, the others can only rely on about 10,000 to 15,000 members.

Religious centres   There exists only one non-catholic association, the Grenoble Evangelica Pentecostale, an indicator of the monopoly held by the Catholic church on religious affairs among Italian immigrants. Altogether, according to the Italian foreign affairs ministry register, there are supposed to be twenty-six Catholic missions and religious charities. Ten were created between the two world wars, twelve between 1948 and 1960 and four between 1960 and 1975.

This is the work of two religious orders founded in the last century by the Archbishops Bonomelli and Scalabrina. The Scalabrinians only became established in France after the Second World War, and they may be differentiated from the others by their social awareness and their distance from political power. (They are rumoured to be close to the left.) The influence of the missions, even if it could never extend to the majority of Italian immigrants in France, was fairly important between the two world wars and until the 1960s. In addition to purely religious activities, the missions did social work. Their influence was more important at the time when they played the role of go-between, between the Italian authorities and the immigrants, thanks to their close links with diplomatic centres during the Fascist period as well as afterwards. This was possible because of the influence of the church on Christian Democracy. From the 1960s onwards, this party begins to become more secularized, reducing the role of the church.

The influence of the church was at one time extended to numerous associations, some of which display openly a religious connotation, for instance Les Amis de la Mission (friends of the mission), Les Hommes Catholiques (Catholic men), Les Mineurs Catholiques (Catholic miners) etc., but all these associations are losing members. There have been recent attempts to strengthen again the influence of the church among immigrants. But although they baptize their children, have church weddings and respect the traditional 'rites of passage', Italian immigrants are generally not practising Christians and follow more the initiatives of regional associations, better rooted among the networks.

However, the prestige of religious figures remains; for example, a priest has been appointed to represent Italians in the Council of Population installed by le Ministère des Affaires Sociales et de la Solidarité Nationale Française (the French Ministry of Social Affairs and National Solidarity).

Para-consular centres and organizations There are twenty consular committees in France which are concerned with immigrant problems. These committees have become more democratic, allowing the participation of representatives of immigrants' associations. There has been a long campaign to achieve the direct election of the immigrants themselves as representatives to the committees. This democratic effort is at its beginning: the stakes are high, since these consular committees allocate state resources to immigrants.

Associations of war veterans Italian immigrants who fought in the two world wars are numerous in France. Associations have actively claimed the allocation of pensions and other rewards. Often these are associations set up at the initiative of a few war veterans linked to Italian politicians. The proliferation of these associations is also related to the desire to obtain allocations distributed by the state. There are between thirty-five and forty associations of war veterans in France. Their membership is rather limited, despite official claims to the contrary. In the future these associations will not be able to rely forever on the maintenance of this often artificial structure. The Garibaldians and old anti-fascist partisans deserve a special mention; although heroic, they are fairly gallicized and isolated from the others.

Sports associations Unlike the Portuguese, Italian immigrants did not create many sports associations. This results from the fact that young Italians rarely promote associations and moreover they tend to socialize and practise sports more with the French. The sports associations that exist are often supporters' clubs of one Italian team or another. Altogether there are about fifteen Italian sports associations in France. Otherwise, sport is an unusual activity within associations.

Cultural associations and associations for the promotion of the language specifically addressed to the French   The most important association is the Dante Alighieri which addresses a primarily French audience, or sometimes assimilated Italians, intellectuals (students, teachers, etc.) in different towns. The participation of immigrants in these associations is practically nil. Altogether there are almost twenty-five associations of this type which generally work within the cultural institutes attached to consulates.

Franco-Italian associations   Associations of this type have been developed in many French towns according to a Franco-Italian formula developed during the 1960s. These have been investigated at times partly upon the advice of the local administration, or the political parties, but also because the law permitting the establishment of associations was rather restrictive for foreigners. Among these associations are those affiliated to the AFI-FILEF, which is a national association close to the French Communist Party and its trade union, the CGT. Associations related to the AFI-FILEF have a restricted clientele, but they constitute a rather efficient means of assimilation.

In the last ten years their membership appears to have dwindled. On the other hand, the Italian FILEF and thus the Italian Communist Party are attempting to establish a direct link with immigrants through their regional sections in Italy, because of existing conflicts between the Italian and French communist parties. Altogether, there are around thirty Franco-Italian associations, of which about twenty are close to the AFI-FILEF. In general, all these associations are more or less in crisis because of loss of membership.

National associations linked to Italian parties   Since 1960, the Italian political system has moved towards 'pluralism' and towards 'social' policies, i.e. the welfare state. Within the framework of these policies, trade unions and associations representative of the workers are participating in the management of resources made available by the state. There has also been what is called the fragmentation of management, and even the proportional distribution of resources between the parties and their affiliates (trade unions, associations, etc.). Hence, in every organization dealing with emigrants (national and regional committees, consular committees, etc.), a post has been granted by right to so-called national associations which deal with emigrants. Obviously these associations have tried to establish the widest structure possible to justify their representativeness and their claims to a significant proportion of the budget allocated by the state to emigration questions.

This has also caused the proliferation of the ACLI (Christian Associations of Italian Workers) linked to Christian Democracy, the FILEF linked to the communist party, the 'F. Sante' institute linked to the socialist party as well as *patronati*, the organizations paid by the state to assist emigrants and regulate their pensions. These national associations have a great deal of power and have been able to achieve a procedure whereby emigrants' representatives in regional committees for emigration should be subject to their approval. This can even mean that this representative has to join their organization. National associations have lost a lot of members, whereas regional associations are increasing their influence considerably. The national ones can rely on their institutional status, which gives them the capacity to maintain a clientele, but the resources at their disposal are engulfed by a heavy and expensive bureaucratic structure, so that little or almost nothing reaches the emigrants.

The credibility of these national associations, as well as that of Italian parties, has been greatly undermined among the emigrants. The competition with regional associations is very serious and national associations are going through a fairly deep crisis, which suggests that they will have difficulty in recovering. This will be discussed again later.

Attempts to infiltrate regional associations will only be successful as long as the leadership from immigrants themselves has not yet acquired the political know-how to handle bickering and clientelism. Numerous leaders of regional associations are faced with the challenge to defeat the 'mafia of national associations'. Between thirty and forty sections of national associations may be registered in France, but statistics very likely exaggerate the number of associations in existence and their respective memberships. The influence of this type of association is still fairly important in areas where there are no regional associations.

Regional associations   As has already been said, the phenomenon of regional associations is fairly recent. Only one of these associations was created before 1914: the Aosta valley in 1913; two between the world wars; six between 1964 and 1969; about thirty between 1970 and 1975; another fifteen between 1975 and 1979; and finally more than twenty-five in the last few years.

The most numerous and widespread regional associations in the whole of France are those created by the Sardinians: there are around fifteen of them federated in the League of Sardinian Associations. They often have their own premises, several activities and a very dynamic relationship with the region of origin. The Sardinian network of associations does not compare with that of other regions and receives substantial support from the regional *consulta* of Sardinia, in which some leaders of immigrants' associations in France participate.

The example of the Sardinians is a model for immigrants of other regions. Indeed, the trend towards co-ordination or federation between associations of the same region is becoming generalized, as is proved by the case of Calabresi, Pouilles, Friulanesi. But of course there are smaller regions or regions with fewer immigrants dispersed throughout France. After the Sardinians, come the Sicilians, with almost ten associations, out of which five are concentrated in the Forbach mining area. But although Sicily has defined the most advanced migration policy among all Italian regions, associations do not enjoy the support of the region, since they are cut off from the clientele structures which operate there.

On the other hand, associations have recently multiplied among the Calabresi, thanks to the links between some immigrant local dignitaries and politicians in the region. Nonetheless, they lack membership because of internal conflicts within the family networks, jealousies and power struggles for the leadership of the group. There are about eight associations from Calabria in France. Another region noted for its associations which have considerably strengthened their links with the region of origin and want to participate in decisions concerning its future is the Friule. In these associations there is a significant participation of youngsters born in France, whereas in other associations younger persons are fairly passive or absent.

The development of associations from the Pouilles is very recent; this is also due to the enthusiasm of youngsters from village networks. Within a three-year period, five associations from the Pouilles have been created in France and a federation has been established.

In other areas, there exist about three or four associations per region. In the current phase of development, regional associations are often encouraged by the independent radio stations as well as French policies favourable to associations in general.

As our analysis indicates, regional associations reflect both localism and cosmopolitanism. The next section will discuss how this factor is reflected in the leadership and activities of associations.

The leaders and the activities of regional associations

Most of those who have created these associations have remained uninvolved in political activities in both the nation of origin and the nation of residence. The new stratum of leaders of regional associations is generally to be found among the immigrants who have been most successful and have made themselves known. They are often businessmen, sometimes children of immigrants: they have been rarely helped by authorities, parties, trade unions; hence their mistrust of these agencies.

It is very significant that nationality, whether Italian or French, is not important for members of the regional association. There are presidents of associations who do not have Italian nationality, and who are city councillors in their municipality of residence, while efficiently representing members in Italy. It is their common origin which unites them, not nationality. The association represents families, not individuals, as is illustrated by the membership card which covers the whole family. Today, membership in associations is no longer a question of defence for immigrants and their offspring. This belongs to the past. It is now a question of obtaining recognition as an institutionalized group.

The new regional associations are very different from the old ones, and so are their activities. It is more and more obvious that the phenomenon of Italian regional associations in France today departs from this model, which is that of the old *amicales* societies (friendship clubs) of the end of the nineteenth century and the beginning of the twentieth. Associations of this category sometimes doubled as regional associations. Today, regional associations tend towards the pressure-group model on the local political and administrative level, in France as much as in Italy.

The few definitive returns to Italy, before and after retirement, show that immigration is irreversible. From then on, what counts for associations is the preservation of the reference to local origins, the preservation of socio-economic links and institutional recognition on the local and regional plane in the two nations. Hence, several kinds of social and cultural activities, in the broadest sense, such as summer holiday camps, to show Italy and particularly the region to immigrant children. These are complemented with school exchanges for language practice, winter holidays for the families, and stays in spas for old people. During the summer, when emigrants come back for holidays, there is always a celebration organized by civilian and religious authorities for emigrants in the village. The immigrants in return respond by paying for a show, a ball, a folk-group, thus demonstrating the symbolic communion of getting together again. On the other hand, in the municipality and the local neighbourhood in the country of residence, immigrants, while organizing some activities such as the yearly ball, a carnival or other activities of this kind for their members, actively take part in festivals, marches and commercial weeks.

Two characteristics are of special importance: on the one hand, investments in property in the homeland are often coupled with business relationships which are interesting for the municipality of residence, and on the other hand, leisure activities have a double symbolic aspect. It is not only a question of asserting one's origins, in the village or in France, but also of involving French friends in all the activities, in both places. One of the old people's wishes when they go to their spa is to bring these along. However, only a tiny percentage manages it, whereas in France, adults and youths encounter no administrative or ideological difficulty in opening up their activities to French friends.

Our limited survey indicates that associations do not place much value on the nation state but instead on diversified social relations between two geographically and administratively distinct places, and they maintain communications between them throughout the year. This is reflected at the level of subjective experience, hence at the expressive level as well as at the institutional level.

From the socio-political perspective we conclude that regional associations arising from networks and communities represent one indication of the decline of the nineteenth-century model of the nation state and the emergence of a transnational and multinational reality with very diverse social and economic activities. Politicians should examine its implications for the existing European order.

Associations and the family—the relationship between generations*

Our central premise is that the success of the family's migration goals are supported by the village networks. These have been adapted to correspond with the new living conditions brought about by immigration. It is this situation which leads to the creation of specific, regionally based associations.

In order to understand the stabilization of any migration flow and the associations which are established, it is necessary to consider the importance of the migratory sequence and of family continuity. These factors are evidenced in the area of expressive relations[26] and consequently in the rearing of children. But beyond expressive relations within the family, the effort devoted to the achievement of the family's goals indicates a common will to work which is expressed concretely in savings. This goes beyond individual ethical or moral values and has become a social fact in itself.

Leaving aside a discussion of the 'generation crisis' during adolescence and the years preceding marriage, it is the family and its decisions which constitute the central point of reference for entry into adulthood and the wider society. The family provides the cultural model to which young persons return once they have 'had their fling'. In some cases, family businesses or trades provide jobs for the 'children', thus helping them find their niche in society, or the father

* by Maurizio Catani

185

'fixes up' something for the hitherto rebellious child, using informal networks. In other cases, the family may help the child to realize plans for upward social mobility, often into the white-collar sector, by the financial support and pocket money they provide.

In all cases, not just during adolescence, but in the years between the ages of twenty and twenty-six, family goals provide the guideline. Each member gives at least part of his earnings to the family, even when pursuing personal plans. In this way the cohesion and the continuity of the family unit is preserved, despite personal differences. Economic and social factors cannot be disassociated from one another, the family consciously strives for social mobility. Its aim is to accumulate a family heritage, usually property, which is generally shared between the place of origin—the village—and the place of residence—town or suburb in France. It is this property in two locales which provides both a certain permanency and a symbolic significance. From this point of view, social success is never individual but rather inter-generational. Although expressive relations play a decisive part, on a subjective level, the crucial factor from the social point of view is the family, which is the determining and solidaric unit. But the family is not cut off from the rest of society. It forms a part of these 'new style' village networks, which have adapted old kin solidarities whether biological or social (*compadrazzo*), to suit the new social reality. It is only after emigration that implicit characteristics of these village relationships assume an importance not felt in the mother country. In the foreign setting, common local origins gain a particular value.[27]

But the importance of local origins does not end there: the whole network of village society is brought to life in the new place of residence. Italian immigrants who are involved in associations have continued to live close to each other, thus 'Italianizing', to a greater or lesser extent, the urban and social environment. Whereas fifty years ago they owned, for example, poor houses in one or two roads in Vitry, today they are the owners of a whole block of land in this area and nearby areas, where they have often built their own homes and other properties to let. Whereas fifty years ago they walked to each other's homes to play cards or to bring each other pieces of handwork for the women to do at home, and walked to various cafés on Sundays, nowadays they take the car, but they still travel only a few kilometres. The difference lies in the quality of life and the value of the property which they have been clever enough to acquire.

Associations also contribute to family socialization, because they allow the local and historical structure of the system of values of the society of origin to be modernized and ritualized.[28]

The anthropological dimension

Value choices   We have developed the term 'bilaterality of references' to refer to orientation towards two cultures. Depending on the circumstances, priority may be given to one system of values over the other, but even then the value system of the other culture is taken into account.

Bilaterality of references thus characterizes inter-generational relationships within the family, the village networks and the life of the associations. Associations are one of the contexts of the socialization of the children, on the same level as the family and the community. Children have in fact many other places of socialization, such as school, and their peer groups. These places of socialization are often viewed with distrust by the family because of their perceived heterogeneity. How do the individuals of the different generations combine their allegiances and loyalties to two cultures? On the basis of specific value choices? It is here that the anthropological dimension comes to the forefront.

Since they are still of working age, the parents' generation attempts to make their presence felt through both the family goals and the association. The grandparents, having successfully completed their migration goals, divide their time between Italy and France, thus cementing the double pole of orientation: their expressive relations and material interests. The generation which is open to question is that of the children and grandchildren because they have been socialized entirely in France. By definition, they would not know what life was like in the country of origin. In fact, for them, Italy is generally nothing more than a place to spend their holidays.

The contradictions between the generations are not clear-cut, as is evidenced by the diversity of cultural features of the associations. Just as the associations take on broad links with the two nation states and relationships within society, so too the solidary family unit recognizes and settles differences between its members, naturally with the help of relatives and village networks.

The family and the associations represent two different levels in this process whose manifestations correspond to each other and are interlinked. In the same way that the activities of the associations are multiple and have two social spheres of reference, so too do relations within the family.

There are a number of individual and subjective choices which form part of the system of bilateral references within associations. This is the institutional reflection of the double system of references within the family. These choices are ethnographic facts, such as the choice of nationality or choice of place of burial. We shall briefly outline these elements and analyse them in order to clarify this line of argument.

A certain number of young second- or third-generation immigrants who were born in France and are therefore entitled to French citizenship choose to forgo this right.[29] In the majority of cases, these are young men motivated by a desire to avoid military service in one or other country. These boys foresee their professional and married life in France. Moreover, the nationality of the future marriage partner is not considered important, although in the parents' generation marriage between Italians and even between those from the same village was common. These two facts amply demonstrate that the three factors which once defined allegiance to a country are no longer valid.

Nationality and place of residence on national soil and place of work and nationality of spouse, are no longer dependent on the same geographical and ideological unity, on the same 'common will' which used to be the narrow definition of national belongingness. To differing degrees, no doubt, the universe of discourse which defined national belongingness is disintegrating. This can no longer be attributed to the 'cosmopolitanism' of tiny sections of the population, such as the wealthy or the very politicized. Inter-generational unity and continuity are apparent when one considers the common characteristics of these choices. In effect, they are choices of society, not of nationality. Associations with their indifference to the nationality of leaders and members, and their ability to 'Italianize' marriages even where spouses are of foreign extraction by sending a bouquet of flowers wrapped with a ribbon in the colours of the Italian flag when a baby is born, are good examples.

Holidays, which are, more than anything else, a personal choice unaffected by daily pressures, are usually taken in the village of origin, or, at least, a part of the holiday is spent there, and this breaking-up of the holiday time is very significant. One submits to certain norms in order to profit from the symbolic resources they provide.

If, in August, sitting at the bar in the village of origin, fellow villagers talk about one of their own, whom they refer to as the 'Irishman', since he has made his millions by selling fish and chips in Dublin, but stress that he is really a man who has remained simple and down-to-earth, they are in reality saying something else: 'The village is a total entity of which you are a member; submit to its authority'. If the successful émigré behaved otherwise, his 'folks back home' would find a way of showing him that he was out of order. For his part, the so-called 'Irishman' could not run the risk of being judged in a bad light. He must remember that his employees and his friends, who may work in Dublin in the same trade as he, share the same origins. To be aloof, to flaunt his success, would cause his holidays in the village and his travels between the village where he was born and the town where he works, to be deprived of meaning. Emigration has reference to *one* universe of discourse: the village, which dissipates any opposition between those who left and those who remain. Everywhere else, the migrant worker, even one who has made good, would merely be a tourist like any other, liable to be criticized because of his origins and distinctive characteristics.

Such is the institutional power of associations which remodel the most different and divergent individual choices by the universal principle of local origins and family descent, which is ultimately seen as an implicit membership. But there is another crucial moment in the emigrant's life, burial arrangements, which shows how young people's personal plans tend to join those of the older generation and of the associations themselves.

Choice of place of burial   Apart from some individual cases, there is a general desire to live in France—preference is given to the society of residence. But this wish to stay is the result of two sets of local roots. This is clear when one considers the choices made by most of the older generation. Their wish, which is usually realized, is to spend the summer in their new house in their home village and to stay in France, where their children and grandchildren live, during the winter. In this way they choose to stay in a society to which they are accustomed and which has satisfied them more than the society of origin in which they no longer feel completely at ease. Nevertheless, some of these older immigrants, whose old homes in Italy are still occupied and who still have relatives living in the village, ask to be buried in the place where they were born. In order to ensure that their wishes are respected, they may set money aside for this purpose. Even more significantly, the families of men who die when still young often ensure that they are buried in the village, and they are helped in this not only by the leaders of the associations as such, but also by the close network of social kinship within their community. Group solidarity manifests itself in the social arrangements surrounding the funeral and sometimes also in the making of commemorative trophies. In such cases, the 'modern' factors cannot be separated from the 'traditional', nor the subjective and expressive elements from the social.

By taking distances and national frontiers into consideration associations modernize a symbolic space which has grown and become *de facto* international, but not on the level of values. The chthonian dimension reveals its fundamental importance when associations intervene to return the corpse home, and in some case commemorate the deceased. This is expressed to a lesser but more common extent when it is the grandchildren who comply with the wishes of their grandparents to be returned. In the Apennines of Parma, some cemeteries have had to be expanded not because of local demographic needs of the actual residents, but because of numbers of *émigrés* wishing to be buried 'at home'.

Although these cases are obviously far from being the norm, they demonstrate that death subordinates references to daily life in France, something one is not willing to do in normal life; and that one of the fundamental customs in any culture, the ceremonial treatment of the deceased, conveys the symbolic significance of family continuity which is sealed in graves in the country of origin.

Whether it be a question of individual plans, the family, or the bi-national reality of the associations, the core around which a whole set of ethnographical facts are organized constantly refers to the relations woven between two societies, localized according to the personal evolution of individuals. These individuals are also social actors who demonstrate that national jurisdictions are inadequate in relation to a new combination of values which arise from international migration.

The two localities and societies overcome the artificiality of national unity. For the descendants of immigrants a national boundary is not an absolute. For them there are specific issues which have to do with plans for life and death which need articulation. Material goods and burial customs follow the inter-generational framework of family plans in which the younger generation's choice of nationality and choice of marriage partner are made within the all-embracing framework of the family's future. (National choice may often, especially for young men, also involve opportunistic motivations.) In this way it is possible to measure the path the family pursues, supported by the immediate network of relations within the structure of the associations.

Family continuity marks the different stages of the life-cycle. This implies the reversal of priorities according to value judgements giving reference, depending on the circumstances, to the symbolic features of the place of residence or the place of origin. These value judgements correspond to the future of the individual who, on a concrete level, considers first the plans of the family and then his social recognition through the association. Both of these factors constitute the conditions for the achievement of his life goals. In this way two elements which otherwise would be contradictory are reconciled: the extreme individualism arising from migration which stresses future goals and the subordination of the individual to the requirements of life in society. This is, then, the meaning of the recent expansion in regional associations: the social, economic and symbolic significance of associations is rooted in the continuity of personal plans and the guiding choices of the family and the community.

It is the vacillation between these choices, articulated as the continuity of origins, and regulated by personal ambition, that we call the 'guided reversibility of references'.[30]

The future of associations*

It is difficult to foresee what will happen to the associations when the older generation of immigrants is dead and their children, the leaders of today, have retired. The future of the associations depends on the way in which the grandchildren and great-grandchildren of the heads of families who took out a membership card will ritualize the affirmation of their future.

What will happen to most of the young people who are a conscious part of the family plans, who take part in activities organized by the associations, but who take French nationality and who will live in France and marry French partners? We can assume that the associations alive today will be able to renew themselves and survive in one form or another, because of the importance still placed on family heritage, the community and the village and regional networks, which is reinforced by the phenomenon of marriages between those originating from the same locality. This is all the more so in Italy since regionalism is a fact which favours this mutual recognition. None the less, questions of cultural heritage can give rise to conflicts between descendants of immigrants and those still resident in Italy.

Although young people born in France are not, except in certain cases, active in the regional associations, and around the age of twenty they begin to grow tired of holidays spent in the village of origin which they may reduce to two instead of their entire four weeks, there are some examples which suggest that there may be a cultural blossoming of young 'Italians' or 'Franco-Italians'. In Grenoble, young people have launched an 'Italian' radio station. This modern means of communication has been successful at least until now with young and old in an area near the Italian border, where there has been large-scale immigration for more than a century. The most popular broadcasts are those concerned with the regions—for example, there is a large group of Sicilians living in Grenoble. At present, this venture, which has only recently begun, proves only the importance of the radio as a means of communication, since it is close to the social representations of the young and adapted to a society characterized by mass communications media. Will they become tired of playing at broadcasting and journalism? Given that the most serious problem facing Italian associations in France is that of modernizing the structure and methods of choosing

* by Maurizio Cantani, Salvatore Palidda and Giovanna Campani

leaders, there is no doubt that ventures such as the radio station can bring about at least a temporary revival. But does an association require more? It is an expression of a continuity in social assertion. Field studies today show, on the one hand, that this is a period of transition and it is difficult to foresee future developments. But on the other hand, our research indicates that the younger generation of Italians has been in many cases 'well educated', at least in the sense that it has been socialized within a framework whose configuration of values has already demonstrated considerable capacities for readaptation.

In any case it is the parents' generation which has founded the association. They are now between the ages of thirty-five and fifty, and even if they complain that the younger generation of twenty to twenty-five is no longer at their side, they still have another ten to twenty years' working life ahead of them, so the future of the association is safe for another ten years or so. Will they find 'real young people born in France' to whom they can pass on the cultural and institutional legitimacy which they themselves received from the generation before them? One thing is certain: the leaders of today have enough time to prepare for this transition. In all probability they will succeed in this because their socio-economic position makes them suitable candidates for representative functions, in the *consulta* of the region of origin and even at French local government level (the municipality). This in itself leads to the assumption that relations with the whole network of family and village structures will be maintained. But this is not the fundamental question. The double references (bilaterality), although based on concrete elements such as property, capital and social networks, are unlikely to resist the erosion of time if they are not supported by the continuity of chthonian origins, signified by burial of forebears. The value placed on these burials demonstrates the personal continuity and loyalty of the emigrants to those still in the village of origin.

It is quite possible that the connections between the two elements—preservation of local ties and the value placed on origins—are not indissolubly linked. The question of expressive ties and therefore the psychological aspect is not necessarily synonymous with 'social identity' (social nomination) or social recognition.[31]

According to an individualist system of ideas the individual would no doubt be evaluated on the basis of the cardinal points of equality and liberty instead of with respect to their place in the social organization and its interdependencies. (We must stress that we are dealing here with values and not with social relations and questions such as man's exploitation of man.) According to this framework, the individual is considered to be the judge and creator of a future which he measures by the yardstick of his own achievement.

The value placed on chthonian origins, through the phenomenon of associations and its familial roots, could be taken to mean that the modern individualist ideology which characterizes our civilization can only be pursued in this case through a valued social identity. Social identity prevents anomie on the subjective level of psychological identity, as well on the social level of origins. The fact that other categories of immigrants and their descendants do not join regional associations to the same extent illustrates that this kind of social identification with a valued cultural heritage is not an absolute but a cultural feature which may disappear on the social, if not the psychological, level. It is nevertheless probable that self-assertion and the rearing of children will be easier if one has not denied, or even tried to forget, the chthonian origins of the family. The re-claiming of local origins is a phenomenon cropping up all over Europe. We believe that its roots and contradictions, notably those related to the weakening of the unifying power of the concept of common good, can be examined on the basis of the scheme which we have just outlined.

Appendix

*A case study of Italian migration: The Laziali di Casalvieri Association**
This association represents the case of a successful local immigration. It was founded in February 1980 following a fête which brought together in the Parisian region emigrants from Casalvieri, a small town in Latium, and the people of the commune of origin. Casalvieri had about 5000 inhabitants in 1936. About fifty years later the inhabitants who remained in the village numbered only 3000, while the same number had emigrated to France. Others went to Ireland and the United Kingdom. Still other Casalvieri natives live in Australia and in America. This migration, which began in the last quarter of the nineteenth century, is characterized by the importance of the links maintained with the commune of origin.

In France, the first immigrants from Casalvieri arrived at the beginning of the century. They have lived through all the difficulties of a first settlement, the delicate experience of family reunion, disorder, and the coming and going of the two world wars. During that period four generations were at first riding the border.

Although the association was founded in 1980, its origins date back much further. It was born after a long period of gestation. The families for dozens of years first had to find their place in French society and the French economy. Through their work they took part in the

* by Salvatore Palidda

modernization and development of France. During that long period they preserved their cohesion which was an asset for their integration in a foreign land.

Almost all of them lived in greater Paris. They knew one another and mixed not only at the place of work, but met on Sundays, at weddings, at funerals. They also worked together and, having saved for years, they would start businesses or become self-employed —generally in building, but also in florists' shops. They would rely on family and village solidarity, on money lent by countrymen who could let them have substantial sums on the strength of their word and without charging interest. Although women have always been classed as housewives in censuses, it would be wrong to say that they did not work. While they rarely went to work in the factory or as cleaners, they worked at home, as homeworkers. From an economic point of view the traditional type of family structure made it possible to accumulate a certain capital and, overall, concentrated the strength of parents and children on the same family project. Still today there are families which say: 'We have only one bank account and several cheque books'. In other words, the consciousness of belonging to *one* family whose cohesion is indispensable, is absolutely clear.

The Second World War meant a rupture in the development of the network. Many came back to Italy, which proves that the bilaterality of references was already manifested then: the place of origin remained the place where one took refuge because one would not be thrown out and because it was possible to produce enough to survive. But people's aspirations are different. The local dimension has burst open spatially and the national one is subordinated to personal prospects. Thus people returned to France. Times were hard, it took several years to achieve again an upward social mobility, and families needed ten to twelve years before they could envisage spending a few days holiday back home.

As the years passed, it became increasingly obvious that migration was permanent. But at the same time, economic success began. In some cases it is very evident; in many other families some measure of prosperity is achieved. All the heads of family have managed to provide their families with a bigger house than in the country of origin. They have sent their children to school and have enough to modernize or build a house back home. But at the same time the support of kin and friends has never failed and their feelings imply a dual loyalty to France where now most of the youth were born and Casalvieri or more exactly the Comino Valley, where the families come from.

When economic conditions improve, people start to go home for holidays: from 1965 onwards, for instance, journeys multiplied and became regular. Emigrants of course got together but they also spent a long time with those who had not left: a glass of wine, a card game, the saints' days, some business, talks with the builders of their house. Festivals for the emigrants were organized. The municipality thus greeted those who came back for holidays. The latter in return organized and offered a meal for those who had not left. This is where, slowly, the consciousness of being a group *per se* was born, a group which belongs to two societies but has its own characteristics. This existence needed to be made official in the home country as much as in the country of residence.

In 1980 'people native of Casalvieri' were in a position to present themselves as a group to French society and the society of origin. It is not any more a case of dispersed meetings of families who know one another, but an assertion of a social whole. The membership card covers the whole family and the association, when it becomes registered, gains the judicial recognition of a collective social phenomenon, i.e. the overall success of a wave of migration.

Indeed showing oneself openly in the face of French society did not happen on its own. Individuals had a hand in it. But although young people (barely beyond thirty) carried out the administrative steps involved, since they had studied in France even if they were not born there, they were helped by the older generation. Not only was there a common desire to get together and be acknowledged as a group but the older generation had to vouch for the younger one to the whole of the families. One can illustrate this. Adults who participated in the creation of the association guaranteed that no one would suffer from their personal address books being turned into membership registers, that on the contrary it even promoted the success of people from Casalvieri.

In France, an association registered under the 1901 law judicially has a national dimension but its area of activity remains local. If the association is French, as its members live in France and most of them have no intention of leaving the country, its activities are necessarily oriented in two specific directions: the place of residence and the place of origin.

Socially and locally associations achieved complete recognition, as is shown by the presence of city councillors from the two nations during the annual festivals. Judicially there is a certain time lag: the association was declared official in France but does not have its counterpart in Italy. In this case, political recognition is achieved through the Consulle Regionali dell' Emigrazione and more concretely through twin towns, and cultural exchanges. The latter occur fairly regularly whilst city exchanges, like participation in the *consulta*, were still in the process of negotiation at the time of writing.

The activities of the association

What has been said above allows for an overall view of the activities of the association which could otherwise appear very diverse. In fact, there are three main ideas. First, the leaders of the association do not forget the difficulties encountered by those who have material or social problems. Knowing that one has made it as an emigrant does not mean forgetting those who still have problems. Hence the constant concern not only to help with administrative problems related to the members' retirement pensions, for instance, but also to participate in international humanitarian help when needed. The association intervened in Italy during the 1980 earthquake (Operation SOS Italy Solidarity); it organized collections for the disasters in Mexico; and even 'humanitarian' journeys to Poland. Whilst the members' participation varied, these initiatives certainly obtained responses.

In this connection, one needs to mention another initiative, the Foundation Louis Carlesimo, which enjoys significant and regular financial support from the members of the association (the aim of this foundation is to help the families from the province and from abroad, who come to be treated in Paris, in particular people suffering from cancer and heart diseases).

The second main theme concerns all the activities which are designed to maintain links with the valley and the region of origin for retired people, families and young people at school. This is a case in point where the idea one usually has of 'holidays back home' is insufficient to define a set of activities which take place throughout the season and are addressed to individuals, to entire families, and to peer groups. That is where it is possible to see the continuity of generations despite age and nationality differences.

Finally, the third main theme is that of constant action towards public authorities, nationally and locally, in France as much as in Italy. It is not only a question of cultural and linguistic exchanges that need to be financed. It is more a case of being accepted as representative as an association, firstly in the two areas of reference and then, when the law makes it possible, on the national plane.

The origin of legitimacy and the institutional game

The annual fête of the association assumes a social importance. This is where the three themes intertwine: (a) consciousness of one's origins and affirmation of upward social mobility, which does not obliterate the memory of very modest social and local origins; (b) continuity of generations; and (c) efforts to achieve the representation of the association on a local national and international level.

The continuation of the activities of the association, the policy geared towards representation can only be guaranteed if a large number of people attend. Out of the 784 families which joined the association, a total number of 3000 people, it is absolutely necessary that more than half be present at this annual event. The fête is rich in contrasts, but it is first and foremost an affirmation of unity, which illustrates a superior all-embracing principle: the recognition of common origins. It is only through this annual reaffirmation that leaders of the association, still the same since it was founded, receive confirmation of their legitimacy and right to representation. They are not elected. Leadership derives from the maintenance of village networks. This is where one observes the flexibility of cultural traits of origin, which are too often hastily referred to as 'traditional' in a contemptuous tone. It is the cohesion between families promoting the relationship between individuals which allowed a relative economic success and today renders social affirmation possible. Undoubtedly, a question remains open: What will be the future? Will the young people who were born in France take over the running from present leaders who were all born in Italy, even if they belong to two different generations? The variety and importance of activities, the ever more evident success of the annual celebration, seems to indicate that the association will be able to find appropriate formulas to renew itself.

Notes

1   In particular, this forms the thesis of Dominique Schnapper, *La Représentation de l'espace urbain pour les italiens immigrés*, Centre de Recherches Historiques, MSH, Paris, 1973; see also the studies by P. Milza for Centre d'études sur l'émigration italienne.

2   For a critique of the concept of integration see M. Oriol (ed.) (1984) *Les variations de l'identité. Etude de l'évolution de l'identité culturelle des enfants d'émigrés Portugais en France et au Portugal*, IDERIC, vol. 1 (vol. II forthcoming). Final report of the ATP CNRS 054. This project is also reported in this volume (Chapter 6) and forms part of the additional activity on migration of the European Science Foundation.

3   Oriol, M. (1984).

4   The concept of 'cultural distance' has always seemed to us to be ambiguous. However, several researchers insist on the 'cultural proximity' between the Italians and the French (D. Schnapper, P. Milza). We prefer to speak of relations with the French 'community' which have been of similitude or contrastive rather than of opposition.

5   It must, however, be noted that 'political' migration has often coincided with 'economic' migration over the last century. Thus at the time of the Risorgimento (struggle for Italian independence) several 'patriots' found refuge in France after Italian unification; anarchists and later socialists fled from police persecution to France.

6   This is one of the episodes of racism which the Italians suffered at the end of the last century. See T. Vetrone (1978) 'Antécédents et causes des événements d'Aigues Mortes', in Duroselle-Serra (ed.), *L'emigrazione italiana in Francia prima del 1914*, F. Angeli, Milan.

7   This information compiled from ISTAT, *Sommario di statistiche storiche dell'Italia, 1861–1975*, Rome, 1976.

8   This information compiled from Institut National de la Statistique et des Etudes Economiques, various census reports on the French population.

9   On the mobility of Italians, see S. Palidda (ed.) (1985), *L'imprenditorialità degli immigrati italiani in Francia*. Santi Editrice; Rome.

10 On this, see A. Annino (1974), 'La politica migratoria dello stato post-unitario' in *Il Ponte*, November–December, and also S. Palidda (1986), 'Aspetti socio-politici dell'imigrazione italiana in Francia', in S.&A. Di Carlo (eds), *I Luoghi dell'identità*. Angeli; Milan.

11 We are thinking particularly of emigrants from the Apennines of Parma and Piacenza and their relations with the Auvergnats, and of the mining regions, see M. Catani and Coll. (1986), *Les Scaldini de Paris: un métier transmis de génération en génération depuis la première guerremondiale*, Ministry of Culture; Paris, and G. Capani (ed.), *L'immigrazione emiliano – romagnola in Francia: scaldini, reggiani e rocchesi*. Région Emilia – Romagna; Bologne.

12 See P. Milza, 'L'immigration italienne en France entre 1870 et 1914', in Duroselle-Serra (1978), see note 7.

13 See L. Gani (1972) *Syndicats et travailleurs immigrés*, Editions Sociales, Paris; G. Noiriel (1984) *Une autre France, immigrés et prolétaries à Longwy*, PUF, Paris.

14 Notable cases are those of members of the Fratellanza Reggiana, a regional organization, most of whom are also members of the French Communist Party or at least the trade union Federation de la Confédération Générale du Travail.

15 J. Ch. Bonnet (1976) *Les pouvoirs publics français et l'immigration dans l'entre-deux-guerres*, Université Lyon II, p. 97.

16 See E. Serra, 'L'immigrazione italiana in Francia durante il primo governo Crispi, 1887–1891', in Duroselle-Serra (1978), see note 7.

17 See E. Temime, 'Les journaux italiens à Marseille de 1870 à 1914', in Duroselle-Serra (1978), see note 7.

18 Jules Guesde (leader of French Socialist Party POF) spoke thus of Italians in 1886: 'Blacklegs . . . from over the mountains . . . come to steal work from our compatriots', quoted by P. Milza, 'L'Intégration des Italiens dans le mouvement ouvrier français à la fin du XIXe siècle et au début du XXe siècle, le cas de la région marseillaise', in Duroselle-Serra (1978) see note 7.

19 See G. Noiriel (1984), *Une autre France, Immigrés et prolétaires à Longwy*, PUF, Paris.

20 Associations composed of both immigrants from one region or town and anti-Fascist *émigrés*. The first disappeared just before the war, the second exists today.

21 See S. Palidda (1985), note 9.

22 See P. Cinanni (1974) 'La Scelta del governo italiano nel se condo dopoguerra', *Il Ponte*, 'La Nuova Italia', Florence.

23 See A. Treggiari, 'Le strutture dello Stato italiano all' estero', in *Il Ponte*, cited above (note 22).

24 See G. Gribaudi (1980), *I Mediatori*, Torino, Rosenberg & Sellier, among others, who has given good descriptions of *clientelismo*, mediation, and power-brokers.

25 There are many publications which discuss these issues (familism, clientelism, etc.); of particular note are: J. Lapalombara (1961) *Clientela e parentela*, Editions Comunita, Milan; R. Catamzaro (1983) 'Struttura sociale, sistema politico e azione collettiva nel Mezzogiorno', in *Stato e Mercato*, no. 8; P.M. Paci (1982) 'Lá Struttura sociale italiana', Bologna, Il Mulino (essay on the social structure and the importance of the family in Italy); F. Piselli (1982) *Emigrazione e parentela*, Giraudi, Turin (study of the importance of family relationships in immigration).

26 'This is the area of pleasure and pain, love and hate. Everyone knows this experience through his own subjectivity in the reverberation and the tonality produced by psychological reactions to changes of any kind in the internal or external environment. Emotions are fundamental to the individual person . . . they are woven closely into the whole of the individual's experience . . . it has, then, an essentially relational character.' G. Chabalier, in *Vocabulaire de Psychopédagogie et de Pyschiatrie de l'Enfant*, PUF, Paris, 1963.

27 Among the earliest immigrants (that is, excluding those in the south) 'popular religion' and, within it, the practice of magic, has virtually disappeared. To be precise: the *immigrants* rarely give up such practices, and their *children* are told of them because they are sometimes the object. But *grandchildren* seem, more often than not, to know nothing of these practices, which, in fact have been abandoned, or more often, modernized, even in the society of origin, where they used to form one of the essential elements of folk culture. Immigration implies this progressive extinction and modernization through 'alternative medicine', for example. In any case, associations are not the best place to observe these practices and their transformation because they are a vehicle for a socialization of conforming to the customs of the new society of residence.

28 It is true that, for a large part of the Italian immigrants, and, in particular, for those who are no longer in contact with the region and village of origin, integration is more common. Nevertheless one should not overlook the subconscious memory of earlier racist attitudes towards Italians, nor the difficulties which southern Italians, who settled in the south of France after the Second World War, still encounter. There, unlike Paris, their social image has not altered in the public eye. No doubt this lives on in people's memory and could be traced through the appropriate methods of data collection, such as the oral history method, but this does not fall within the scope of our study.

29 M. Catani, G. Campani and S. Palidda (1984) *Analyse des motivations des jeunes qui déclinent la nationalité française par le jeu de l'article 45*, Paris, Ministère de la Solidarité, November.

30 These considerations could doubtlessly be applied to other groups of immigrants. But the basic question is not exhausted by a description of ways in which each wave of immigrants maintains links with national culture. The stage of socio and ethnographical enquiry, although necessary, is only a preliminary. We must relate the combinations of traits specific to each culture to a global anthropological interpretation.

31 The French text uses the term 'social nomination' in the sense of Selim Abbou. This use refers to the child's nominal heritage through its identification with the name of the family of origin. In this context it means social identification or recognition as a member or descendant of a certain village of origin. Selim Abbou (1981) *L'identité culturelle*, Editions Anthropos, Paris.

References

Abbou, Selim (1981) *L'Identité culturelle*, Editions Anthropos, Paris.

Annino, A. (1974) 'La politica migratoria dello stato post-unitario', *Il Ponte*, November–December, A. XXX, no. 5.

Beteille, R. (1981) 'Une nouvelle approche géographique des faits migratoires—champs, relations, espaces relationnels', *L'Espace géographique*, no. 3, 1981, pp. 187–95.

Bonnet, J. Ch. (1976), *Les Pouvoirs publics français et l'immigration dans l'entre-deux-guerres*, (Thèse) Université Lyon II, Lyon, p. 97

Bonnet, J. Ch. (1978), 'Notes sur les dossiers de naturalisation des Italiens dans le Rhône de 1880 à 1915', in J.B. Duroselle and E. Serra (eds).

Catanzaro, R. (1983) 'Struttura sociale, sistema politico e azione collettiva nel Mezzogiorno', *Stato e Mercato*, no. 8.

Chabalier, G. (1963) *Vocabulaire de psychopédagogie et de psychiatrie de l'enfant*, PUF, Paris.

Cinanni, P. (1974) 'La Scelta del governo italiano nel secondo dopoguerra', *Il Ponte*, November–December, A. XXX, no. 5.

Ciuffoletti, Z. (1978a), L'emigrazione nella storia d'Italia. Vallechi; Florence.

Ciuffoletti, Z. (1978b), 'Sfruttamento della manodopera infantile in Francia alla fine del secola XIX' in J.B. Duroselle and E. Serra (eds).

D'Atorre, P.P. (1974), 'L'evoluzione storica dell'emigrazione italiana attraverso alcune analisi del movimento operaio italiano', in *Affari Sociali Internazionali*, nos 1-2.

Dumont, L. (1983) *Essai sur l'individualisme. Une perspective anthropologique sur l'idéologie moderne*, Seuil, Paris.

Duncan, D. and Leiberson, S. (1959) 'Ethnic segregation and assimilation', *American Journal of Sociology*, 64.

Duroselle, J.B. and E. Serra (eds) (1978), *L'emigrazione italiana in Francia prima del 1914*. F. Angeli; Milan.

Faidutti-Randolph, A.M. (1964), *L'immigration italienne dans le Sud-Est de la France*, (Thèse). Gap; Lyons.

Galasso, E. (1986), *Italiens d'hier et d'aujourd'hui*. Impr. du Bâtiment; Lyon.

Gani, L. (1972) *Syndicats et travailleurs immigrés*, Editions Sociales, Paris.

Garasci, A. (1953), *Storia del Fuoruscitismo*. Laterza; Bari.

Gribaudi, G. (1980), *I Médiatoré*. Rosenberg et Sellier; Turin.

Guillen, P. (1983), 'Le rôle politique de l'immigration italienne en France dans l'entre deux guerres', in *Risorgimento*, nos 1-2.

Gut, Ph. (1978), 'L'immigration italienne en France de 1830 à 1870' in J.B. Duroselle, and E. Serra (eds).

Herskovitz, M.J. (1950) *Acculturation: A study of culture contact*, Peter Smith, Gloucester (Mass.).

ISTAT (1976) *Sommario di statistiche storiche dell'Italia 1861–1975*, Rome.

Lapalombara, J. (1967) *Clientela e parentela*, Editions Comunita, Milan.

Mastellone, S. (1978), 'L'immigration italienne en France sous Louis Philipe, 1830-1848', in J.B. Duroselle and E. Serra (eds).

Miliza, P. (1978a), 'L'immigration italienne en France de 1870 à 1914', in J.B. Duroselle and E. Serra (eds).

Miliza, P. (1978b), 'L'intégration des Italiens dans le mouvement ouvrier français à la fin du XIX et au début du XX siècle', in J.B.Duroselle and E. Serra (eds).

Miliza, P. (1981), *Français et Italiens à la fin du XIX siècle*, Ecole Français de Rome, Rome.

Miliza, P. (1983), 'Aspects politiques de l'immigration italienne en France de 1861 à 1914', in *Risorgimento*, nos 1-2.

Miliza, P. (1985), 'Un siècle d'immigration étrangère en France', in *Vingtième Siècle*, no. 7.

Nobile, A. (1974), 'Politica migratoria e vicende dell'emigrazione durante il fascismo', in *Il Ponte*, November–December, A. XXX, no. 5.

Noiriel, G. (1984) *Lonwy, Immigrés et prolétaires*, PUF, Paris.

Oriol, M. (ed.) (1984) *Les variations de l'identité*. IDERIC, Nice.

Paci, P.M. (1982) *La struttura sociale italiana*, Il Mulino, Bologna.

Piselli, F. (1980) *Emigrazione e parentela*, Einaudi, Turin.

Reyncri, E. (1979), *La Catena Migratoria*, Il Mulino, Bologna.

Schnapper, D. (1974), 'Les immigrés italiens, in *Annales*, no. 5.

Schor, R. (1980), *L'opinion française et les étrangers en France 1919-39*, (Thèse); Aix en Provence–Nice.

Sori, E. (1979), *L'emigrazione italiana dell'Unità alla seconda guerra mondiale*. Coppelli; Bologna.

Treggian, A. (1974) 'Le Strutture Stato Italiano all' estero', in *Il Ponte*, November–December, A. XXX, no. 5.

Vetrone, T. (1978), 'Antécédentes et causes des évenements d'Aigues Mortes', in J.B. Duroselle and E. Serra (eds).

8 Informal Networks and Formal Associations of Finnish Immigrants in Sweden

Magdalena Jaakkola

Social networks as a basis for organization

Finnish immigrants in Sweden are primarily to be found in the industrial and service sectors. As workers they contribute to the Swedish economy: they make use of services offered by Swedish society, and recent (1975) enfranchisement in local elections has made it possible for them to participate directly in Sweden's political processes.

This, however, does not imply that Finnish immigrants have been integrated into Swedish society on an individual level. Despite their proximity to native Swedes, both at work and at leisure, ethnicity has a major impact on informal interaction (cf. Barth 1969). Many Finnish immigrants have little social contact with Swedes. Chain migration and the concentration of Finnish immigrants in particular occupations and in particular regions increase their opportunities for coming into contact with other Finns and lay the foundation for the creation of a Finnish subculture in Swedish cities. It has been suggested that the Finns practise a sort of 'passive self-segregation', that is they do not deliberately isolate themselves, but naturally come into contact with other members of the Finnish subculture (Kuusela 1974). In a situation such as this, it would require a conscious effort to learn Swedish and make contacts with Swedes.

There are also other reasons for the poor motivation to learn the Swedish language and for the maintenance of ethnic boundaries. For many people, Finland is still an 'active community' in the sense that their social networks extend into their native country. As a consequence of the short distance and the good communications, contacts with Finland are regular, and the bulk of Swedish Finns spend their summer holidays there. Most Finns are not certain whether they will remain in Sweden and view their stay as temporary.

The maintenance of ethnic boundaries may also be a consequence of the internal homogeneity of the social networks. A study of friendship networks and life-styles among Finnish immigrants in one industrial town in Sweden (Västeras) in the 1970s found notable homogeneity

(Jaakkola 1983a) according to length of residence in Sweden and linguistic ability. This may have led to the persistence of poor knowledge and the maintenance of ethnic boundaries among newcomers. The ethnic boundaries may also be a consequence of 'status degredation' which a number of Finns suffer when migrating to Sweden. Many Finns in Västerås tended to believe that Swedes have negative attitudes towards Finns (Trankell 1974; Westin 1984). They suffered from feelings of incompetence and inferiority, or even guilt or shame in their relations with Swedes. The main reason for this was reported to be an inability to speak Swedish fluently.

This has lead to 'cumulative passivity' in closed networks: immigrants are passive even in situations in which they would have just as good opportunities to be active as other people. The life-style of people with a poor knowledge of Swedish was privatized, and they were the least active in sports and leisure time activities organized by the local Finnish society. Material values were central for these newly arrived immigrants who planned to return to Finland in the future.

On the other hand, an accumulation of linguistic resources in social networks by those who had lived longer in Sweden led to cumulative activity among immigrants. This did *not* imply that Swedish was used in these activities. Indeed, many people in the bilingual networks tended to engage in sports and other activities organized by the Finnish society. Nevertheless, the ethnic boundaries of the networks tended to weaken, at least in more distant relations. The life-style of bilingual immigrants is, in other words, more open and active. It does not, however, lead to a rejection of their own ethnic community and assimilation into Swedish society.

Some people in these networks—especially women—already enjoyed living in Sweden and felt that their roots were there. Some no longer think of returning to Finland, because their children go to school in Sweden. In a situation such as this, integration at least into the local Finnish community and organizations seems to be a 'rational choice' (cf. Banton 1977).

Ethnic mobilization
The ethnically limited social networks and the generation of Finnish associations in industrial areas of Sweden have also created the prerequisites for organized interaction and for the establishment of associations for the immigrants. However, this is not a sufficient explanation for the ethnic mobilization of Swedish Finns at the end of the 1970s and the beginning of the 1980s. It was during this period that the 'quiet Swedish Finns'—who previously had felt themselves helpless in the face of difficulties, tended to blame themselves for these difficulties, or rationalized any inequality that they experienced

(Jaakkola 1983a; 1984)—became a notable and demanding group which dares even to demonstrate civil disobedience in fighting for issues that it considers morally justified. This is demonstrated by the school strikes that have already spread to several localities in support of an improvement in the position of the Finnish language (Jaakkola 1987). The ethnic mobilization of Swedish Finns is also apparent in their association activity. Typical features of this activity during the 1970s were: a considerable increase in the number of associations; a strengthening of pressure-group activity and a fight for linguistic rights; and a specialization of associations, in that various occupational groups, leisure-time activity groups and pressure groups established their own associations (Jaakkola 1983b; 1987a).

This ethnic mobilization was not limited to Swedish Finns, although it is unique in comparison to other immigrant groups in Sweden and elsewhere in Europe. An increase in ethnic self-awareness and in ethnic organization was typical of many European minorities during the 1960s and the 1970s. However, these minorities were generally well-established territorial minorities (Allardt 1979). With the increase in the time-span of immigration, and the growth in the proportion of second-generation immigrants, the Swedish Finns also began to resemble these well-established linguistic minorities. Already today almost 40,000 Finnish-speaking children attend comprehensive school in Sweden, and there is about an equal number of Finnish-speaking children below school age in Sweden.

Various, in part diametrically opposing, explanations have been presented for the ethnic mobilization of minority groups. Some believe that a considerable weakening of the position of a minority leads to an ethnic revival, organization and protests. Others believe that an improvement in the position of a minority is the reason for ethnic movements. It is, however, a fact that an increasing number of states have begun to grant funds to reforms easing the position of minorities, for example to bilingual services. It has been suggested that this development is connected with the attempt of states to regulate conflicts: in order to avoid conflicts, the states have considered it best to grant at least some concessions to minorities (Allardt 1979; 22–6).

It is scarcely a coincidence that the ethnic organization and pressure-group activity of Swedish Finns strengthened during the second half of the 1970s, after the Swedish parliament unanimously passed in 1975 an immigration policy programme which, in comparison to the other countries of Europe, was unique. According to this programme, the state was to safeguard the right of minorities to protect and develop their language and culture on a level equal to that of the native population (Widgren 1980). The decision had been preceded by a lively public discussion of research results bearing out the linguistic and educational difficulties faced by Swedish Finnish children (for example, Skutnabb-Kangas and Toukomaa 1976). The discussion was opened in 1968 by Nils-Erik Hansegard in his book on bilingualism, semi-lingualism and alingualism; this book emphasized the significance of an education in the native language of children for their linguistic, social and emotional development.

It is probable that both this public debate and the consequent shift in immigration policy roused Swedish Finns to protect their linguistic rights. Another essential factor behind this was that the children of those who had come to Sweden during the years of peak migration were now coming to school age, and their problems became more acute. As a consequence of the expansion of Finnish-language education in Sweden, furthermore, there are now about 1500 Finnish teachers in Sweden, and they are active in the defence of Finnish-language education and communicate to the parents information on the linguistic problems and the rights of their children in school.

Among the rights brought by the new immigration policy was the right to receive education in one's native language in school (1976). Since then, the teaching of Finnish in the school system has essentially improved—in 1983 it was taught in 163 localities and two-thirds of Finnish speakers attending comprehensive school chose it as a subject. As many as seventy-five localities have Finnish-speaking classes, in which other subjects are also taught in Finnish. There are over 600 such Finnish-speaking classes in the first to sixth grades of comprehensive school in Sweden; in some schools, there are such classes also in the upper comprehensive school level and in senior secondary school. However, the establishment of such classes is not mandatory, this is open to the discretion of the municipality in question. Because of this, Swedish Finns have had to fight for the establishment of such classes, in some cases even by calling school strikes.

From the point of view of the possibility that migrants have of influencing matters, an important reform in 1975 was the enfranchisement and possibility of standing for office granted to all migrants who have lived in Sweden for at least three years. The shift in immigration policy also facilitated ethnic organization: from 1975 on, the state has subsidized national associations of migrants.

The growth and differentiation of Swedish–Finnish associations
The growth and functional differentiation of the network of Finnish organizations during different phases of immigration and Swedish immigration policy has been described in greater detail elsewhere (Jaakkola 1983b). Today, however, there are approximately 630 Finnish associations with various goals in Sweden. Of these, 216—of which 179 were active during 1983—are local multipurpose Finnish

societies ('Suomi societies') with a total membership of 52,000. Roughly 19,000 of the members are less than twenty-five years old.

The increase in the number of, and membership in, local Suomi societies belonging to the Central Association of Suomi Societies was notable during the years of peak immigration at the end of the 1960s and during the 1970s (see Table 8.1). However, the first Suomi society was established in Stockholm as early as 1894. In 1985 this was the largest of all Suomi societies, with nearly 2500 members.

The functional differentiation of the network of organizations is also a new phenomenon. During the 1970s, various pressure groups were organized. New occupational groups—immigrant teachers, clergy and church officers, students and radio reporters—established their own special organizations. When the children of immigrants reached school age, their Finnish parents organized themselves; today there are Finnish-language parent–teacher associations in over thirty localities. Artists—writers and painters—have their own associations. In the social sector, war veterans and war invalids became organized, as did Finnish alcoholics in their Alcoholics Anonymous groups. Both the Lutheran and the Orthodox church, as well as various free-church groups, arrange activities in the Finnish language. Finnish Karelians, Finnish Ingrians and Finnish gypsies have their own organizations in Sweden, as do Finns whose mother tongue is Swedish (see Table 8.2).

The role of the traditional Suomi societies has also changed. Suomi societies are multi-purpose organizations which used to arrange dances, sports and cultural activities for Finnish immigrants. Today they are also pressure groups in Swedish society, interested in questions of language policy and the political rights of immigrants. As

Table 8.1   The increase in the number of, and membership in, Suomi societies

	Number of local Suomi societies	Total number of members
1960	14	n.a.
1970	107	30,000
1980	197	56,000
1983	216[1]	52,000
1984	217	49,000
1985	218[2]	45,000

[1] The number of functioning (living) organizations was 179.
[2] The number of functioning (living) organizations was 170.

mentioned above, even school strikes and demonstrations have been arranged by immigrant organizations with the aim of improving the status of the Finnish language in schools, in the social sector and in services.

In other words, organizations do not only maintain the language and ethnic identity of Finnish immigrants in their own activities, they also serve as pressure groups which fight for the status of their language also outside their organizations.

Paradoxically, ethnic organization may also indicate the integration of immigrants into Swedish society. On the individual level,

Table 8.2   Voluntary organizations of Finnish immigrants in Sweden

Year established	Organization	Organizations today (1981 or 1982)	
		Number of (local) organizations	Total number of members
1725	Finnish parish	110	
1894	Finnish multi-purpose society	212	53,589
1939	Swedish-speaking Finns	23	3,630
1947	Finnish Ingrians[1]	9	369
1966	Social Democrats	82	8,000
1969	War veterans	9	1,000
1971	Finnish Karelians[1]	10	3,500
1971	Teachers[2]	13	746
1971	Communists	37	1,000
1971	Clergy and church officers	1	n.a.
1972	Gypsies	8	n.a.
1974	War invalids	1	760
1975	Writers	6	151
1977	Painters	1	150
1977	Radio reporters	1	32
1978	Students	5	1,500
1979	Parents[3]	30	n.a.
1983	Librarians	1	
1984	Social workers	1	n.a.

Notes:
1   The main part of Karelia and the whole of Ingria were Finnish provinces until 1917. Today they are part of the Soviet Union.
2   The number of local organizations totalled seventeen in 1985.
3   The number of local organizations totalled thirty-one in 1985.

participation in organizational activity indicates integration at least into the local community in Sweden. In addition to material goals—which are individual—members of organizations share common interests and collective goals. The organizations, on the other hand, have become more integrated into Swedish society; they are represented in various committees and working groups founded as a consequence of the new Swedish immigration policy (cf. Jaakkola 1983b).

Today many immigrants are even members of Swedish political parties. Finnish chapters of the socialist parties have been founded after immigrants were granted the right to vote in municipal elections in 1975. Today, there are eighty-two Finnish associations in the Swedish Social Democratic Party, and thirty-seven Finnish sections in the Communist party (see Table 8.2). Several members of municipal councils—253 ordinary members and 163 alternates in the 1979 elections— were born in Finland (Hammar 1982). Even two members of parliament (in 1983 and 1984) are Finnish immigrants, although they are Swedish citizens.

The leaders of immigrant organizations

Even though the ethnic self-awareness of immigrants grew during the 1970s, and there was considerable informal interaction among immigrants, organization did not come about spontaneously. As with other minorities in Europe (cf. Allardt 1979: 19–20), the initiative for ethnic organization in Sweden has come from those who had received a higher than average education. It is indicative that it was precisely the teachers, students and reporters who were the first to establish their own professional organizations.

According to a study carried out between 1982 and 1986 (cf. Jaakkola 1983b), the current leaders of the Finnish central organizations are from the middle class. Some have an academic degree. Many have previous experience in various organizations and hold political office. Education and experience in the running of an organization are advantages when a pressure group expands. Already today, one-fifth of the labour output in the larger central organizations is devoted to participation in various commissions established by the authorities and in the preparation of position papers.

The leaders of the local multi-purpose Finnish organizations resemble more 'ordinary' Finnish Swedes than do the leaders of national organizations and differentiated organizations. Of the members of the boards (N = 1230) of 161 Finnish multi-purpose organizations responding to my questionnaire in 1983–4, about half were workers and one-fifth worked in the lower service industries. One in every seven was either an upper white-collar worker (5 per cent), a teacher (5 per cent) or a student (6 per cent). Eight per cent of the members of the boards were pensioners and 2 per cent were housewives. Ninety per cent of all currently active Finnish organizations (161 of 179) responded to the questionnaire; the forms were filled out by the chairman of the board (Jaakkola 1987a).

First-generation immigrants are at the head of organizations of Finnish immigrants. The bulk have lived for a long time (ten to twenty-five years) in Sweden. Women are under-represented in the organizations; for example, only a quarter of the boards of the local multi-purpose organizations are chaired by women. The only specialized organizations chaired by women are those for radio reporters and artists. The activity within organizations tends to be cumulative: many of the same people are at the head of different Swedo-Finnish organizations, which tends to increase co-operation among the organizations.

Financial resources
The creation of parallel networks of Finnish organizations is costly. Because of the marginal position of the immigrants, both Finland and Sweden provide financial support for the organizations. The annual budget of one of the largest organizations, the Central Association of Multi-purpose Suomi Societies, totalled 9 million Swedish krone (1.5 million US dollars) in 1982. The subsidy provided by the Finnish state, however, is limited to the payment of the salaries of the officers of national organizations. The local Suomi societies function with the aid of Swedish subsidies and their own revenue. There is considerable variation in the financial strength: one-third of the 161 local Finnish organizations studied reported that their annual income during 1982 was less than 3650 US dollars, one-third had an income ranging between 3650 and 10,950 US dollars, and one-third had an income above this range. As the state and municipal subsidies depend on the number of members and the activity, the larger organizations were, as expected, better off than the smaller organizations: the correlation between the number of members and income was .77 (see Table 8.4).

The financial resources of all the specialized organizations are limited, their income is irregular, labour input voluntary and unpaid, and they lack various facilities.

Functions of multi-purpose associations
Contrary to the situation with differentiated organizations, the multi-purpose organizations reach people of different ages, belonging to different occupational groups and interested in different activities. The large majority of the members of Finnish organizations, however, are workers, and the second largest group is formed by those

*Table 8.3   The ethnic boundaries of Finnish multi-purpose
organizations (%)*

	Number of members				Total of all organizations
	0–99	100–199	200–499	500+	
	%	%	%	%	%
Organization has Swedish members	72	86	98	96	89
Organization has members from other countries	12	24	33	37	27
Sports teams of organization compete with Swedish teams	25	42	70	43	51
Cultural groups of organization perform for Swedish audiences	11	18	32	53	28
Number of responding organizations	28	50	50	30	158

outside of the pool of labour, by the youth, students, housewives or pensioners. In about four-fifths of the Finnish organizations, the proportion of white-collar workers was estimated to be about one-tenth. The organizations did not have sharp ethnic boundaries, as the majority (89 per cent) had at least some Swedish members and one in four had members from other countries. However, generally there were not more than thirty non-Finnish members (see Table 8.3).

The number of members in and the financial and personnel resources of the organizations are correlated with each other and with the number and variety of activities. In the larger and better-off organizations there is a greater tendency to have paid personnel. Their boards of directors also more often have teachers as members and those who are young who came to Sweden after the peak years of immigration, at the end of the 1970s or even later. Also, the rotation among board members is generally more rapid in the larger organizations (see Table 8.4).

The activity of the large organizations, furthermore, is well-rounded; in addition to informal get-togethers, parties and dances, this activity includes many types of athletics and cultural activities as well as pressure-group activity in educational, language and social policy and retirement matters (see Table 8.5). The ethnic heterogeneity of the members of these organizations is also greater than average (see Table 8.3).

The most common cultural activity undertaken by the Finnish organizations was drama: 45 per cent of the organizations had theatrical activity. The next most common forms of cultural activity were folk dances (41 per cent), choir (33 per cent) and other music (33 per cent). These cultural activities uphold Finnish traditions. Most common types of sports were volleyball (76 per cent), gymnastics (62 per cent), table tennis (51 per cent) and football (37 per cent). In athletic activity, Swedish is used in addition to Finnish, as many of the participants are second-generation immigrants, and especially many native Swedes or immigrants from other countries participate. The cumulation of activity in the organizations is demonstrated by the fact that the correlation between the numbers of cultural activities and the number of types of athletics is positive, .58.

In addition, the pressure group activity is connected with the size of the organization and the amount of athletic activity ($n = .52$) and cultural activity ($n = .47$). Three-quarters of all, and as many as 90 per cent of the largest organizations had attempted, during the preceding two years, to influence municipal decisions. These attempts at influence primarily dealt with the position of the Finnish language, or

Table 8.4   *Financial and personnel resources of Finnish multi-purpose organizations (%)*

	Number of members				Total of all organizations
	0–99	100–199	200–499	500+	
Income under US$ 3650 per annum	92	48	11	–	34
Income over US$ 10,950 per annum	–	16	69	90	24
Full-time personnel	4	6	42	80	31
White-collar workers on board of directors[1]	44	56	70	81	63
Teachers on board of directors[2]	22	26	27	48	30
Persons under twenty-five years old on board of directors[2]	16	38	34	37	33
At least four new board members[3]	28	72	72	90	71

1   At least one white-collar worker on board of directors. This category includes upper white-collar workers, teachers and students.
2   At least one teacher/one person under twenty-five years on board.
3   Members who have been on board for three years or less.

Table 8.5   Purposes of Finnish multi-purpose organizations (%)

| Forms of activity | Number of members | | | | Total of all organizations |
	0–99	100–199	200–499	500+	
Dances	43	85	98	97	84
Sports activity	92	96	100	100	95
—at least four types of athletics	32	50	83	97	71
Cultural activity	58	55	82	97	72
—at least three activities	6	15	36	70	31
Own newspaper	4	42	62	86	50
Social welfare project (alcohol, narcotics, etc.)	15	16	36	70	33
Pensioner activity	11	16	45	70	34
Interest-group activity[1]	52	67	78	90	72
Tried to influence the improvement of the position of the Finnish language in the municipality	19	41	53	82	47
Co-operation with Swedish organizations	42	50	66	80	60
Co-operation with Finland[2]	15	15	29	60	28

1 Organization has tried to influence municipal activity during recent years.
2 Organization has co-operation with municipalities, organizations or enterprises in Finland.

with attempts to receive subsidies or meeting facilities. Of the large organizations, 82 per cent had attempted in this way to improve the position of the Finnish language in Sweden. Table 8.5 shows that in addition, over one half of the organizations with less than 100 members had attempted to influence municipal decisions. However, only one-fifth of these had attempted to have an influence in the improvement of the position of the Finnish language in their municipality.

The large organizations are older ($r = .45$) and are to be found in localities where there has long been a number of Finnish immigrants. Paradoxically enough, the presentation of ethnic demands can be seen as a demonstration of their integration with their environment: it shows that the organizations are familiar with Swedish society and

Table 8.6   Channels of influence of Finnish organizations (%)

	Number of members				Total of all organizations
	0–99	100–199	200–499	500+	
Contacted municipal authorities	52	50	62	76	59
Contacted a municipal politician	26	36	43	76	44
Contacted a political party	7	20	23	41	22
Written to a newspaper	11	8	11	24	12
Participated in action group	3	10	8	24	11
Arranged demonstration	–	–	2	10	3
Responded to request for official position on some issue	4	20	32	59	28

dare to act in Sweden in promotion of their own interests. This is also shown by contacts with Swedish organizations and the larger variety of the channels of influence used by the larger organizations (see Tables 8.5 and 8.6). Over three-quarters of them had, within the preceding two years, contacted municipal authorities, and as many had turned to a municipal politician. In the larger organizations, it was also quite common to have responded to an enquiry regarding an official position, written to the newspapers, participated in action groups and arranged demonstrations (see Table 8.6). The correlation between the number of channels of influence and the size of the organization was .39.

Table 8.7   Contacts of Finnish organizations with authorities and politicians (%)

	Number of times during preceding two years					
	0	1–2	3–4	5–9	10+	Total
Sent letter to authorities	55	15	11	9	10	100
Visited authority	47	16	11	8	18	100
Sent letter to politician	74	14	6	4	2	100
Visited politician	65	17	5	7	6	100

Table 8.8   Representation of Finnish organizations (%)

	Number of members				Total of all organizations
	0–99	100–199	200–499	500+	
Society representatives elected to regional level of Finnish society activity	25	57	78	87	63
Society representatives elected to national level of society activity	11	22	40	67	34
Society represented in municipal immigration council	29	24	41	73	40
Board members of society have elected municipal position	18	42	32	52	37
Board members of society have elected position in labour unions	39	58	47	56	40
Board members of society have elected position in other Swedish association	33	46	51	54	43

In attempting to influence municipal decisions, the Swedish Finns turn more often to the authorities than to political parties. Table 8.7 shows how actively the organizations on average have been in contact with the authorities and political parties. Also the number of contacts is correlated with the size of the organization; for example the correlation between the number of members in the organization and the sending of letters to the authorities is .43. Two-thirds of the organizations believed that they had succeeded at least in part in influencing municipal decisions.

The potential that the larger organizations have for influencing matters is increased by the fact that, first of all, they have the most representatives in the higher levels of the organization itself, on the regional and national levels. Three-quarters of the largest organizations were also represented in the muncipality's advisory board, the immigration council. Their boards more often have members who also hold elected municipal positions or elected positions in trade unions or other Swedish organizations (see Table 8.8).

Moving on to the federation board level, which represents the Finnish societies on the national level, one can see also that there the positions are generally filled by middle-aged men who have been in Sweden for over fifteen years. There are only two women on the twelve-member federation board. The members of this board have normally worked their way up from the factory floor to white-collar occupations or to special 'immigrant occupations' such as director of an immigrant affairs office, language teacher, office head or so on; only a quarter of the members were workers at the time they were on the board. They have a well-rounded organization career, and most have also been active in leftist parties. The majority (eight out of twelve) were members of their municipal council or of the educational, cultural or immigration affairs board of their municipality.

The influence of the federation is increased by the academically trained personnel who, in addition to the federation board, represent the organization in the many committees and commissions resulting from the new immigration policy. The amount of such participation has increased greatly during the 1970s and the beginning of the 1980s (Jaakkola 1983b; 44). It shows, on the one hand, an increase in the interest that the organization has in many social sectors and, on the other hand, a recognition of the position of the organization as a Swedish Finnish pressure group in Swedish society.

The federation and the district organizations have arranged cultural and athletic competitions for Finnish societies and have helped train personnel. They also attempt to mobilize the pressure activity of the local Finnish societies. A demonstration of this is the Finnish-language campaign arranged during 1981 and 1982, together with other Swedish Finnish organizations. During the campaign, as many as sixty-three Suomi societies delivered their proposals in different municipalities in Sweden for the improvement of the position of the Finnish language in different social sectors. When the budget cut in 1982 threatened to limit the teaching of Finnish, a large demonstration was arranged in Sergel Square in Stockholm, and within a week over 10,000 Swedish Finns had signed a petition on behalf of the teaching of Finnish.

Also, in order to retain Finnish-language classes, school strikes were arranged at the beginning of the 1980s in many localities—Gothenburg, Mölndal, Västerås, Koping, Kalix and Stockholm. The strike by the children of Finnish-speaking families in Stockholm in 1984 lasted for almost two months, and almost all the pupils in the first to sixth classes (a total of 120 children) took part. This strike received an exceptional degree of attention in the mass media, and it was even the subject of ministerial-level discussions between Sweden and Finland. The strike ended in a compromise between the school and the strikers. Although the strikes were arranged by the parents of the pupils, the Finnish-language parent–teacher associations and the local Suomi societies also gave them their support.

Contacts with Finland
Finnish immigrants in Sweden differ from those who come from further away in that it is possible to obtain both material resources and intellectual and cultural stimulation from their former homeland. In some cases, it has been possible to recruit people from Finland to take charge of immigrant organizations in Sweden. Cultural exchange and visits by leading politicians have been common.

One new feature has been the establishment of contacts with organizations of Swedish speakers in Finland. The rights of Swedish speakers in an officially bilingual country such as Finland are a useful bench-mark for pressure groups in Sweden, despite the obvious historical and social differences. The number of Swedish speakers in Finland is about the same as that of Finnish speakers in Sweden. Although the drawing of parallels between these two minorities has been a source of irritation for many, prominent Swedish-speaking politicians and cultural figures in Finland have recently begun to support actively the linguistic demands of Finnish speakers in Sweden. Their views have been given much attention in the Swedish mass media.

Because of the Nordic cultural agreement (1971) and the Nordic language agreement (1981), Finnish speakers in Sweden are in a special position when compared to non-Nordic minorities. According to the language agreement, Nordic citizens have the right, at least in principle, to use their mother tongue when dealing with the authorities in other Nordic countries. Freedom of movement among the Nordic countries also provides the possibility of returning to Finland, a phenomenon which has become more common recently, precisely due to the schooling difficulties of the children of immigrants, despite the improvement in the position of the Finnish language in the Swedish school system. Also, Swedish Finns can receive, on request, Swedish citizenship more rapidly than other immigrants, after having lived in Sweden for two years. It is also easy to have Finnish citizenship restored after returning to Finland.

Own institutions
Voluntary organizations are in themselves not enough to make up for the absence of cultural facilities and economic institutions. The creation of such facilities is of considerable significance for the future of the Finnish-speaking minority in Sweden. A few institutions already

Table 8.9   Own institutions of Finnish immigrants in Sweden

Year established	Type of institution
1967	Educational council
1969	Finland Hall Foundation
1972	Advanced education institute (in Haparanda)
1975	Finnbook Publishers
1975	Swedo-Finnish language board
1977	Archive
1981	Art gallery
1981	The President Urho Kekkonen Scholarship Fund
1982	Advanced education institute (in Axevalla)

exist. Most of them were created during the 1970s, the decade of ethnic organization by Finns in Sweden. There are two advanced education institutes (one in the northern and one in the south-western part of Sweden) as well as a multi-purpose building in Stockholm which houses the Swedo-Finnish Educational Council, the Swedo-Finnish Archive, and an art gallery (the Suomi Galleria). The Swedo-Finnish Linguistic Board has devoted its attention to the language needs of Finns living in Sweden. Finnbook Co-operative Publishers and the President Urho Kekkonen Scholarship Fund are two economic institutions (see Table 8.9).

The short-term goals of Finnish organizations in Sweden are the establishment of a Swedo-Finnish cultural foundation, a professional theatre and a daily newspaper to be published in conjunction with their own papers, which appear less frequently.

Summary
In the late 1970s and the beginning of the 1980s, the community of Finnish immigrants in Sweden acquired the characteristics of a permanent ethnic minority. It has not become assimilated with its new environment, but has instead developed into an ethnically self-aware minority group acting in pursuit of its own interests. This development has taken place, from an international perspective, in favourable circumstances such as:

1   the short distance and good communications with the country of departure;
2   the slightness of cultural, socio-economic and political differences;
3   the special Nordic agreements;

4 the exceptionally progressive immigration policy adopted by Sweden, recognizing the rights of immigrants to the maintenance of their language and culture;

5 the fact that the Swedish Finns are the largest immigrant group in Sweden, a fact which at least in principle makes it possible to arrange Finnish-language services in at least the largest Finnish localities.

The ethnic mobilization of Swedish Finns during the 1970s and the beginning of the 1980s has, in this paper, been construed as a consequence of

1 the heightening of the problems of immigrants following the reaching of school age by the children of immigrants and of second-generation immigrants;

2 the lively discussion on the school difficulties of these children and on 'semi-lingualism' and 'alingualism';

3 the increase in the level of demands of immigrants after the new immigration policy (adopted in 1975) recognized the immigrants' rights to the maintenance and development of their own language.

Paradoxically enough, the defence of their own ethnic identity and linguistic rights led the organizations to closer contacts with the decision-makers. The organizations have become mediators between the decision-makers and 'ordinary' Swedish Finns. It is also interesting that along with the growth of Swedish state and municipal subsidies to the organizations, the demands related to language policy have also increased. It remains to be seen whether the school strikes which have been so sharply condemned by the Swedish authorities will affect their attitude towards the organizational activity of Swedish Finns.

References

Allardt, Erik (1979) 'Implications of the ethnic revival in modern, industrialized society. A comparative study of the linguistic minorities in western Europe', *Commentationes Scientiarum Socialium*, vol. 12, Societas Scientiarum Fennica, Helsinki.

Banton, Michael (1977) 'Rational choice: A theory of racial and ethnic relations', *Working Papers on Ethnic Relations*, no. 8, SSRC research unit on ethnic relations, University of Bristol.

Barth, Fredrick (1969) 'Introduction', in Fredrick Barth (ed.), *Ethnic groups and boundaries*, Little, Brown & Co, Boston.

Hammar, Tomas (1982) *Invandrarkanddiater i 1979 ars kommunala val*, Expertgruppen för invandringsforskning (Commission for Immigration Research, Sweden), no. 20, Stockholm.

Hansegard, Nils-Erik (1968) *Tvasprakighet eiler halvsprakighet?*, Aldus/Bonniers, Stockholm.

Jaakkola, Magdalena (1983a) *Finnish immigrants in Sweden: Networks and life styles* research group for comparative sociology, University of Helsinki, research reports no. 30.

Jaakkola, Magdalena (1983b) *Sverigefinlandarnas ethniska organisationer*, Expertgruppen för invandringsforskning (Commission for Immigration Research Sweden), no. 22, Stockholm.

Jaakkola, Magdalena (1984) *Siirtolaiselamaa. Tutkimus ruotsin-suomalaisista siirtolaisyhteisona* (English summary: Immigrant life: Networks, life styles and ethnic mobilization of Finnish immigrants in Sweden), doctoral dissertation, University of Helsinki.

Jaakkola, Magdalena (1987a) *Sverigefinnovras ethniska mobilisering* (English summary: The ethnic mobilization of Swedish Finns), Centrum för Invandringsforskning (Center for Research in International Migration and Ethnicity), Stockholm (forthcoming).

Jaakkola, Magdalena (1987b) *Skolstrejken i Rinkeby* (English summary: School strike in Rinkeby, Stockholm), Centrum för Invandringsforskning (Center for Research in International Migration and Ethnicity), Stockholm (forthcoming).

Kuusela, Jorma (1974) *Sex Slags liv. Ett försök till systematisk analys av invandrarnas an passning*. D-uppsats, sociologiska institutionen vid Stockholms Universitet, Stockholm.

Reinans, Sven (1982) 'Finsksprakiga i Sverige. Seminaraiet Sverige-finnar och finlandssvenskar', *Hanaholmen*, 15–16 November.

Skutnabb-Kangas, Tove and Toukomaa, Pertti (1976) *Teaching migrant children's mother-tongue and learning the language of the host country in the context of the socio-cultural situation of the migrant family*, The Finnish National Commission for Unesco, Helsinki.

Trankell, Arne (1974) 'Svenskarnas fordomar mot invandrare', *Invandrarutredningen*, 4, Statens offentliga utredningar (SOU) 1974: 70, 121–73, Stockholm.

Westin, Charles (1984) *Majoritet om minoritet. En studie i etnisk tolerans i 80-talets Sverige*, Liber, Stockholm.

Widgren, Jonas (1980) *Svensk invandrarpolitik*, Liber, Lund.

Wiman, Ronald (1975) *Tyovoiman kansainvalisen muuttoliikkeen mekanismis* (English summary: *The mechanism of international labour migration*), Elinkeinoelaman tutkimuslaitos (ETLA) (The Research Institute of the Finnish Economy), B 9, Helsinki.

218

9 Spanish Immigrant Associations in the Netherlands and Switzerland and the Problem of Ethnic Identity[1]

A. Verdonk, S. Mancho, C. Peredo, M.A. de Prada, J.L. Recio, L. Seoane and R. van Soest

This study was based in the first place on a study of associations and secondly on young people's conceptions of ethnic identity.

The study of associations was based upon a census of associations having the following characteristics: that they were constituted by or on behalf of migrants, that they were voluntary, stable, active, formalized, without commercial interests, legally recognized and that they covered various fields of a migrants' life, such as culture, recreation, education and sport.

On this basis 124 associations were found amongst 24,000 Spanish immigrants in the Netherlands (one association for 200 immigrants) and 177 associations amongst 100,000 Spanish immigrants with 'permission B and C' (that is, excluding temporary contract workers) in Switzerland (one association for 564 immigrants).

After the construction of a list, a sample of thirty associations was chosen, fourteen from the Netherlands and sixteen from Switzerland. These were chosen according to the criteria of origin of the association, type of principal activity (for example sport, culture, education, political or trade union activity, simple conviviality) and regional distribution (see Figure 9.1) to ensure a representative cross-section.

The questionnaire used in the Franco-Portuguese study was applied to these thirty associations. Information was collected on the following topics:

—location
—history

219

*Figure 9.1(a)   Density of Associations of Spanish Emigrants
in the Netherlands*

Figure 9.1(b)   Density of Association of Spanish Emigrants in Switzerland

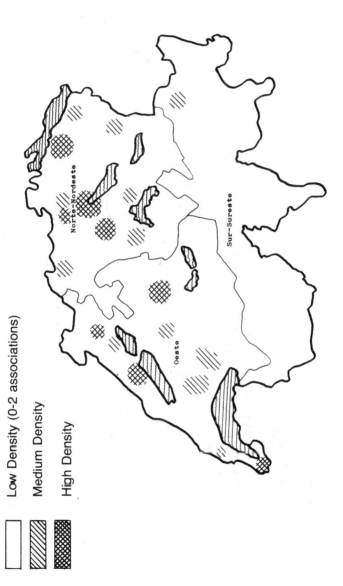

Low Density (0-2 associations)

Medium Density

High Density

—structure and functioning
—evolution
—network of relations
—activities
—cultural activities
—relations with youth
—equipment.

Methods for the study of young people's identity involved a combination of material derived from the study of associations and other material, including interviews with qualified informants about migration, the analysis of discourse in fourteen discussion groups, forty-one personal interviews, bibliographical research and the life-histories of six Spanish families.

The history of Spanish associations

The Netherlands
This history starts with the first migration at the end of the 1950s and the beginning of the 1960s.

The situation of associations in the Netherlands is unusual in that, at first, factories organized many Spanish centres (especially sporting groups). On the other hand, there have been very few instances of organization by Catholic missions.

A second stage was the creation of centres for convivial reunions and recreational purposes, again funded by the factories. Political parties and trade unions also existed, but clandestinely because they feared reprisals from the Franco administration. Such groups sometimes took the initiative in making claims on behalf of the centres.

From the end of the 1960s Spanish centres were funded increasingly by the Dutch government via the so-called foundations for help to foreign workers. These foundations established organized social work with both Dutch and foreign employees.

Since 1983, welfare work for immigrants has become the task of general institutions with concomitant changes in the functions of immigrant associations. With family reunions and the birth of new children in the host society, a need for new organizations arises. Typical of these are the Padres de Familias (associations of parents) intended to defend Spanish culture and to start classes in Spanish language and culture especially for the children. These associations asked for and obtained Spanish teachers from the Spanish government. The Padres de Familias formed a European confederation which was recognized as a representative body by the Spanish government.

The Padres de Familias have not developed relations with Dutch institutions and culture. As a result the children of Spanish immigrants are not completely identified with them and are inclined to form their own associations. New youth clubs arise which are ambivalent with respect to the Padres de Familias because they fear that attempts will be made by parents to control the clubs. These clubs are the latest development in the history of Spanish associations.

Two other points need to be made. One concerns the demand of the European confederation to make structures democratic. This led to conflict between the Communist and Socialist parties and to a schism in the organization. The second is that Spanish associations have remained disconnected from other immigrant movements. They direct themselves towards the Spanish rather than the Netherlands government. Only in the last few years have the associations been represented in the LSOBA, the national board of the organizations of foreign workers.

Switzerland

The first fundamental difference from the Netherlands is the absence of any organization on behalf of immigrants created by Swiss institutions. The associations had three roots:

—a spontaneous movement to organize sport and recreational groups (some of these groups are regionally based, especially Galician ones);

—organizations promoted by migrants with a hidden political ideology, normally sponsored by militant members of the Communist party;

—groups formed under the influence of Catholic missions to which immigrants came for multiple reasons during the first years of migration and which were vivid centres of immigrant life.

Later development was different in these various types. The recreational and sports clubs flourished during the early 1970s and were strongly supported by the Spanish Institute for Emigration, which was disinclined on the other hand to support political groups. Such political groups started to organize in 1965, and in 1969 founded the Association of Spanish Workers in Emigration in Switzerland (ATEES) to defend the rights of Spanish workers.

At first the ATEES received the collaboration of many immigrants of diverse ideological tendencies in its fight for the democratization of official Spanish institutions in foreign countries, in its fight for workers' rights and as an alternative to simple convivial and recreational associations. Because of its close connection with the Communist party, however, it lost members and, with this, much of its vitality. Another type of political organization was represented by the Federation of Associations of Spanish Emigrants in Switzerland (FAACS) which was founded to co-ordinate immigrant associations in 1980.

Associations of Padres de Familias appeared at the end of the 1960s and expanded all over Switzerland after the First Congress on Education in 1975.

Also founded at this time was a Confederation of Associations and School Councils of Spanish People in Switzerland (CAEES). This now has seventy associations and various regional groups. Some minority groups of the association of Padres de Familia, mainly in the French part of Switzerland, rejected CAAES because of their Communist political links. The most notable of these is the APLA Autonoma de Lausanne which has an impressive educational record in connection with the school 'La Baracca' of Renens.

Casas de España or other centres organized by the Spanish government such as are found in the Netherlands do not exist in Switzerland except for the welcome-centre in Geneva and the one now being founded in Zurich. Another organization, though not strictly an association, was Ateneos Populares which appeared on the scene at the end of the 1960s with cultural and educational objectives. ATEES and CAEES are indirectly represented in the consultative councils for foreigners at local level. In the federal consultative commission, ATEES represents the Spanish immigrants and UGT the trade unions.

The category of 23,000 temporary workers (with permission A) participate very little in the associations though they go to the centres for social and recreational purposes.

Results of the questionnaire survey

Findings may be summarized under the headings location and equipment, history and functioning, membership, network of relations and activities.

About one-third of the thirty associations studied (fourteen Dutch and sixteen Swiss) are associations of Padres de Familias whose principal activity lies in educational and school issues. About one-third are centres which promote convivial relations, recreation and sport. This category includes three regional centres especially for the people of Galicia and Andalucia. Three centres are more polyfaceted such as the Casa de España which encourages relations and friendships and provides certain informative and cultural activities accessible to the whole Spanish population. Finally three centres have a political or trade union character, and one association is concerned with social assistance.

Location and equipment

Two of the thirty associations do not have their own premises (both in Switzerland), four own their buildings, and the rest either rent or have the use of rooms. Renting occurs more in the Netherlands, ownership in Switzerland. In the Netherlands the foundations for help of foreign workers in the municipal administration provide premises which are also used by other ethnic groups including Dutch people. In Switzerland there is only one case in which Spanish immigrants use buildings also used by other groups of foreigners. In the Netherlands one finds the headquarters of associations in areas of dense foreign concentration, not necessarily of Spaniards. In Switzerland they are to be found in areas of Spanish concentration.

The great majority of associations have a room for reunions and two-thirds have a room for recreation (more in the Netherlands than in Switzerland). Two-thirds have a secretariat (more in Switzerland than in the Netherlands). Twenty per cent of associations reserve a room for the use of youth. Two-thirds of the associations have telephone, typewriter and card-indexes of members. More than half have a television and a film projector (mostly in the Netherlands). Twenty per cent have a slide projector and 40 per cent loudspeakers and amplifiers. Eighty per cent have packs of Spanish cards and the usual games. Two-thirds have a bar and sometimes a kitchen where typical Spanish dishes are prepared. Seventy per cent have a library, but only 50 per cent a reading room. Books are given by Spanish institutions, such as the Institute of Emigration and the Ministry of Culture. Apart from a few centres dealing with populations from particular regions, nearly all the books are in Castilian. Some of the books are about literature, geography and history, but most are for recreation and diversion. More than 50 per cent of the libraries have a special shelf for children and youth.

History and functioning

Seven of the twenty associations analysed were founded before 1965, eleven between 1965 and 1975 and the others later. Two-thirds are recognized officially by authorities of both states, eight by Spain only. In 80 per cent of cases migrants themselves have been the founders, but four associations were created by Spanish institutions, for example Casas de España. Nearly all of them carefully follow rules and norms in relation to change of directorate, tasks assigned, the obligation to hold meetings and so on. The directorate in nearly half of the associations has seven or fewer members; more than two-thirds have less than eleven members. Directors can be re-elected without limits. Forty per cent of associations have a general assembly three to four times a year.

Regarding funding, the Swiss state does not pay anything whereas the Netherlands offers significant support via the foundations for help to foreign workers. The Spanish government gives small contributions in both countries. All this, however, is not sufficient to pay for the associations' activities and two-thirds of the associations receive money from their members or from activities such as the running of a bar or bingo. The Casas de España have their costs completely covered by the Spanish administration.

Membership
In spite of lists of members it is difficult to know exact numbers, sometimes because the counting unit is different (it may be individuals or it may be families). Our questionnaire shows that the majority of the associations have 100 to 150 members, 20 per cent have between fifty and 100, two have less than fifty members. The Casa de Espana does not have members. Everyone can use its services.

One-third of those interviewed say that they have fewer members than before, mainly because of return migration. Half, however, say that they have more members now. Sixty per cent have more men than women, the remainder have equal numbers of the two sexes. The associations of Padres de Familias usually have equal proportions. Ninety per cent say that young people do not participate, though 30 per cent think that they have an interest.

Participation is highest in festive celebrations but lower in recreational activities and lowest in conference-type activities. Only 10 per cent of the associations claim that the majority of members are interested in the association.

People of the country of residence do not participate in the associations' activities except on special occasions. Those who do are the workmates, friends or neighbours of members.

Members of the associations do not differ much in occupational activity, region of origin, and years in country of residence. Most of them are in low occupational categories. They come generally from Galicia, Andalucía and Extremadura. Nearly 60 per cent say that their members have lived between fifteen and twenty years in the country of settlement, 23 per cent between ten and fifteen years. Half of the associations have members of an average age of between thirty and forty, while 30 per cent have members of an average age of between forty and fifty years.

Networks of relations
Associations and centres are not co-ordinated or federated on local or regional level, but on national or European level. It is a hierarchical system with a delegation of duties and powers which are re-

cognized by the Spanish administration as representing Spanish emigrants. It is very rare to find cases in which relations are maintained on local level with professional organizations, trade unions, political parties and organizations for the help of immigrants amongst other immigrant communities. Only 20 per cent of associations have some relations at the local level. These are limited to the subjects of education and school organization (in the case of one-third) or funding (in another third).

Activities
Around 30 per cent organize traditional recreational and sport activities or give room for recreation and friendship among the Spaniards themselves.

Around 35 per cent (mainly the associations of the Padres de Familias) work to promote a Spanish school for a better education of the children and the adult population.

Sixty per cent organize films either fortnightly or during feasts and on special occasions. Most of the films are in Spanish, but some are in regional languages. The main objective is diversion but in four associations films were seen as imparting information (four cases) or knowledge of a regional Spanish culture (two cases). Only in one case was the film intended to improve knowledge of the culture of the country of residence.

Nearly half of those interviewed say that they organize theatre, but only a quarter has its own proper theatre groups or dance-groups. Two-thirds say that they sometimes organize encounters, seminars and symposia on migration themes open to the whole immigrant colony.

All the interviewed organize feasts which mostly coincide with Spanish ones. Two-thirds of the youth participate, together with parents and friends of the country of residence (in 40 per cent of cases) and immigrants of other nationalities (in seven cases).

Slightly more than one-third have their own football team participating in a self-organized competition. Apart from this, only four of the thirty analysed associations organize anything specific for youth, though a third organize classes in Spanish and the language of the country of settlement. Excursions and travelling form an activity of 80 per cent of the associations.

Though the second generation's fate is much in the minds of parents and though there is a young man or woman in the electorate of half of the associations, in fact they do little for youth. One-third of the associations receives queries from young people but only eight are able to give effective answers.

The associations and the significance of identity for Spanish migrants
To answer this question we will define one concept of identity and the methods used for studying it, and then give an account of our results.

The concept of identity and ethnic identity as an ideology
A review of the literature revealed two important approaches to the study of cultural and ethnic identity, a primordialist and a situationist one (R. van Soest and A. Verdonk 1984). The first one sees identity implicitly as something quasi-objective, a stable set of traits which individuals receive via enculturation by parents and kin. The second one rejects this quasi-objective character and claims the actual situation to be the primary factor in the awakening of ethnic conscious-ness.[2] Ethnic identity is a social construction by members of ethnic in-groups and outside society as a result of their interaction.

Literature is unequivocal in linking ethnic identity and ideology. An ideological component is considered to be present in the 'new ethnicity' (Stein 1975) or 'ethnic identity is ideology' (Aronson 1976).

Combining elements of the primordial and situationist app-roaches, we take the view that ethnic identity can be defined as ideo-logy for pursuing social and psychological interests of an ethnic group and its members, coming out of and materialized in social practices of the group and its members (R. van Soest and A. Verdonk 1985: 13).

Primordial interests refer to primary inclusive affective bonds people have with their family and kin. Ideology therefore includes patterns of opinion and affects.

> Collective ethnic identity is a dynamic whole of explicit and implicit vague and outlined conceptions, images and feelings of an ethnic group, which refer to society, the ethnic group and its position in society, coming out of and realised in social practices of the group.[3]

Individual ethnic identity is defined likewise, *mutatis mutandis*.

Methods used in the study of identity
Consequent on the above, analysis of ethnic identity can be done by unravelling the ideologies of ethnic groups or of their members, which is exactly the method the Spanish members of our team have used in the discourse analysis of discussion groups of Spanish youth and their parents. Though these discussion groups did not treat specifically the relations between associations and ethnic identity, the discursive structures of the discourses are relevant for our sub-ject. These include self-retreat and integration.

We also present interviews with Spanish individuals of which two types will be reproduced, one of a daughter of an 'association family' and one of a son of an ordinary Spanish family without any contacts

228

with associations. The daughter chooses to identify with Spain, the son with the Netherlands. This qualitative material cannot provide the basis of a generalization, but is nonetheless illustrative of types of second-generation response.

Results from the study of associations
Associations certainly serve as conditions for the construction of identity by their members. This is clear from a summary of findings about associations:

1 Associations have fulfilled an important role for the first generation as providing an opportunity for social relations and as a forum for claiming rights both in Spain and in the country of settlement. In the beginning many associations played an active political role against Franco's Spain. Afterwards, in the middle of the 1970s the children's need for Spanish education and culture became the most urgent concern. Now the problem of youth needs attention.
2 Associations have been harbours of traditional Spain, though already in collision with modern secularized and industrial contexts.
3 With few exceptions, Spanish associations have no relation with other ethnic groups. Thus isolation has prevented effective negotiation with the host country.
4 Young people do not participate in associations very much. This is probably because these young people have partly assimilated the language and culture of the host country, including its leisure-time pursuits. There is also criticism by young people of the politicization of associations and the rivalry and jealousy which exist amongst their leaders. But these are probably given as a justification of their stand rather than being the cause of it.[4]

We conclude that political issues (for example, the opposition to Franco, the fight for democracy at all levels) have been of importance, but educational goals, cultural goals and simple conviviality have also been objectives of the associations.

All these elements have shaped the ethnic identity described as ideology. In terms of our definition: associations have offered the sort of social practices which are expressions of and which enhance ethnic identity, considered as a bundle of ideas, feelings, formulations for pursuing material and primordial interests of the ethnic group and its members.

Discursive structures in the discussion groups[5]
Our Spanish colleagues conclude that two discursive structures give

229

coherence to the several discourses. All discourses are marked by a vivid consciousness of being a foreigner in a host country. Within that there are two reactions, being an outsider and trying to integrate by being an insider. These two reactions are called discursive structures because they give focus to the discourses of several discussion groups. They are fundamental forms of ethnic-identity construction.

The option of being an outsider suggests an ideal of communication with other people in the same situation. Within the ethnic minority community the Spaniard does not have the sense of being stigmatized. Communication between Spaniards goes to the heart, without a sense of being excluded. The following are some examples of relevant discourse:

> I am going there every summer and I may choose two friendships because my brother-in-law is Dutch, married with my sister. I have two milieus for choice. But I am going always to the Spanish milieu. Naturally! And what do I find? I see a lot of Spanish men and women who are completely outsiders. And, for instance, when I go to a Spanish group, I am Spanish, and I am at a margin too like they are, because we are *all* Spanish. When I go to a Dutch group it is different, because I am the Spanish girl but all the others are Dutch. It is completely different whether you go with a group of Spaniards or with a group of Dutch.

> You have to change your coat very much being Swiss.

> There is no Dutchman who likes the foreigners, but other people than we don't dare say it.

> You are talking with him and he is. . . Yes, yes, he argues with you. Then you turn your back and he has got to speak.

The logic of integration manifests itself in the nearly obsessive need to deny discrimination or to explain it in terms of the 'self-marginalization' of the immigrant versus the native-born. It is the family which imposes the mark of being a foreigner on the youth, impeding its liberty to decide for or against integration. In order to integrate, the youth has to deny his family and the internal codes of the immigrant group. The young person who chooses to integrate seems obsessed with dissimulating the marks of his Spanish origin, including language, habits and even his physical appearance: 'In Switzerland', as one participant in a discussion group put it, 'the major mistake one may commit is trying to be a Spaniard in Switzerland'. And, 'If one isn't fair and tall, the chance of integration does not seem that good. I speak German and I am like a German.' Not surprisingly the strongest advocates of integration in both meetings were fair.

If in the logic of marginalization the most determining factor was the group of equals, in this case what is important is the relationship between unequals. In the view of the Spanish, the Dutch and the Swiss place emphasis upon order, work, nationality, and these qualities are important for those who want social recognition:

> But if you, for instance, if you prepare yourself enough, that for instance you can be better than a Swiss person; if you are prepared better than he is, they will accept you, though you are an immigrant and you, naturally, you have to adapt yourself.

One might say therefore that the option for adaptation is the opposite of that for setting oneself on the margin. The option of adaptation means putting one's ideal in a communication determined by law and regularity.

Both attitudes, nevertheless, have the same goal: to wipe out the national mark, or the stigma of inferiority. One revitalizes the Spanish identity to do this, the other the Swiss/Dutch.

Two examples: Jiminez the all-in Spanish family and Juan the Spanish Dutchman

A life-history of the Jiminez family[6] illustrates fairly well the orientation towards Spanish society and the chance of a Spanish identity and the use of association membership to express that attitude.

The contrasting case of Juan, the Spanish boy, who ran away from his family at the moment they obliged him to return to his country illustrates the 'logic of integration'.

The Jiminez family

This family emigrated twenty years ago from Andalucia to the Netherlands for economic reasons—to save money to buy a flat. The family has four children. The mother considers the unity of the family their supreme value (the interpreter, J.L. Recio, suggests that it is the key to their symbolic universe).

The information which the Jiminez family exchange with one another to establish a congruence of images within the family goes back to the childhood of the parents. By doing this they contribute not only to accentuating the continuity of the family and all of its members, but to demonstrating in a subtle way the superiority of Andalucian values, reinforcing in this way the will not to acculturate within the country of residence, but to 'save' oneself for reintegration into the original society.

As regards the boundaries of the migrant and family system the eldest daughter (nineteen years old) observes that her parents are always busy; they participate very actively in the association of Padres de Familias of which Jiminez was one of the founders. Because of the network of friendships, created via the association, the children were in a natural way introduced within it, accepting various roles in the association. In this way the parents have produced two effects; first, an extension of the family system via the network of relations and friends in the association and, secondly, the creation of internal bonds, which facilitate continued affiliation to the culture of the society of origin. This has, of course, only been possible because of the simultaneous actions of other families, members of the association. These together laid the foundation of a youth club and for cultural and festive encounters especially at weekends.

Though the association stimulates the development of socio-cultural identity and helps towards reintegration in the parents' country, it may at the same time foster isolation from Dutch society. In fact, the eldest daughter describes Spanish young people she knows as much more acculturated than herself. They have adopted Dutch habits and customs and would have to make a considerable effort to re-adapt if they went home.

In general, the parents steer and limit the experiences of their children indirectly, via successful cultivation of Spanish cultural identity. They see their dances (*Sevillanas*) as something natural. They have typical regional costumes, apparently made by the mother, and are invited to dance at feasts of other immigrant associations and even Dutch groups.

It is not surprising that the eldest daughter has built up a strong preference for Spain. She has made her choice, identifying completely with Spain like the rest of her nuclear and 'association' families. She has not identified with Dutch society: 'These people I cannot digest'. In spite of this she admits to feeling somewhat strange both in Spain and in the Netherlands and that she

> will need time. I cannot get used to being here . . . well, I know that returning to Spain, I shall get slowly accustomed there, naturally being Spanish, and that is that, and the day will come . . . that I forget those habits that I had here.

Seen here is an explicit 'voluntary' identification with Spain, which nevertheless admits to some ambivalence, because of the expected long process of reintegrating in Spain again.

Concluding remarks on the Jiminez family   We have in this abstract of a life-history the following:

—The use of a more cultural-anthropological vocabulary for identity (socio-cultural identity, acculturation, cultivation of Spanish identity) which is in clear contrast with ethnic identity as ideology.

—A declaration of preference for Spain against the Netherlands which is, in terms of our concept of identity as a subjective social orientation, a bundle of ideas and feelings related to the ethnic

group itself or in comparison with the natives, that is as ideology.
—The inseparability of behaviour, interaction and verbal reflection. Identity manifests itself as much in what people do as in what they say. Ideas and practical actions go hand-in-hand.
—The negative effects of associational active life for acculturation to Dutch ways of life and isolation from Dutch society.

Juan and the Netherlands option

In Juan we find the contrasting case of a nineteen-year-old boy who ran away from home because he refused to return with his parents to their very poor region of origin. He was only five and a half years old when he came with his mother to the Netherlands to be reunited with his father. He went to infant school, elementary school, then to a school for slow students and finished in a low technical school. He got a certificate as a metal worker in 1979. He works now in a big shipyard. His parents were unable to read or write. His father did all types of work in the factory, his mother worked in agriculture in Spain and in office-cleaning in the Netherlands.

Juan admits to being a Spaniard but doesn't regret his inability to speak Spanish very well. During our interview he spoke Dutch. Next year he will receive Dutch nationality and do his military service. He will stay in the Netherlands and only return to Spain for holidays. In the life of this boy constant beating up by his father has had a great influence:

> If you are hurt, humiliated and beaten up for such a long time, then you choose your own point of view. There are other boys who say they have to stay with their parents, but I think they haven't chosen for their own life.

He is glad not to have returned to a place where he could not have used his technical skills and would have had to work in agriculture to earn money for his parents. They are without work in Spain now and live by the help which they receive from their children.

Juan says that he doesn't feel Spanish, but more Dutch. He has had that feeling since his ninth or tenth year. Then he thought: 'Either here or there and I decided to stay here because things were better here'. Asked what it meant for him to be a Spaniard he answered: 'Not much, not even 50 per cent'. If there were a possibility of having two nationalities he would accept that, though he has heard that such people don't know at a given moment what they are, Spanish or Dutch:

> This will not happen to me. I choose to be a Dutchman though inside myself I am a Spaniard. . . Well, God, it's like a man in space with his space-suit. On the outside he is a spaceman, on the inside he is on earth. On the outside I am simply Dutch, you don't see it.

His option for the Netherlands for his work and future expresses itself in Dutch friends and in his work and membership of a Dutch trade union, in which he became a militant. Nevertheless he speaks Spanish from time to time with his cousins and has frequent contact with them. He has five Spanish friends. He normally goes to his cousins or meets them in the Spanish centres every four to six weeks.

This is the only thing Juan said about his Spanish associational life. But, as we have said, he restructured his life after running away. He went to a youth centre and thereafter lived with a Dutch family for a year and a half. The wife of this family was at that time working in the youth centre. He has built up a trusting relationship with her and talks with her when he feels awkward or thinks about home.

> When I feel awkward I go to J and we talk about it. Or I go to my cousin. My cousin says, 'Well they are your parents', but I say 'I have to build up a life of my own'. They think that you simply have to love your parents. Well I do it too, but in another way.

Though his words are reasonable, there is much emotion behind them.

> Sometimes I am upstairs in my room and then. . . Goddam, I like to hit somebody. Sometimes I dream about it, that I hit him [father] on his head . . . but most times I wake up against the walls of the bedroom.

Asked whether he would like to see his parents again, he answers, 'Yes, but there is a big wall which one has to pass through first, which has to go first'.

The boy has gone through very bitter and intense experiences which contrast sharply with the ideal of family love and unity of which the Jiminez family gave such an eloquent testimony. These experiences have shaped his expressions about himself at that time. His activities in the trade union are, apart from living with a Dutch family, his instruments for building a new conscious orientation towards Dutch society. He has been a member of the National Trade Union Youth Contact for two years now. They have ten members and have among other things tried to convince foreign youth to be members too. They have informed them about their rights as workers.

This boy has accepted a Dutch life-style and ideology about the roles of men and women to a great extent. He likes to be Dutch though he does not deny being a Spaniard. His continuous and dramatic fight with his brutal, illiterate and traditional father has been a strong influence in determining this, but has not been the only factor. As important is the possibility of achieving occupational advancement and training in the Netherlands. Associational life is not completely absent for him, but it has not been an acculturating channel for Juan as it has for the Jiminez family.

These interviews show that associational life may have a very different impact on the identity formation of youth and also that this membership of associations should always be interpreted against the overall background of the family-context.

Conclusions on the case of Juan   In summary the following points may be noted:

—Ethnic identity as ideology means in practice *talking* in a rather loose way about oneself and one's own actions and behaviour. This talking includes emotions, bitter ones in Juan's case and pleasant ones in other cases.

—What primordialists claim to be important in the formation of ethnic identity, namely the relations with the basic group, is clearly present in this case, though in the form of a fight between father and son.

—Identity and self-construal leads to action: in this case a readiness to integrate into Dutch society leads to a factual membership of a Dutch trade union, to a request for Dutch citizenship, etc.

—Spanish associational life has not had much influence on the construction of identity of this boy; membership of Dutch groups like the trade union is, on the other hand, referred to in his conversations.

Summary of relations between association and ethnic identity

The foregoing sections suggest a wide range of relations between associations and identity:

1   Although young people of 17 to 21 years of age do not participate in the associations of their parents, according to our survey, the conclusion that associational life has no influence on their construction of ethnic identity is not warranted. Many of them participated as children in the activities of associations; a small group has built its own associations in reaction to those of their parents; and there are still occasions when youth actually participates in associational activity.

2   Associational life provides facilities for mutual social relations and revitalization of Spanish cultural forms (folk-dances, languages, etc.). Associations defend the rights of migrants *vis-à-vis* the home country and the country of settlement. They convey a message of 'Spanishness' to the outsiders and construct a certain ethnic identity. From this identity it becomes legitimate and valuable to develop all sorts of activities from language courses to negotiations with external forums.

3   Associations and their members construe their opinions and feelings about many aspects of 'Spanishness' within a context of migration. Thus ethnic identity can be considered as an ethnic ideology to pursue social and primordial interests.

4   In spite of this, our qualitative material leaves open the possibility of analysing identity in terms of revitalizing a cultural heritage or in terms of the socialization of children in parental traditions. In that case it is a question of whether the possibility of defending oneself in societies of settlement diminishes in argument over time.

5   Ethnic ideology is considered to be 'everyday ideology' in Weinreich's sense, although belonging to the working class has shaped the content of this ideology. But this is not to say that it can be reduced to working-class ideology.

6   Ethnic identity is very difficult to delineate in its most important and less important features. It is thus difficult to measure. Even our own definition is so broad that it resembles such general concepts as personality, *Gestalt*, organization of various traits—too much to be captured in one precise measurement.

7   Identity is a concept which is attractive for many groups and individuals: it acts in their speech as a principle of organization of various scattered, and not mutually linked, elements of life-histories of individuals, belonging to ethnic groups etc. In this sense the word identity with all its related terms such as 'identity-crisis', 'collective and individual identity', 'maintenance of identity' and so on have a certain heuristic value: we know more or less where to look to explain phenomena of migrant individuals and groups. And the term is a flag, an invitation not only to organize a system of ideas and feelings, but to pursue collective goals, that is to act as an ideology.

Notes

1   Several Spanish ministries funded the Spanish part of the investigation; the Erasmus University, Department of Preventive and Social Psychiatry, funded the Dutch part. The investigation is officially accepted as an element of the Agreement on Cultural Exchange for 1982/1983 between Spain and the Netherlands. The European Science Foundation funded various meetings in distinct cities in Europe.

2   Dutch literature, including this article, prefers the word 'ethnic identity' rather than 'cultural identity' to avoid the connotations of a primordialistic, cultural and static approach and to accentuate the importance of a situationist, social and dynamic perspective (Vermeulen 1983: 3).

3   Spanish members of our team do not have exactly the same idea about identity as ideology. They write:

> We choose Pizarro's outline definition of 'ideology' (Pizarro 1979: 152–95). 'The production of discourse (or, according to Saussurean terminology, "speech") is not an individual act of will and intelligence. This production, like the whole of social production is structured. The modes of transformation of enunciates, that is to say, application procedures, are defined and limited by ideological models. Ideological models can be defined

236

as recurrent types of temporarily fixed and privileged transformations within the set of possible transformations. The recurrence of certain particular application procedures ensures the production of similar speech products, and this recurrence is ensured by the more or less homogeneous upbringing within a social class, of the agents of speech practice, as well as by repression' (Pizarro 1979, p. 213) (Pereda *et al.* 1981: p. 85).

'. . . the only way to root the problem of identity in social processes is from the notion of ideology. . . In so far as the individual and the collective subject are indispensable elements for the reproduction of social processes, we can establish that one of the principal functions of ideology is the constitution of subjects' (Equipo Español 1983: 106).

4 An interview with two Rotterdam Dutch officials for migration affairs corroborates some of these findings: for example, the splitting-up of the community in many clubs and associations for reasons of personal envy and need of prestige, or financial reasons (interview June 1982).

5 Spanish team members have much experience in analysing the discourse of groups (Pereda *et al.* 1981). They have found inspiration in the French Groupe d'Entrevues (1979) and in the work of the Dutch linguist T.A. van Dijk (1980) among many others. They start always with a proper semantic analysis of the text of a discourse. By this is meant: the identification of several themes and their connectedness (syntagmatic level): the identification of semantic fields which points to diverse discursive elements related with each other because of the enunciation of the same type of predicates. Such a semantic field is then given a name, for example, 'democracy-authoritarianism'. For example, relations between unequals (parents/children, teacher/pupil, man/woman, boss/servant) can get the same type of predicates which all belong to the semantic field of democracy-authoritarianism (Equipo Español 1983: 40). The third moment in this semantic analysis is the uncovering of the 'isotopes' in the discourse. These isotopes guarantee the coherence of the discourse (Pereda *et al.* 1981: 42). More or less synonymous terms are: 'ideological complexes' which interrelate the several themes of the discourse (Equipo Español 1983: 23) or 'discursive structures' (Equipo Español 1983: 286).

Apart from this strict semantic analysis which stays *within* the text, there is another analysis which connects the former results with the world outside the text. This is called the analysis of the symbolic function of the group text or the pragmatic function. The analysis of the Spanish teams have translated these three approaches in the following way:

—semantic analysis of the discourses of the discussion-groups
—the discursive structure of the discourses
—the social genesis of these discursive structures.

The object of the study has been investigated in the following ways:

—bibliographical research on concept and theories about cultural or ethnic identity
—discourse-analysis of several discussion-groups
—semi-structured interviews with Spanish families, Dutch persons
—life-histories of six Spanish families
—quantitative and qualitative analysis of associations in Switzerland and Holland.

As regards interviews, the following were undertaken:

—12 semi-structured interviews of Spanish qualified informants, 2 of Dutch officials of immigration policy
—11 discussion groups of which: 2 of Spanish youth in the Netherlands; 2 of Spanish youth in Switzerland; 1 of Spanish fathers in the Netherlands; 1 of Spanish mothers in Switzerland; 1 of returned youth in Spain; 1 of Spanish youth living in Spain; 1 of Dutch mothers; 1 of Dutch boys; 1 of Swiss youth
—48 interviews of Spanish young people in Holland and Switzerland
  4 interviews of Spanish young people in Holland who have been in contact with

psychiatric wards or other problem-oriented institutions
9 interviews with Dutch young people
—life histories of 6 families (3 Spanish families in Holland, 3 in Switzerland).

6   J.L. Recio (1984: 27) has written a text about the methodology of the history of
    family life and added six cases, three Spanish families in the Netherlands and three
    in Switzerland. We have given a summary of one of these cases.

   In contrast with our usage of 'ethnic identity' in the rest of the text, we follow in
the summary of the Jiminez family the terms, as Recio has used them, to indicate
the various conceptions about identity within the Spanish-Dutch team.

References

Aronsons, D.R. (1976) 'Ethnicity as a cultural system: an introductory essay', in F.
    Henry (ed.) *Ethnicity in the Americas*, Mouton, The Hague.
Dijk, van T. (1980) *Texto y contexto, Semántica y pragmática del discurso,* Catedra,
    Madrid.
Equipo Español (1983) 'Evolucion de la identidad cultural de los jovenes de la segunda
    generacion de emigrantes espanoles en Suiza y Holanda', Informe Intermedio,
    Calle Martin de Los Meros, Madrid, December.
Groupe D'Entrevues (1979) *Analyse Sémiotique des Textes*, Presses Universitaires de
    Lyon, Lyon.
Mancho, S. *et al.* (1983) 'Red Associativa de los Emigrantes Espanoles en Holanda y
    Suiza', *Informe Intermedio*, nos. 5, 10, Calle Martin de Los Meros, Madrid, Sep-
    tember.
Pereda, C. *et al.* (1981) *Approach to the analysis of the problem of young Spanish
    immigrants in Holland from the methodology of discussion groups*, Calle Martin de
    Los Meros, Madrid.
Pizarro, N., (1979) *Metodología sociológica y teoría lingüística*, Alberto Corazón,
    Madrid.
Recio, J.L. (1984), *La metodología de la historia de vida*, Calle Martin de Los Meros,
    Madrid.
Seoane, L. *et al.* (1983) *Avance de conclusiones del estudio sociologico sobre la evol-
    ucion de los jovenes y adolescentes pertenecientes a la segunda generacion de los
    emigrantes espanoles en Suiza y Holanda*, Calle Martin de Los Meros, Madrid.
Soest, R. Van and Verdonk, A. (1984) *Etnische identiteit, begrip en theorieen; een
    literatuurstudie*, Instituutspublicatie, no. 61, Instituut Preventieve en Sociale Psy-
    chiatrie, Erasmusuniversiteit, Rotterdam.
Soest, R. Van and Verdonk, A. (1985) *Etnische identiteit is een ideologie* (Ethnic ident-
    ity is an ideology), in preparation (20pp).
Stein, H.F. (1975) 'Ethnicity, identity and ideology', *School Review*, (83) pp. 273-300.
Verdonk, A. (1986) Interviews with Dutch officials, Spanish and Dutch young people,
    Institute Preventieve en Sociale Psychiatrie, Erasmusuniversiteit, Rotterdam.
Verdonk, A. (1983) *Identiteit van Spaanse jongeren in Nederland: een semantisch-
    structurele analyse van discoursen van enige discussie-groepen,* (The identity of
    Spanish youth in the Netherlands: an analysis of the semantic structure of dis-
    courses of some discussion groups), paper for the congress on minorities, Erasmus
    university. Abstract of six pages published in *Congresboek EUR*, Etnische Mind-
    erheden. 1983 paper, published in *PS*, 1984, no. 18, pp. 34–53.
Vermeulen, H. (1983) *Verkenningen in etnische identiteit. Onderzoek van de
    Chinezen, Surinamers en Turken*, Universiteit van Amsterdam, Antropologisch-
    Sociologisch Centrum, Euromed, Amsterdam.

Index

dramatics clubs, Portuguese
145-6
Dressmakers' Association
(Cypriot) 54
Duncan, D. 168
Durham Road Residents'
Association 73
Durkheim, Emile 16-17, 18, 19
Division of Labour in Society
(1973) 16
Suicide (1952) 16, 17

East Birmingham Parents'
Association 77
education 9, 219
Asian attitude to 27-8, 29
Greek Cypriot attitude to 38
Pakistani 74-5
Portuguese 158-9
Turkish 90, 91
see also schools
Education Nationale (France)
147
educational associations, Cypriot
48
EFEKA 46
Elfi 103
Elif Gida 104, 105
Emigration, Institute of
(Spanish) 225
Emigration Affairs, Ministry of
(France) 142
employment 9
Cypriot 44
Pakistani 67
Turkish 90
see also business;
unemployment
ESEKA 39, 50, 55, 58
Espirito Santo 133
'ethnic identity' 42
Spanish **219-39**
Pakistani 78-81
see also identity
'ethnicity' 42
Cypriot 51, 54-7, 59

see also identity
European Community 5, 177
European Science Foundation
10, 11, 22, 24
ex-servicemen's associations
(Pakistani) 78
Ex-Servicemen's Society
(Pakistani) 71

F. Sanit Institute 177
FAACS 224
Facism 168, 170, 171, 175
Faith Moshee 112
Fatima, Our Lady of 138
FIDEF 108, 118
FILEF 177, 181, 182
Finland 215
Finnbook Co-operative
Publishers 216
Finns 1, 6, 24
ethnic mobilization of 202-16
multi-purpose organizations of
208-15: channels of influence
212; financial and personnel
resources of 210; purposes of
211; representation of 213;
and social networks 201-2
food habits 28
Cypriot 50-51
Pakistani businesses 64
Portuguese 149-50
Turkish 99-101
Foreign People, First Law on
(Switzerland) 7
formal organizations 8, 19-20
Cypriot 46-50
Turkish 107-13, 114, 115-21
Foundation Louis Carlesimo 196
Franco, Francisco 229
Franco-Italian associations 181
Fratellanza Reggiana 175
Fratellanza Romagnola 175
'function', definition of 20
'funeral associations', Pakistani
71
Furnivall, J.S. 19

izzat 31

Jamaati Islami of Pakistan 69, 80
Jamiat Ahl-e-Hadith 74, 77
Jews 27, 30, 79
Journal di Fundao 152

Kafeneion 45, 50
Kashmiris 11, 21, 23, 26, 67, 80,
    81
kinship 8-9
KOMKAR (Association of
    Kurdish Workers) 108, 109,
    118
Kurdish Cultural and Counselling
    Centre 117
Kurds 94, 96-7, 109, 110, 113, 118

Labour Party, British 26, 40, 70,
    73, 78
Landmannsschaften (hemseri) 98
languages 24, 112-13
    Arabic 75, 81, 113
    Bengali 24
    Cypriot 35
    Finnish 203-4, 205, 206, 210-11
        214-15, 217
    Greek 33, 34, 35, 52-3, 56-7
    Gujarati 24
    Italian 181
    Kurdish 110
    Pakistani 75-6, 81
    Pashto 24
    Portuguese 145, 146-7, 154,
        158-9
    Punjabi 24, 75, 81
    Spanish 227
    Swedish 201, 202
    Turkish 35, 98, 115
    Urdu 24, 75, 76, 77, 81
Laziali di Casalvieri Association
    193-7
leadership
    of Italian regional associations
        184-5

of Finnish associations 207-8
    Pakistani 66, 68-70
    Portuguese community 151-6
    Turkish 113
Lebanese 34, 35
Lévi-Strauss, Claude 12
Lieberson, S, 168
local associations, Cypriot 48
Local Government Act (1966)
    (Britain) 70
LSOBA 223
Lynx, the 81

MacIver, Robert 18
madrasa 68, 74-5
Malinowski, Bronislaw 20
Maronites 34
marriage 27, 31, 33
    arranged 29
    endogamy 197
    Greek Cypriot 36-8, 45-6, 57
    Italian 188
    Pakistani 64, 77, 80
    Turkish 95, 97, 98, 99
Marrucho, Antonio 138
Marxism, Indian 25
Mauritians 134
MHP Party 108, 119
Mietskaserne 91
migration 1
    chain 88, 92-3, 94-6, 129
    Finnish to Sweden 1, 6
    to France: Italian 1, 4-5, 11,
        166-74; Portuguese 1, 4-5,
        11, 129-30
    to Great Britain 2-3: Cypriots
        43-4; Irish 2; Pakistanis 1,
        62 4
    motives for 8
    Spanish to Switzerland and the
        Netherlands 1, 6-7, 10
    Turks to Germany 2, 3-4, 86,
        87, 88, 89-90, 91, 92
Milli Görüs 105
Mineurs Catholiques, Les 180
Ministère des Affaires Sociales et

243

expansion 104-7
social interaction and ethnic
boundaries 96-9
social relations 95-6
wholesale trade
development of 103-4
Tyler, E.B. 15

UGT 224
umma 66
unemployment
Pakistani 64, 71, 72
Turkish 107
Union Musicale Italienne 174
unions *see* trade unions
Unita 103

Vema 46
VEPIFM 121
village associations, Cypriot 48
virginity 36

war veterans, associations of
(Italian) 180
Weber, Max 12, 13
Weinreich, Peter 22, 23
welfare 51, 52, 72, 114, 137, 222
women
Greek Cypriot 36-7
Kurdish 96
Pakistani 67, 75
Portuguese 148

Women's Association (Turkish)
117
women's groups
Cypriot 49
Pakistani 67, 71
workers' associations
Asian 25, 26
Italian 181-2
Turkish 107, 108
Workers' Youth Association
(Turkish) 117
'working parties', Cypriot 53-4
World War
First 7, 43, 129, 169, 175
Second 6, 43, 62, 168, 170, 175,
176, 179, 194

Yemenis 76
Yezidi 94
youth
clubs, Cypriot 47, 48
culture 31-3
Italian 185-6
Pakistani 23, 65, 74-5
Portuguese 149, 150, 156-60
Spanish, and ethnic identity
219-39
Yugoslavs 3, 6, 89

Zaouia 74
Zia Ul Haque, General 74, 79